THE ELEMENTS OF
REASONING

Second Edition

David A. Conway
University of Missouri—St. Louis

Ronald Munson
University of Missouri—St. Louis

Wadsworth Publishing Company

I(T)P® An International Thomson Publishing Company

Belmont, CA • Albany, NY • Bonn • Boston • Cincinnati • Detroit
Johannesburg • London • Madrid • Melbourne • Mexico City • New York
Paris • San Francisco • Singapore • Tokyo • Toronto • Washington

Philosophy Editor: Peter Adams
Assistant Editor: Clay Glad
Editorial Assistant: Greg Brueck
Marketing Manager: Dave Garrison
Project Editor: Jennie Redwitz
Print Buyer: Barbara Britton
Permissions Editor: Jeanne Bosschart
Advertising Project Manager: Joseph Jodar
Copy Editor: Adrienne Armstrong
Cover Design: Laurie Anderson
Page Compositor & Illustration: Margarite Reynolds
Printer: Malloy Lithographing, Inc.

Printed in the United States of America
1 2 3 4 5 6 7 8 9 10

For more information, contact Wadsworth Publishing Company, 10 Davis Drive,
Belmont, CA 94002, or electronically at http://www.thomson.com/wadsworth.html

International Thomson Publishing Europe
Berkshire House 168-173
High Holborn
London, WC1V 7AA, England

International Thomson Editores
Campos Eliseos 385, Piso 7
Col. Polanco
11560 México D.F. México

Thomas Nelson Australia
102 Dodds Street
South Melbourne 3205
Victoria, Australia

International Thomson Publishing Asia
221 Henderson Road
#05-10 Henderson Building
Singapore 0315

Nelson Canada
1120 Birchmount Road
Scarborough, Ontario
Canada M1K 5G4

International Thomson Publishing Japan
Hirakawacho Kyowa Building, 3F
2-2-1 Hirakawacho
Chiyoda-ku, Tokyo 102, Japan

International Thomson Publishing GmbH
Königswinterer Strasse 418
53227 Bonn, Germany

International Thomson Publishing
Southern Africa
Building 18, Constantia Park
240 Old Pretoria Road
Halfway House, 1685 South Africa

Library of Congress Cataloging-in-Publication Data
Conway, David
   The elements of reasoning / David A. Conway, Ronald Munson. —2nd ed.
      p. cm.
   Includes index.
   ISBN 0-534-51672-6 (pbk.)
      1. Reasoning. I. Munson, Ronald. II. Title.
BC177.C67   1996
160—dc20   96-22769

D.C.

To the memory of Harold Tresize—
great friend and amateur philosopher extraordinaire

R.M.

To the memory of my father Callen Lemuel Munson

CONTENTS

PREFACE

We wrote *The Elements of Reasoning* (*ER* for short) because we felt a need for it and believed others did also. Even though many excellent informal logic and rhetoric texts are available, they tend to be more discursive than absolutely necessary. We wanted a book that would do for informal logic what Strunk and White's *Elements of Style* did for English composition. That is, we wanted a book that would present the basic concepts of critical reasoning and analysis in a brief, straightforward way and yet would be clear and accurate.

ER is that book, and no other is quite like it. The job turned out to be harder than we expected; Strunk and White came to serve more as an inspiration than a model. Sentences are more familiar to people than arguments, and rules of usage are more precise and easier to employ than rules of evaluation. Hence, we had to do more explaining than did our predecessors.

Despite such difficulties, we believe *ER* is successful in presenting clearly and concisely the principles, methods, and concepts important in guiding our own reasoning and in analyzing the reasoning of others. The discussions of such basic topics as identifying and evaluating arguments, testing causal claims, detecting and resolving vagueness and ambiguity, and framing acceptable definitions follow traditional lines and focus on practical interests. We don't aim to offer novel ideas, but we do aim to show how traditional ones can be important. As we say in the Orientation, "Little here is new, but much is useful."

This edition of *ER* contains a great many minor and two major changes from the first edition. One major change is the addition of a chapter on the use of Venn diagrams to evaluate validity in categorical reasoning. The first edition offered only the informal and generic "thought experiment" method (Chapter 3) for evaluating such reasoning. The importance of categorical reasoning in everyday thought amply justifies the introduction of the more precise evaluative method of Venn diagrams.

The other major revision is that the number of exercises has been expanded by a factor or 3 or 4. Since the text itself remains concise, the "handbook" character of *ER* is not affected, but it is now suitable for use as the sole text in an introduction to informal logic or critical thinking. We will say more about this below.

Some instructors may notice that we do not employ any distinction between "linked" and "convergent" arguments. This is neither an oversight nor an attempt at brevity. Rather, we do not find any of the many versions of the supposed distinction to be of much real conceptual or pedagogical use. (See David A. Conway, "On the Distinction between Convergent and Linked Arguments." *Informed Logic* XIII. 3 [Fall 1991]: 145–158.) Nothing in the text, however, is incompatible with some such distinction, should an instructor wish to introduce it.

ER may be used in several ways. First, it may be read straight through by anyone wishing to become familiar with the standard tools and operations of practical logic. Alternatively, *ER*'s chapters are written to stand alone so the book may be used as a reference and consulted for information on particular topics.

However the book is read, it is written to be accessible to everyone and requires no previous knowledge of philosophy, logic, or any other specialized subject. Its nontechnical character and short length make it suitable for use in a variety of courses in several disciplines.

Certainly *ER* can be used as a secondary text in any philosophy course. For example, an introductory survey of philosophy could include a logic component and explicitly cover the topics in *ER*. In contrast, courses in ethics, philosophy of religion, metaphysics, or the philosophy of science could simply assign *ER* as background reading or make it a reference work.

At this point in the preface to the first edition, we said: "*ER* can also serve as a primary [logic] text. Many longer logic books have no more content than *ER*, and exercises are crucial in a course designed to improve analytical skills. Thus, an instructor willing to provide more exercises can employ *ER* to teach an excellent course in critical thinking."

The number of exercises included now should make it unnecessary for the instructor to provide more in order to have enough material for an entire course in introductory logic or critical thinking. (In fact, one of us, D.A.C., has frequently taught an introductory course in logic/critical thinking, using the text of the first edition of *ER*, handouts with about the same number of additional exercises as are included here, six or seven quizzes, and two exams. Allowing ample time for discussion, he has never succeeded in covering all ten chapters of the first edition of *ER*. More material is certainly not needed.) Alternatively, if *ER* is not the sole text in any sort of course, it is by no means necessary to assign or discuss all of the exercises provided.

ER may also be used in areas besides philosophy and critical reasoning. It could be helpful as a supplementary text in various courses in the social sciences. For example, political science, history, sociology, psychology, and anthropology often offer courses discussing research techniques in conjunction with general principles of reasoning. Since *ER* presents these principles concisely and employs many examples from the social sciences, it fits easily into such courses. Further, social science courses dealing with theory and systems may also find *ER* a useful adjunct.

English composition, both beginning and advanced, is another area in which *ER* may be used. Skills in writing and thinking are not separable, and *ER* can play a valuable role in any composition course that aims at more than drill. Not only does *ER* present information about topics like definition, ambiguity, and fallacies, it provides a vocabulary to talk about rational analysis and persuasion. *ER* has an obvious place in courses teaching persuasive writing.

In summary, *ER's* compact size and the general usefulness of its principles make it a help to instructors in a variety of courses in a variety of disciplines. Its clarity and accuracy make it a help to an even wider variety of students.

Throughout the book, we have tried to make every discussion clear and accurate. We would appreciate hearing about any errors, confusions, or unclarities that may remain. We would also be grateful for any suggestions for improvement so that we can take advantage of them in the next edition.

Acknowledgments

We would like to thank the following reviewers for their input: Deen K. Chatterjee, University of Utah; Paul Gregory, University of Illionois at Chicago; Walter H. O'Briant, University of Georgia; and Kirke Wolfe, Portland Community College.

ORIENTATION

Reasoning is an ancient subject but an everyday practice.

We are all able to reason. Someone totally unable to assess claims and arrive at conclusions would believe anything and act in wild and arbitrary ways. That we do not generally behave in this fashion shows how we rely on reasoning to guide our actions and ground our beliefs.

This book aims to improve reasoning skills and to enhance effective thinking. Although everyone is able to reason, not everyone reasons perfectly. The skills of reasoning can be improved by experience and instruction. Even a practiced and capable tennis player can become better through proper coaching. We are concerned with what we do when we reason well and with some of the ways we can go wrong. We are also concerned with what to look for when we are attempting to understand and evaluate the reasoning of others.

More precisely, this book presents a set of intellectual tools to employ in the process of establishing, understanding, and testing claims. These tools are the principles, distinctions, and methods that have been developed by generations of philosophers, logicians, essayists, scientists, critics, and thinkers of all kinds. Little here is new, but much is useful.

Basic Assumptions

Five basic assumptions have guided and shaped this book:

1. Everyone is already skilled to a degree in the rational process of analyzing, defending, and evaluating claims.

2. Everyone can improve such skills by becoming aware of the principles behind them and by doing deliberately what is usually done unreflectively.

3. The principles are not imposed from the outside but are implicit in the ordinary practices of defending and evaluating claims. We are rational creatures, even though we do not always act ratio-

nally. We have found that these principles, when followed, produce the best overall results.

4. It is good to have some general guidelines in defending, analyzing, and evaluating claims—even if the guidelines are not always strictly accurate and reliable.

5. These guidelines can be presented in a brief but still useful way.

Organization

The book begins with a discussion of argument in general, moves through discussions of more specific kinds, then examines the ways in which arguments can be flawed. In the final three chapters, it focuses on the background of argument and on aspects of language useful in rational analysis.

Arguments are the main instruments of rational persuasion, and it is crucial to be able to recognize them and distinguish them from similar forms of prose. In Chapter 1 we define the term *argument* and discuss ways of identifying an argument. In Chapter 2 we present ways of analyzing arguments and displaying their structures. In Chapter 3 we distinguish deductive from nondeductive arguments and present some general techniques for evaluating both. In Chapters 4 and 5 we introduce some valid argument forms and discuss constructing proofs of validity.

Chapter 6 focuses on causal arguments and analysis and discusses various meanings we assign to the word *cause*, depending on our interests. We sketch conditions for causal explanation and state and illustrate the four traditional methods of experimental analysis. Chapter 7 describes ways we argue from analogies and models and presents criteria for evaluating such arguments.

We conclude the focus on argument in Chapter 8, which is devoted to describing common errors in reasoning. We identify and name frequent fallacies.

In Chapter 9, "Reasonable Beliefs," we face the question of how to establish the beliefs we use as premises in arguments and employ them in assessing claims offered for our approval. In the last two chapters we focus on language, rather than arguments and beliefs. Chapter 10 describes basic types of definition, methods of defining, and the standards definitions should meet. Chapter 11 describes and illustrates how to identify and deal with specific sorts of vagueness and ambiguity.

Using This Book

The book may be read straight through, but it is not necessary to do so. Each chapter may also be read by itself. Those people not interested in technical matters may want to skip the chapters on valid argument forms, and those concerned mostly about rational arguments may wish to ignore the chapters on definition and on vagueness and ambiguity.

The book does not presuppose any specialized knowledge. Each topic should be accessible to anyone, although some topics are inherently difficult and require more effort to understand than others. Technical terms are explained as they are introduced, and references to additional discussions of a topic are scattered throughout the book.

The book's compact size should make it possible for someone to gain a quick grasp of a wide range of topics connected with rational analysis and argument. The book aims to be accurate as well as brief. Yet keep in mind that each topic here has itself been the subject of more than one book, and many important distinctions and qualifications have been passed over silently.

The justification for this approach is both simple and powerful: This book is intended to be useful in an immediate and practical way. It is more a handbook than an encyclopedia.

Chapter 1

RECOGNIZING ARGUMENTS

Arguments are the instruments we use in rational persuasion. Whenever we want to convince someone to accept a position we consider correct, we present arguments in its favor. We also use arguments to express our reasoning even when we have no concern with persuading others. In this chapter, we define the concept of an argument, explain how to recognize an argument, and introduce some standard terms for discussing arguments.

What Is an Argument?

To give an argument is to make a claim and to offer other claims as reasons for its acceptance. Thus, an **argument** is a set of claims, one of which is meant to be supported by the others.

This is not an argument:

> By the end of September in New England, the leaves are already changing to beautiful browns and reds. The nights are cooler, and the days are noticeably shorter. Some inhabitants begin to feel a sense of dread as they think of the long winter to come.

Several claims are made in this passage, but as no one of them is offered as a reason for any other, we have no argument.

This, however, is an argument:

> Every person in the United States is entitled to a decent minimum of health care. But thousands of people in need of health care must go without it because they cannot afford it. Clearly, then, justice demands that we change our health care system.

This, too, is an argument:

> She's armed, so she's dangerous.

In both passages, some claims are offered as support for another claim. That means both contain arguments.

A **conclusion** is a claim meant to be supported by reasons offered in the argument. A **premise** is a claim put forth as a reason for a conclusion. Using these terms, we can say that an argument is a set of claims that can be divided into a conclusion and one or more premises. (Argument = conclusion + premises.)

The two arguments above are made up of premises and conclusions in the following ways:

PREMISE 1: Every person in the United States is entitled to a decent minimum of health care.

PREMISE 2: Thousands of people in need of health care must go without it because they cannot afford it.

CONCLUSION: Justice demands that we change our health care system.

PREMISE: She's armed.

CONCLUSION: She's dangerous.

We infer or make an **inference** each time we draw a conclusion from a premise or set of premises. In the last example, an inference is made to "She's dangerous." In the first, we infer from premises 1 and 2 that "Justice demands that we change our health care system." Each of these arguments involves a single inference.

Three General Considerations

1. Length of Arguments

Our examples of arguments have been brief, but an argument may be any length. Some books are best regarded as giving one elaborate argument for a single conclusion. For instance, the whole point of some books is to make a case that the earth was visited by creatures from outer space thousands of years ago, while others argue that capitalism is an evil economic system or that eating meat is immoral. Yet, despite its brevity, "She's armed, so she's dangerous" is no less an argument than these.

Arguments may occur in any context and involve any subject matter. We find arguments in mathematical treatises, newspaper editorials, sociological or philosophical or literary journals as well as in barroom conversations, exchanges between sports fans, familial discussions about how to budget a limited income, and in other everyday situations. Further, the subject matter can be trivial ("You had better get your feet off the coffee table. Mother's coming.") or profound ("Innocent children suffer and die every day in this world. That shows life has no meaning.").

2. Arguments and Disputes

An argument in our sense is not a dispute. ("Neighbors called the police because the newlyweds were having a terrible argument.") People disputing might use arguments in an attempt to bring about agreement (or they might just yell), but the *arguments* they might offer would not be the same thing as the *dispute* they are having.

3. Arguments and Bad Arguments

An argument can fail for any number of reasons. Its premises may be false, or irrelevant, or provide inadequate support for the conclusion. For example, the premises in this argument give little or no support for its conclusion:

It hasn't rained in weeks. That means it is sure to rain tomorrow.

In later chapters we discuss ways in which arguments can be flawed. For now we want to emphasize only that whenever a set of claims is given, one of which is meant to be supported by the others, then an argument is given. If the claims offered as support are false or if they do not support the intended conclusion very well, the argument is a bad one. The argument may be so bad that we are led to exclaim, "That's not an argument at all!" Nevertheless, a bad argument is just as much an argument as a bad boy is a boy.

Recognizing Arguments

We first consider in this section some useful markers for identifying premises and conclusions. These help us both in recognizing arguments and in analyzing them. We then show how parts of arguments may be implicit, intended even though not explicitly stated. Finally, we consider the role that questions, commands, and other nondeclarative sentences can play in arguments.

Inference Indicators

"Today is the 5th. Yesterday was the 4th." Is this an argument? If it is, what is the premise and what is the conclusion? No straightforward answers are possible because the passage can be understood in three different ways.

a. The first sentence might be meant as a premise and the second as a conclusion:

PREMISE: Today is the 5th.
CONCLUSION: Yesterday was the 4th.

b. The first sentence might be meant as a conclusion and the second as a premise:

PREMISE: Yesterday was the 4th.

CONCLUSION: Today is the 5th.

c. The sentences might be meant as just two related observations with no inference intended:

Today is the 5th, and yesterday was the 4th.

Many cases are of this sort. Here is a more serious one: "All people are corrupt by nature. Everyone around me is corrupt." Is the first claim meant as a reason for the second or the second as a reason for the first? Or perhaps there is not any argument here and neither claim is intended as a reason for the other.

In both these examples, unless we are given more to go on, we have no grounds for choosing among the different interpretations. All we can do is note the possible interpretations and leave matters at that.

Suppose the first example said: "Today is the 5th. And *so* yesterday was the 4th." Or this: "*Since* today is the 5th, yesterday was the 4th." Either of these additions makes clear that an argument is being offered and that "Yesterday was the 4th" is its conclusion.

Similarly, the second passage would not be puzzling if it said, "All people are corrupt by nature. *Thus*, everyone around me is corrupt." Nor would there be a problem if it said, "*Because* all people are corrupt by nature, everyone around me is corrupt." Here too the added words remove the ambiguity. We do have an argument, the first sentence being the premise, the second the conclusion.

The words we added help by "flagging" premises or conclusions. Words or phrases that do this are called **inference indicators**. There are two sorts of inference indicators. **Conclusion indicators** are words used to indicate that a conclusion is about to be drawn. Here are some conclusion indicators:

So	Thus
Therefore	Hence
Consequently	We may conclude
It follows that	This entails that

Premise indicators are words used to indicate that a premise is about to be given:

Since	Because
For	The reason is that
Seeing that	As is implied by

These lists are not exhaustive, and generally we must rely on our knowledge of language to recognize when other inference indicators are present.

Also note that the occurrence of one of the listed words is not an infallible indication that an inference is being drawn:

Since lightning struck his bedroom, he has been acting peculiarly.

Starting with the Ace, she played next the King, then the Queen. *Thus*, she played the entire suit until the deuce was reached and the game was won.

"Since" and "thus" do not serve as inference indicators in these cases. "Since" as used here means "ever since" and tells us about a temporal relationship. The "thus" in the second case means something like "in this way," rather than "therefore." Being sensitive to language and context is the best guide to recognizing when an argument is intended.

Unstated (Implicit) Premises and Conclusions

Arguments can have premises or conclusions that are implicit—that is, not openly or explicitly stated. An implicit premise or conclusion is a genuine part of an argument if it is clear that the person giving the argument *meant it to be* understood this way. Arguments that have implicit premises or conclusions are called **enthymemes**.

Realizing when a sentence is implicit is seldom difficult. Consider this advertisement:

The bigger the burger the better the burger.
The burgers are bigger at Burger King.

The intended but unstated conclusion is obvious:

The burgers are better at Burger King.

Advertising copywriters count on our being able to see the unstated conclusion, and they are right to do so.

Similarly, suppose someone argues that

Herman cannot be the person who robbed the lingerie emporium, because Herman does not have a snake tattoo on his left arm.

We can be sure the unstated premise is

> The robber of the emporium has a snake tattoo on his left arm.

At times we cannot be sure if there is an unstated premise or conclusion. At other times we are sure *something* is intended, but we cannot be sure what that something is. In either case, we simply consider the argument as it is explicitly stated. The job of the author of the argument is to make it tolerably clear what her intentions are.

Questions, Commands, Exclamations, and Exhortations

Arguments are sets of *claims*, so questions, commands, exclamations, and exhortations cannot be parts of arguments because they make no claims. But we need to be aware that in everyday language grammatical questions, commands, and so on may have the force of making claims. You ask a friend to meet you at the beach at 3 a.m. to watch the underwater submarine races and the friend indignantly replies, "What kind of a fool do you think I am?" This is not really a question. (*You* would look the fool if you tried to give a serious answer.) It is a statement denying being a fool or being the sort of fool who would fall for such a suggestion. When a football player makes one incredible play after another and a fan shouts out, "What a great quarterback!" the fan is saying that the player *is* a great quarterback.

This means that passages like the following should be recognized as giving arguments:

> Clouds are rolling in, and the wind is picking up. Go check the boat *now!*

> Don't you know that no decent poetry has been written since T. S. Eliot died, and even he wasn't in the same class as Yeats? How can you possibly say that poetry is getting better?

In any ordinary situation each of these cases would be understood as offering reasons for a claim. It would be natural and correct to represent them this way:

PREMISE 1:	Clouds are rolling in.
PREMISE 2:	The wind is picking up.
CONCLUSION:	You should go check the boat *now*.

PREMISE 1:	No decent poetry has been written since T. S. Eliot died.
PREMISE 2:	Eliot was not in the same class as Yeats.
CONCLUSION:	Poetry is not getting better.

At times we must look beyond the literal forms of sentences. If the real point of what is said is to make claims meant to be understood as premises and conclusion, then what is said should be regarded as an argument.

Multiple Conclusions and Complex Arguments

Arguments sometimes appear to have more than one conclusion. In addition, some long arguments seem to have small arguments as components. How can we reconcile these features with our characterization of an argument as consisting of a single conclusion and one or more premises? We begin by considering the matter of multiple conclusions, then look at the distinction between simple and complex arguments.

Single or Multiple Conclusions?

We said earlier that an argument can be book length. Do these book-length arguments really have just one conclusion? Also, length aside, aren't there cases where we would want to say a single argument is offered even though more than one conclusion seems present?

Here is one sort of case where it may seem we have a single argument but more than one conclusion:

> Erlich forgot to pay his gas bill again. It looks like the poor guy is obsessed with finishing the novel he has been writing. Anyway, he sure will be cold this winter.

We might take this to be a single argument with two conclusions:

PREMISE: Erlich forgot to pay his gas bill again.

CONCLUSION 1: Erlich is obsessed with finishing the novel he is writing.

CONCLUSION 2: Erlich will be cold this winter.

If we understand the argument in this way, the result is not disastrous. Yet what we really have here are two essentially independent inferences (two conclusions being drawn) with the same premise. And, in terms of sense or worth, the inferences have little to do with one another. Such independence indicates that a case like this is better thought of as involving two different arguments, not a single argument for two different conclusions.

The argument is best understood in this way:

PREMISE: Erlich forgot to pay his gas bill again.

CONCLUSION: Erlich is obsessed with finishing the novel he is writing.

And separately:

PREMISE: Erlich forgot to pay his gas bill again.

CONCLUSION: Erlich will be cold this winter.

Thus, if we draw multiple conclusions from a single premise (or set of premises), we are dealing with several different arguments. We are not dealing with one argument with several conclusions.

Simple and Complex Arguments

Now consider a different sort of case, another one where a single argument seems to contain more than one conclusion:

> Now look, everyone who has read Marx knows that capitalism cannot possibly survive into the twenty-first century, and Sanchez has read more than his share of Marx. So he is well aware of that. And if he is well aware of that, he's lying to you when he says you should start a florist shop. The man's a liar.

Clearly we have two inferences:

PREMISE 1:   Everyone who has read Marx knows capitalism cannot survive into the twenty-first century.

PREMISE 2:   Sanchez has read Marx.

CONCLUSION: Sanchez is well aware capitalism cannot survive into the twenty-first century.

Furthermore:

PREMISE 1:   Sanchez is well aware capitalism cannot survive into the twenty-first century.

PREMISE 2:   If Sanchez is well aware of that, he's lying to you when he says you should start a florist shop.

CONCLUSION: Sanchez is a liar.

Although two inferences are present, the intention in the original passage is clearly to present a single uninterrupted chain of reasoning aimed at concluding that Sanchez is a liar. Thus, in considering either the sense or the worth of the reasoning, we must treat this passage as a single unit. It is one argument, not two joined together.

⌊With such cases in mind, we can distinguish two types of conclusions. First, there are conclusions used as premises in a continuing chain of reasoning. ("Sanchez is well aware capitalism cannot survive into the twenty-first century" is such a conclusion.) We will call these **intermediate conclusions.**⌉

Second, there is the conclusion that is not itself a premise for anything else but is the argument's final point. ("Sanchez is a liar" is such a conclusion.) We will call this the **final conclusion.**

Arguments with no intermediate conclusions we will call **simple arguments.** When an argument has at least one intermediate conclusion, we will call it a **complex argument.** A complex argument can have any number of intermediate conclusions, but no argument can have more than one final conclusion.

Since to draw a conclusion is to make an inference, a simple argument can also be characterized as an argument that consists of only one inference; a complex argument consists of more than one inference.

Exercises

A. *Determine whether each passage contains no argument, one argument, or more than one argument.*

For each argument, determine whether it is simple or complex (whether it contains only one or more than one inference), pick out any premise or conclusion indicators, and identify each premise and conclusion.

The exercises marked with an asterisk (*) are addressed at the end of the book.

*1. The snow is making driving conditions very dangerous. But I must still go out and vote even though my candidate has no chance of winning.

*2. Smallpox is no longer a threat to anyone in the United States. And the vaccination against it is unpleasant and, in rare cases, life-threatening. We were wise when we ceased the routine vaccination of our children.

*3. Herbert had the highest score on the qualifying exam, and so he will get first consideration for the job. The person who gets first consideration almost always does get the job. Thus, it is pretty sure that the job will go to Herbert.

4. Someone accused of selling obscene videos has three possible defenses: The accused did not know the content of the videos; the videos that were sold are not really obscene; the law regarding obscenity is unconstitutional. None of these defenses is likely to be successful in the short run against a zealous prosecutor.

5. Since yesterday's editorial cartoon succeeded in making the mayor look silly, the cartoonist must have finally regained his touch. And the mayor probably won't be re-elected.

6. It is not difficult to program computers so that they "learn" from their mistakes. Thus, soon computers will exceed the abilities of humans at complex games such as chess or bridge. That makes it obvious that computers *think*.

7. The Mighty Mite Heater features 1500 watts of power, an adjustable thermostat, and automatic shutoff if it should tip over. It is on sale now at your local hardware or discount store.

*8. A woman complained to "Dear Abby": "My husband works for an oil company offshore. There are seven females who are now working side by side with the men on that rig, thanks to the government and women's lib! There are plenty of jobs for decent women on land, so why would a decent woman want to work on an oil rig with a bunch of men?" —*St. Louis Post-Dispatch* (August 20, 1990)

9. I know Thompson used to be a chef in a five-star Parisian restaurant. But if his béarnaise sauce doesn't improve, he's fired. And that's final.

10. You should stop killing every spider you see. Spiders help keep down the insect population, and most of them pose no threat to people.

11. Duchamp's "Urinal" is considered an important work of modern art. The thing is nothing you can't find in any men's room. Modern art is garbage.

12. Stop disagreeing with everything the boss says! I can tell she is getting angry. And you don't want to lose your promotion, do you?

13. An Oregon man said his wife had the right to commit suicide: "It's not a matter of how long you live but the quality of life you live, and it was her life and her decision and she chose. She could not do the things she loved most anymore."

14. What an idiot you are! Trying to cheat by copying from the worst student in the class!

15. As much as I hate to be on the side of the liberals, we definitely should not have a constitutional amendment banning flag burning. Such an amendment would be the first ever to affect a freedom guaranteed by the First Amendment. Besides, flag burners may think they are showing disrespect by burning the flag of their country, but by being allowed to do so, they prove to the world that this country practices the freedom it preaches.

B. *Each passage contains an argument that can plausibly be understood as having an unstated conclusion or premise(s). Determine what the argument is and supply the unstated premise(s) or conclusion.*

*1. Duchamp's "Urinal" deliberately leads us to see an ordinary object in a new and interesting way. Thus, it is rightly regarded as a genuine work of art.

2. Tomorrow is Thursday, because today is Wednesday.

*3. It is entirely right that everyone who was arrested in the raid be publicly disgraced. Melvin is a nice enough guy, but—let's face it—he *was* arrested in the raid.

4. No pit bull can be trusted around children. So we certainly can't trust Tiny with the baby.

5. It is very sad considering all her years of practice. But Hovey has used steroids, and if a person has used steroids, there is no justification for allowing that person to compete.

*6. Abortion kills a living human being. So it's murder.

7. Many philosophers have tried to distinguish between what they called *just* and *unjust* wars. But all war causes the suffering of innocent people. So there can be no such thing as a just war.

8. You spilled it. Whoever makes the mess cleans up the mess.

9. Golf is a very difficult game to play well, but it is not a sport. It does not require foot speed, stamina, or quick reflexes.

10. If the god of the Christians and Jews existed, there would not be massive amounts of evil in the world. But we all know evil does exist in huge quantities.

11. We may not like Mr. Whewell wearing the American flag as a skirt, but it is a form of expression. Thus, it is constitutionally protected.

*12. The film *Debbie's Down Duo* must be regarded as pornography. It has a lot of nudity and almost no plot.

13. You should not eat that greasy hamburger. It is loaded with fat.

14. The fraternity-sponsored "Sexy Legs Contest" must be outlawed at once. It is just plain offensive to a lot of us.

*15. Fellow jurors, we have a simple choice. As reasonable people, we can't believe this defendant should not be convicted.

16. We should all seek happiness. For we should seek that which is desirable. And happiness is desirable since it is desired by everyone.

*17. "If everything can not-be, then at one time there was nothing in existence. Therefore, if everything can not-be, even now there would be nothing in existence." —St. Thomas Aquinas, *The Third Way*

18. The police detective lied to the jury, and no one who lied to the jury should go free.

19. "A child who has received no religious instruction and has never heard about God, is not an atheist—for he is not denying any theistic claims." —Ernest Nagel, "A Defense of Atheism"

20. When I look at the coffee table, what I see changes. Looking straight down on the table it looks to be of a certain size and perfectly square. As I move farther away the size diminishes and the angles I see are no longer 90 degrees. The color is a dark and uniform brown from one side but a washed-out shiny brown from the other side as the sun reflects from the surface. What I really see then is not the table itself but something else.

21. Many of us become very attached to our animal friends and come to think of them as reasoning in the way we do. But the fact remains that without language nothing can reason in the full sense, and dogs, cats, horses, and other animals do not have genuine language.

22. Abby replied to the woman who complained about women on the oil rig (exercise A #8 above): "Any woman who works alongside a man on an oil rig is earning her bread the hard way. If she wanted to cash in on her femininity, I can think of several other jobs she could have chosen."

Chapter 2

ANALYZING ARGUMENTS

Once we have decided a passage contains an argument, we want to identify its premises and conclusion and the relationship between them. This task is not always an easy one. Arguments may deal with difficult subject matter, be stated in obscure language, or be long and complex. Nevertheless, with practice we can become skilled at analyzing arguments. In this chapter we discuss some useful techniques for dealing with difficult arguments.

Showing the Structure of Arguments

For both understanding and evaluating arguments, it is important to have clear ways of exhibiting how their sentences are related to one another.

Simple Arguments: Standard Form

So far we have shown the structure of arguments by labeling premises and conclusions. Other ways of showing the structure of arguments are more clear and more efficient. Some are variations on what is frequently called **standard form**.

We can put simple arguments (arguments with only one inference) into standard form just by listing the premises one after another, drawing a line, then stating the conclusion:

> Strikes by public employees are illegal.
> The teachers at PS 197 are public employees.
> _____
> The strike by the teachers at PS 197 is illegal.

An equally good alternative is to list the premises and conclusion, then instead of drawing a line under the premises, write three dots in a triangular pattern ∴ in front of the conclusion. The pattern of dots is the conventional symbol for "therefore."

Complex Arguments: Standard Form

We need a more sophisticated way to exhibit the structure of complex arguments. Consider this argument:

> Congress refuses to raise taxes, and so the deficit will continue to increase. Furthermore, consumer interest rates will be high for the indefinite future because the Federal Reserve Board is maintaining tight-money policies. Things do not look bright for future generations of Americans.

To exhibit the structure of this complex argument in standard form, first arrange the claims so the premises come before the conclusion they support. Do this for both the intermediate conclusions and the final one. Then number the premises and conclusions in the order in which they are written down. Finally, after each conclusion, write the number of the premise (or premises) that supports it. The structure of an argument represented in this way is immediately clear. A line without a number on its right is a premise; a line with a number on its right is a conclusion; the numbers on the right tell us the premises for that conclusion.

Applying this procedure to our example, we get the result:

1. Congress refuses to raise taxes.
2. The deficit will continue to increase.   1
3. The Federal Reserve Board is maintaining tight-money policies.
4. Consumer interest rates will be high for the indefinite future.   3
5. Things do not look bright for future generations of Americans.
   2, 4

This shows that line 2 is an intermediate conclusion supported by line 1, and that line 4 is an intermediate conclusion supported by line 3. The final conclusion is expressed in 5, and the intermediate conclusions 2 and 4 support it.

Diagrams

Diagramming is an alternative method for exhibiting argument structure. Using arrows to represent inferences, we can clearly display the connections among claims even in complicated arguments.

Consider this simple argument:

> Most people classified as *poor* are employed. Thus, talk of "welfare chiselers" is unjustified.

The argument has one premise for its conclusion. We can show that in this way:

Most people classified as *poor* are employed.

↓

Talk of "welfare chiselers" is unjustified.

The arrow indicates that the first statement is given as a reason for the second.

A more concise way of diagramming an argument is to bracket each claim in a passage, assign each one a number, and use the number in the diagram. Our example is represented:

[1][Most people classified as *poor* are employed.] Thus, [2][talk of "welfare chiselers" is unjustified.]

1

↓

2

This method also can easily show that more than one premise leads to a conclusion. An argument with two premises

[1][Computers do not feel pleasure or pain.] And [2][they have no sense of right and wrong.] Clearly, then, [3][it would be a serious mistake to treat computers as moral agents.]

can be diagrammed in this way:

$$\frac{1 + 2}{}$$
↓
3

The plus and the arrow show that both [1] and [2] are premises for [3].

If an argument contains more than one inference (if it is a complex argument), its diagram has more than one arrow.

[1][Almost all U.S. Senators, throughout the history of the Republic, have been far wealthier than the average citizen.] Thus, [2][the Senate has not been, and cannot be, representative of the needs and aspirations of the common citizen.] [3][A legislative body so out of touch should not be allowed to continue with its present power.] So, [4][the Constitution should be amended to restrict the Senate to an advisory role.]

The inference indicators *thus* and *so* make the intended structure of this argument quite clear: [1] is the premise for [2], and [2] and [3] are premises for [4]. Here is the diagram of this structure:

$$
\begin{array}{c}
1 \\
\downarrow \\
\underline{2+3} \\
\downarrow \\
4
\end{array}
$$

The same techniques can be used to build up a diagram of any argument, no matter how complex.

Strategies of Analysis

Decision procedures exist for many sorts of problems. For instance, we can give a set of rules that, if followed, will produce the right answer to any problem in long division. Unfortunately, we have no such decision procedure for analyzing arguments, no set of rules that guarantees a correct analysis. Even so, we can offer some practical advice that will increase our chances of analyzing arguments correctly. We present the advice here in the form of eight strategies to use in making an analysis. The strategies are divided into three categories.

1. Indicators and Context

a. Identify Inference Indicators Inference indicators are the best clues to understanding an argument. So the first step in an analysis should be to go through the passage being analyzed and pick out the words indicating premises and conclusions. If the argument is a long one, drawing circles around the indicator words is useful.

b. Consider the Larger Context In Chapter 1, we noticed that we cannot be sure which of the three possible interpretations of "Today is the 5th. Yesterday was the 4th." is appropriate unless we have additional information. Often the context in which something occurs provides the information we need to make such a decision. In a situation where someone expresses uncertainty about the day's date, and someone else utters these sentences, we can be sure the intention is to present the argument that "Today is the 5th *because* yesterday was the 4th." In a different context, a different interpretation might be justified.

The larger context in which a passage occurs often is enough to enable us to interpret it properly. However, in many cases we get no such help because we don't know the context. For instance, if we are unsure about what a newspaper editorial means, we are not likely to have access to information outside the editorial itself that will help us understand what its author intends. What we hope is that a passage containing an argument is clear enough so that we see what is meant.

2. Dealing with Claims

a. Identify Each Claim in a Passage Each claim in a passage should be identified. (Putting each claim in brackets is helpful.) This identification is important because any claim could turn out to be a premise or conclusion with respect to any other. Thus, if we mistakenly take two or more claims to be a single one, then we won't notice whether a premise–conclusion relationship holds between them.

"He is destitute and utterly without hope and so will end up on the streets" is a single sentence with a single subject. Yet it contains three separate claims and is an argument:

> He is destitute.
> He is utterly without hope.
> _____
> He will end up on the streets.

No harm would be done if we treated the first two lines as making a single claim and wrote them as one premise, but failing to see that "He will end up on the streets" is a separate claim would result in missing the inference. (Notice how the inference indicator *so* calls attention to the claim.)

It is important to recognize when claims are separate, but it is just as important not to divide up what are really single claims. As we will see below, it is particularly important to remember that explanations, conditionals, disjunctions, and "unless" sentences make only single claims.

b. Reformulate Claims When Necessary Sometimes we must reformulate sentences to clarify them. As we discussed in Chapter 1, questions and commands ("Don't you think you should apologize?") may need to be restated as assertions, but reformulation is necessary in other sorts of cases as well. For instance: "I don't think Dworkin is competent to stand trial. She seems entirely confused even about her own identity." This case is not just a report about what someone thinks but an argument that should be understood as follows:

> Dworkin seems entirely confused even about her own identity.
> _____
> Dworkin is *not* competent to stand trial.

Language is far too complex and subtle to allow a reasonable sampling of all the ways claims may be made. But if we are careful and sensitive, we can find and understand claims correctly, provided we do not expect them to come stated in just the way they should appear in an analyzed argument.

c. Discard Elements That Do Not Belong to an Argument If we recognize that an argument is being given, we may try to fit everything said into an analysis. The following example shows how this would be a mistake:

> Come on now. Pay attention. Marriage is an institution that should be discarded. I was married for six months myself, you know. You shouldn't listen to "Dear Abby" and those other moralists. All marriage does is make it too hard to get out of a bad relationship.

Stripping away the excess wordage, the argument is simply:

> All marriage does is make it too hard to get out of a bad relationship.
> _____
> Marriage is an institution that should be discarded.

Although the comments about the speaker's marital history, "Dear Abby," and so on look at first as if they should be parts of some argument, they are not. They serve as neither premises nor conclusions.

Statements that are not part of any argument often surround the claims making up arguments. When we analyze a passage, we must identify and discard any part of it that is neither a premise nor a conclusion. What we must discard is sometimes obvious, but deciding is often part of the further task of actually picking out premises and conclusions.

3. Structures

a. Identify the Main Argument Every argument has exactly one final conclusion. This conclusion and the premises that directly support it can be called the **main argument**. Since the final conclusion is the point of the whole argument, it is crucial to identify it and its supporting premises as soon as possible.

b. Identify Any Subargument The premises of the main argument may themselves be supported by other premises. Those premises may in turn be supported by yet others, and so on. That is, any premise may be an intermediate conclusion in a given argument. An intermediate conclusion together with its supporting premises constitute a **subargument**. We have to understand each subargument to understand the argument as a whole.

c. Identify Any Replies to Objections Subarguments that counter objections to the central argument often play an important role in supporting a conclusion. For example, in the course of arguing that addictive drugs should be legalized, someone might attempt to reply to the obvious objection that legalization would increase the number of addicts. Such a reply indirectly supports the main conclusion by removing an objection that stands in the way of accepting either the main conclusion or an intermediate one.

We need follow no special order in picking out parts of an argument. In some cases, the final conclusion may be obvious, whereas the subarguments are difficult to find. In other cases, the subarguments may be clear, while the overall point of the argument is at first obscure. The only rule here is *Do what you can as you can*. In short, start with what is clear and build from there.

Analyzing an argument is something like doing a jigsaw puzzle. Looking at the collection of pieces, we may have no idea how they form a whole. But if first we put together those pieces that clearly fit, we find we can gradually join more and more pieces until the entire puzzle has come together.

Two Special Problems

1. Arguments and Explanations

Arguments and explanations are importantly different. Explaining *why* she murdered her children is not the same as arguing *that* she murdered her children. Arguing that she murdered them must involve other claims that *give reasons for accepting* the claim. By contrast, an explanation of why she murdered them assumes that she did—takes it as a given fact that she did—then accounts for her doing it. In general, when the point of a passage is to explain *why* (rather than *that*) something is the case, we are dealing with an explanation, not an argument.

Arguments and explanations often resemble one another, and words that serve as inference indicators can also serve as explanation indicators. For example, despite the presence of indicator words, each of the following is far more likely to be meant as an explanation than as an argument:

> I don't love you anymore *because* you always make fun of me.

> *Since* you stayed on the beach all day, your nose is peeling in that ugly way.

> We are sitting in the dark *because* you forgot to pay the electric bill.

If anyone doubts that the above examples are explanations and are different from arguments, notice that what they are saying, in order, is

> The reason I don't love you anymore is that you always make fun of me.

> The cause of that ugly, peeling nose of yours is that you stayed out on the beach all day.

> The reason for the darkness here is that you forgot to pay the electric bill.

Put in these ways, the explanations do not resemble arguments at all and would not be mistaken for arguments. Each example contains a *single statement* about a cause or reason, not two statements, one of which is offered as a premise for the other.

It is not always easy to tell whether something is an argument or an explanation. Consider "Teachers assign students more work than they can do, because, if they don't, students won't do the minimal amount." Is this an argument to the effect that teachers overassign work, or is it an explanation of *why* teachers overassign work? We need to know more about the context before we can answer this question.

Even though it may not be obvious whether we have an argument or an explanation, which one we have can be of the utmost importance. Whether she killed her children and we are explaining why she did it, or we are giving a reason in favor of believing that she killed them, can make all the difference in the world in a great number of ways.

To deal with cases in which an explanation forms part of an argument, we can adopt the following rule: *An explanation that occurs within an argument should be treated as a single claim.* It can be represented as, in effect, one long premise or conclusion.

2. Conditionals ("If . . . then . . ."), Disjunctives ("Either . . . or . . ."), and "Unless"

A simple sentence like "Income rose in June" makes just one claim. Compound sentences like "Income rose in June, and unemployment declined" make two claims (or more in some cases).

But how are we to treat **conditional sentences** (sentences of the form "If . . . then . . .")? Sentences like "If the battery is charged, then the car will start" play a crucial role in many arguments, and to understand the arguments correctly, we must interpret the sentences correctly.

It may seem that a conditional sentence is an inference itself—that it makes two distinct claims, one a conclusion, the other a premise. This tempting interpretation is wrong; a conditional sentence makes only one claim. To see why this is so, reconsider the conditional sentence about the car battery. It does not assert "The battery is charged" or "The car will start." Whether the battery is charged or the car will start has nothing to do with the only claim made: *If* the battery is charged, *then* the car will start. A conditional sentence always makes a single claim (a conditional one). Thus, as a part of an argument, a conditional sentence must be treated as a single unit, as a premise or as a conclusion.

A **disjunctive sentence** presents alternatives in some version of an "Either . . . or . . ." form. The sentence "Either the roof will be patched or the documents will be damaged by the rain" is a disjunctive one. Like conditionals, disjunctive sentences contain other sentences as components, so they too may appear to be making more than one claim.

Despite appearances, such sentences make only a single claim. Our example does not claim that "The roof will be patched," and it does not claim that "The documents will be damaged." Its only claim is that one or the other of these events will occur.

Similarly, compound sentences using "unless" make only a single claim. The sentence "There will be no tomatoes in the garden unless fertilizer is applied" claims neither that there will be no tomatoes nor that fertilizer will be applied.

We can now state another rule for analyzing arguments: *A compound sentence that is a conditional or a disjunction, or whose components are joined by "unless," makes a single claim. Thus, it is always a single unit (premise or conclusion) in an argument.*

Analyzing a Complex Argument: An Example

Complex arguments may look confusing, but often they are not difficult to understand. Consider this one:

> There is a bill before Congress, S. 143, that would allow diacetyl-morphine, a form of heroin, to be dispensed for the relief of intractable pain due to cancer. This bill should be passed.
>
> The case for passing the bill cannot be denied. Diacetylmorphine (DAM) is the one drug that would best relieve the agony many cancer patients suffer. And whatever drug would best prevent this agony should be available. For such agony often leads to a severe deterioration in the quality of life of the patient and heartbreak for the patient's family.
>
> There is one objection to this bill that seems especially callous. This is that a cancer patient might unexpectedly survive and turn out to be addicted. There would be time to worry about addiction if the terminally ill patient surprised his doctors.

Three times I have seen loved ones die of cancer, and two of them were in such pain they could neither weep nor scream. Injections of heroin might have let them go in relative peace. It's not a great deal to ask.

(Adapted from a syndicated article by James Kilpatrick, *St. Louis Post-Dispatch*, June 15, 1987)

The overall point of this passage is clear: the drug DAM should be made available to cancer patients. (Bill S. 143 should be passed.) The main argument for this claim is clearly signaled by the first sentence of the second paragraph, which all but says "Here is the main argument."

DAM is the one drug that would best relieve the agony many cancer patients suffer.
Whatever drug would best relieve this agony should be made available.

DAM should be made available. (The bill should be passed.)

Furthermore, the last sentence in the second paragraph begins with "for," a premise indicator. The premise that follows *for* is clearly intended to support the second premise in the main argument. We insert this new premise, and we have

1. DAM is the one drug that would best relieve the agony many terminal cancer patients suffer.
2. Such agony often leads to a severe deterioration in the quality of life of the patient and heartbreak for the patient's family.
3. Whatever drug would best relieve this agony should be made available. 2
4. DAM should be made available. 1, 3
5. The objection that a cancer patient might unexpectedly survive is callous.
6. There would be time to worry about addiction if a patient unexpectedly survived.
7. This is not a serious objection to the conclusion (4). 5, 6

Line 7 is not explicitly stated in the original passage. Still, it is obvious that the inference from 5 and 6 to 7 (or something like it) is intended.

Since 7 is a response to an objection to 4, we can think of it as part of the overall case being given for 4. That means we could insert 5, 6, and 7 between 3 and 4, renumbering as appropriate.

On the other hand, we can leave 5, 6, and 7 in a separate group, indicating that it gives a subargument responding to an objection to the conclusion. Either method is acceptable, so long as the structure of the overall argument is unambiguously represented.

The final paragraph of the passage contains a moving personal testimonial about the pain terminal cancer patients endure. We do not see this as a further argument. (There may be room for disagreement about this.)

The argument expressed in this passage did not prove difficult to analyze. A careful, patient reading does much to ensure that even long, complex arguments become understandable.

Exercises

A. *Determine whether each passage is most likely meant to give an argument, an explanation, or neither.*

* 1. I dislike smoking. It smells bad and makes my asthma worse.

* 2. You should not smoke anywhere. It smells bad and makes other people's asthma worse.

3. The law against spitting on the sidewalk was passed because spitting is unsightly and unsanitary.

* 4. Hobart was kept in solitary confinement for over seventeen years. Then he was released and was expected to become a completely normal member of society.

5. He will surely kill again because his hatred of others has increased.

6. Herbert walks his dog every day because the dog is getting too fat.

7. Several states have passed laws allowing citizens to carry concealed weapons. And they are entirely right to do so. Law-abiding people have to be able to defend themselves against the lawless.

8. I hate the way you eat. You put ketchup on steak and have peanut butter for breakfast.

9. You have no taste at all. Your apartment is full of pictures of big-eyed children and dogs playing poker.

10. Don't move that brick! There may be a brown recluse spider underneath it, and they are quite poisonous.

* 11. Jan has been sleeping in a tent ever since her house burned down in April.

12. That truck in the ditch is there because it was going too fast in the snow.

13. Since your philosophy essay is unclear and apparently trivial, you are almost certain to flunk the course.

14. I prefer the steak to the lobster. I believe the lobster is over-cooked.

15. She has never called me since we had our only date.

16. If Fermat's Last Theorem has really been proven, many mathematicians will have to find new projects, and some-how the world will be a less interesting place.

17. She abused her children because she was herself an abused child.

18. Since an adult chimpanzee is more intelligent that a one-year-old human, the life of my chimpanzee has more value than the life of your one-year-old human.

*19. In the following, is the *first sentence* best understood as an argument or an explanation? Explain.

Allen is very ill because he was bitten by a rattlesnake. So he will survive only if snakebite antitoxin serum is made available immediately.

20. I believe that God exists because that is what my parents and my teachers in religious school always told me when I was growing up.

*21. I believe that God exists because the universe is a wonderful place of great beauty that could not have come about by chance.

22. In the following, is the *first sentence* best understood as an argument or an explanation? Explain.

Since farmers are still using sixteenth-century irrigation meth-ods, thousands are starving in the countryside. So the govern-ment should immediately begin an educational program on water management.

B. *Analyze the following arguments. Circle inference indicators and show the argument structures in standard form.*

You should not add any unstated premises or conclusions, but you should treat questions, commands, and so on that, in effect, make claims as making those claims.

1. No matter what the fast drivers think, higher speed limits will result in more needless deaths on the highway. So the speed limits should not be raised.

*2. The Cat90 is the best lawn mower you can buy. Since you want the best, you should buy the Cat90.

*3. Without a tax increase there will soon be runaway inflation. But Congress refuses to raise taxes. Thus, before long there will be runaway inflation. That means that you should borrow all the money you can right now.

4. Because Henry has started on a weight-lifting program and weight lifters are very strong, it follows that Henry will soon be very strong. And anyone who is unusually strong can make the football team. So Henry will make the team this year.

5. People who study history are wiser than those who do not. Studying history makes a person less likely to repeat the mistakes of the past, and not repeating past mistakes is a sign of wisdom. And because the primary aim of education is producing wisdom, all universities should require the study of history.

6. Never, never pass up a four-leaf clover! They are very rare because a clover normally has three leaves, and the four-leaved ones bring good luck.

C. *Analyze the following arguments. Circle inference indicators; bracket and number each statement; construct the appropriate diagrams.*

Here again, you should not add any unstated premises or conclusions, but you should treat questions, commands, and so on that, in effect, make claims as making those claims.

1. AIDS may be the most horrible disease in the world's history. It is always lethal. There is no cure. And it is most often transmitted through pleasure.

2. Higher education should increase our ability to think critically and to appreciate a greater variety of experiences. Thus, it is good to take courses in the humanities, science, and social science. So, students who take the advanced-level course in twentieth-century American poetry have made a wise choice.

*3. We should go for a hike in the canyon this weekend. The air is crisp, and the leaves are turning to lovely reds and yellows. And the exercise will be good for us, since we haven't been out all week. So, let's take the hike.

4. The hike has been nice, but we must be pretty far from civilization, because the only people we have seen in the last

three hours have been toting big backpacks. So we had better turn around before we get lost in the middle of nowhere.

5. The fate of the hikers will forever be a mystery. The *Weekly World News* said they were devoured by army ants, but not much in *WWN* is true, so probably they weren't. If they weren't, we just don't know what happened to them. So, we will always be wondering.

*6. A meter is longer than a yard. Therefore, since this ship is 100 meters long, it is longer than a football field.

7. The detective is unlikely to be a convincing witness because he has the reputation of being a racist. Probably, then, the defendant will be acquitted.

*8. If the detective really is a racist—which he is—then he never should have been allowed to testify at all, since white racists are especially unreliable witnesses when the accused is a person of color. So, the detective should not have been allowed to testify at all.

*9. The eighteenth-century philosopher David Hume was undoubtedly a finer thinker than his even more celebrated successor Immanuel Kant. Hume was by far the more lucid writer. His contributions were more diverse than Kant's, for he was a first-rate historian as well as a philosopher. Further, Hume's ethical thought did not suffer from the rigidity of Kant's. Hume, unlike Kant, would never have said the duty not to lie is so absolute that we should answer truthfully even when a would-be murderer asks where his intended victim is hiding. Thus there can be little doubt that, of the two, Hume was the superior thinker.

10. How can anyone claim that we should outlaw guns? Guns don't kill people. People kill people.

11. Dozens of people have claimed to have seen Elvis Presley since he was supposed to have died in 1978, so he must still be alive, since that many people wouldn't be wrong. On account of the fact that Elvis is alive, "Hound Dog" will soon again be a best-selling single.

12. Elvis must surely still be very fat because he is usually spotted buying food in supermarkets and so is eating a lot. If he is to be a hit on the stage now, he will need to be thin. So he will not be a hit on the stage once more unless he loses weight.

13. Here are some reasons why you should stop sniffing cocaine: Cocaine is addictive; it is likely to lead to the use of even

harder drugs, because the user will always be looking for an even greater high; rightly or wrongly, it is illegal; and it is actually quite bad for your nose.

14. John Lennon outraged many people when he said that the Beatles were more popular than Jesus. But there are real similarities between the way rock figures and religious leaders are treated. Many think Elvis is alive despite overwhelming evidence of his death. Elvis's home, Graceland, is visited as if it were a religious shrine. And the day of his death is commemorated in a nearly holy way by his followers. Obviously, then, we should reconsider the value of both religion and rock music.

15. It is superfluous to suppose that what can be accounted for by a few principles has been produced by many. But it seems that everything we see in the world can be accounted for by principles other than God. For all natural things can be reduced to one principle, which is nature; and all voluntary things can be reduced to one principle, which is human reason or will. Therefore, there is no reason to suppose God's existence. —Adapted from St. Thomas Aquinas

16. If the economic picture does not improve soon—and it won't—there will be large-scale unemployment within the next few months. So, many people will be out of work before the end of the year. That means that it will be a bleak Christmas.

17. The increase in the inner-city infant mortality rate will continue unless the government does something to improve the quality of medical care for the poor. But the current Congress is not likely to do anything effective because it opposes any intervention in the process of supplying medical care. And so the infant mortality rate will keep going up. Because many people are poor or are genuinely concerned with the well-being of the poor, this climb will be intolerable to a significant proportion of the population. Thus, under the policies of the present Congress, there will eventually be large-scale demands for socialized medicine in this country.

*18. Most people are surprised to learn that, overall, capital punishment is *more* expensive than life imprisonment. The main reason for the greater expense is that people who are sentenced to death are entitled to many sorts of money-consuming appeals of the sentence. Of course we could make capital punishment much less expensive by greatly limiting the number of possible appeals for someone sentenced to death. A result of limiting the number of appeals would be that more innocent people would be executed. This is not acceptable in a civilized society. So appeals cannot be limited much. Capital punishment must, then, remain the more expensive alternative if it is kept at all.

19. Several times the U.S. Congress has come close to passing a constitutional amendment that would allow for the prosecution of political protesters who burn the American flag. As of early 1996, cooler heads have prevailed and the amendments have failed to receive the needed two-thirds majority. This is entirely a good thing. Such an amendment addresses a nonproblem, since there have been only a handful of cases of flag-burning in recent years. The Constitution has served us well for 200 years. So, there is always a very strong presumption against changing it for any other than the most pressing of reasons. Nor can we be sure what might count as unlawful burning of a flag. Burning a T-shirt with a flag stencil might count. Disposing of a tattered flag by burning it could count, particularly if the person happened to be complaining about high taxes at the time. And a law is always a bad law if citizens cannot know for sure in advance what would count as breaking it. In short, there should be no amendment regarding burning the flag.

20. Pornography harms young people, because it presents a false and ruinous view of human sexuality. In pornography, sex is mere animal coupling, whereas in reality it must be combined with love and marriage or it is empty, meaningless, and sterile. Women are always victims of pornography. Men see the wanton actions of the women on-screen and go home and expect, even force, their wives to do the same things. Women are kidnapped and made to be "actresses" in the films. Pornography always presents women as objects, objects to be used for the pleasure of men. Since pornography damages our youth and makes victims of women, it must be stopped before it is too late.

Chapter 3

EVALUATING ARGUMENTS

The worth of any argument depends on two considerations: (1) the truth or falsity of its premises and (2) how much support its premises provide the conclusion. In this and the next five chapters we concentrate on the latter issue, considering how we can evaluate the degree of support the premises give the conclusion in various sorts of arguments.

[Deductive arguments are meant to be valid; that is, their premises are meant to guarantee the conclusion] In **nondeductive arguments**, the premises are meant to make the conclusion likely. In this chapter we discuss deductive arguments and validity first. Then we describe common types of nondeductive arguments, discuss in some detail the types most common in ordinary life, and consider ways to evaluate their worth. In the penultimate section, we discuss evaluating complex arguments, those involving more than one inference. In the last section, we broaden our concern to overall argument evaluation.

Deductive Arguments

Deductive arguments are characterized as valid or invalid. We begin with a discussion of validity then consider an informal way of testing for it.

The Concept of Validity

The word *valid* has a technical use in logic. We speak of "valid criticisms" and "valid results," but in logic, only an *argument* can be valid or invalid. A **valid argument** is one in which there is no possible way for the premises to be true and the conclusion false. *If* all of its premises are true, the conclusion would *have* to be true. The combination of true premises and false conclusion is literally *inconceivable* in a valid argument. Thus, the truth of the premises of a valid argument *completely guarantees* the truth of the conclusion.

Each of these arguments is valid:

If whales are mammals, they have lungs. Whales are mammals. Therefore, whales have lungs.

Everyone in the ward yesterday was exposed to the virus, and you were there then. That means that you were exposed.

James I was monarch before Charles I. And Charles I was monarch before Charles II. Thus, James I was monarch before Charles II.

Harold is this woman's son. So this woman is Harold's mother.

This argument is *invalid*:

Crombie was stoned, stabbed, shot, and scalped. So Crombie is dead.

It is possible, no matter how unlikely, that Crombie was treated in these horrible ways and yet survived. The truth of these premises does not guarantee the truth of the conclusion. That makes the argument invalid.

Validity, Truth, and Soundness

Validity is a matter of the support that a set of premises lends to a conclusion. It is a question of whether a certain relationship holds between premises and conclusion. (*If we grant the premises, must we grant the conclusion?*) Hence, validity does not require the premises of an argument to be true. Yet if they are true and the argument is valid, the conclusion must be true also.

Given what it means for an argument to be valid, a valid argument can have: (1) false premises and a true conclusion, or (2) false premises and a false conclusion, or (3) true premises and a true conclusion. The only combination incompatible with validity is true premises and a false conclusion.

This argument is valid despite the false first premise:

All fish read Russian novels, and tuna are fish. So tuna read Russian novels.

Although the argument is valid, the false first premise renders it worthless. It is crucial to avoid thinking that a valid argument must be a good one overall.

The following argument is valid, has a true conclusion, but is also worthless:

Idaho is east of the Mississippi River.
Every state east of the Mississippi is famous for producing potatoes.

Idaho is famous for producing potatoes.

This conclusion is true even though both premises are false. With respect to the premises, the truth of the conclusion is obviously just a matter of luck. If an argument has false starting points, we cannot expect to arrive at a true conclusion, although sometimes it may happen. In sum, we should not place any reliance on arguments with false premises even if they are valid.

By contrast, we can place the greatest reliance on valid arguments with true premises. Because the truth of the premises in a valid argument guarantees the truth of the conclusion, we do not have to count on any lucky coincidences. Valid arguments, all of whose premises are true, are called **sound arguments**. These are the valid arguments we are most interested in establishing.

Validity and Added Premises

A surprising characteristic of valid arguments is that if an argument is valid, it remains valid no matter what other premises are added. Here is a simple valid argument:

All platypuses are mammals.
Nadine is a platypus.

Nadine is a mammal.

Suppose we add new premises, getting this result:

All platypuses are mammals.
Nadine is a platypus.
Almost no mammals lay eggs.
Nadine lays eggs.

Nadine is a mammal.

We now have premises within the argument that give strong reason for rejecting the conclusion, and the argument no longer has a valid look. Nonetheless, it is still valid. If Nadine is a platypus, and *every* platypus is a mammal, we *must* conclude that Nadine is a mammal.

Another way of adding premises may still seem to render the argument invalid:

All platypuses are mammals.
Nadine is a platypus.
Nadine is a duck, not a platypus.

Nadine is a mammal.

An argument is valid if the premises cannot be true and the conclusion false. The condition is met here, because it is not possible for all the premises to be true. They involve a contradiction. The second premise asserts that Nadine is a platypus, but the third asserts that she is not. Nadine cannot both be and not be a platypus, so the two premises cannot both be true. In short, we cannot have all true premises *and* a false conclusion because we cannot have all true premises.

In general, any argument with premises that involve a contradiction is valid. Thus, even adding a premise that produces a contradiction does not threaten the principle that a valid argument remains valid no matter what premises are added. As we often find valid arguments nested in a context of additional premises, this principle tells us that we need not be concerned about these premises if our concern is only with validity.

Checking Validity

In Chapters 4 and 5 we will present formal ways of determining whether some arguments are valid. Here we will consider a useful, informal way of thinking about whether any particular argument is valid.

Since an argument is valid if there is no possible way its premises can be true and its conclusion false, one way we can check validity is by conducting thought experiments to try to determine whether there are any possible circumstances in which the combination "true premises and false conclusion" would occur. If we discover a possible case, then the argument is not valid. We can think of this as trying to "tell a story" in which the premises are true and the conclusion is false.

To see how this procedure works, consider this simple example:

Ninety-nine percent of students in the course will pass.
Patrick is a student in the course.
_____

Patrick will pass the course.

Obviously, these premises would be true and the conclusion false if, for instance, there were 100 students in the course; ninety-nine pass; one fails; the one who fails is Patrick. So the truth of the premises does not guarantee the truth of the conclusion, and the argument is not valid.

Consider a slightly more difficult example:

All the relatives of the deceased were at the funeral. So there's no denying everyone at the funeral was a relative of the deceased.

Suppose the deceased had exactly five relatives, and they were all at the funeral. Suppose, too, that several unrelated friends of the deceased were also present. Under these circumstances, the premises are true and the conclusion false, and so this argument is also invalid.

Here is one more invalid argument:

> The thimbleful of water has been in the 10° Fahrenheit freezer for twenty-eight hours. Thus, it is frozen.

Clearly, there are *possible* circumstances under which these premises are true but the conclusion false. For instance, the thimbleful of water is placed in the 10° freezer; it remains there for twenty-eight hours; *water has no freezing point— no water ever freezes*; the thimbleful of water (of course!) is unfrozen.

In evaluating the validity of this or any other argument, we must be careful to distinguish what is true from what is possible. It is not *true* that the water would not be frozen, because the freezing point of water is in fact 32°. But the given premises do not include this fact; they do not rule out the possibility that water never freezes. And since the premises of a valid argument must rule out any possibility that the conclusion is false, this argument as it stands is invalid. (If we add premises about the freezing point of water and how long it takes certain quantities to freeze, we will get a valid argument. But that does not mean this argument as stated is valid.)

In contrast, consider this valid argument:

> Some vegetarians are malnourished.
> All malnourished people need vitamin supplements.
> _____
> Some vegetarians need vitamin supplements.

We can assure ourselves that there are no circumstances in which the premises are true and the conclusion false by imagining certain possibilities. Suppose the first premise is true because there are three malnourished vegetarians. For the second premise to be true, each of these three, being malnourished, must need vitamin supplements. Thus, we have three vegetarians who need vitamin supplements, and the conclusion is true. Since the reasoning would be the same no matter how many malnourished vegetarians there might be (as long as there are *some*), we can be confident that it is not possible for the premises to be true and the conclusion false.

This informal method has limitations. If we can imagine a situation in which the premises are true and the conclusion false, we know the argument is not valid. But failing to imagine such a situation does not rule out the possibility that one exists. We may just lack the imagination to think of it. (It is unlikely we have missed any possibilities in the vegetarian argument, but not all cases are so simple.) The rigorous methods for assessing validity given in the next two chapters are helpful in dealing with some arguments that are hard to handle using the thought experiment procedure.

Exercises

A. *Decide whether each argument is valid. Explain your decision in each case.*

  *1. Harvey's mother has read Kant's *Critique of Pure Reason* many times. Herbina has never read a word by Kant. Herbina is not Harvey's mother.

  2. Everybody who watches daytime TV has a corrupted mind. Herbert's mind is just incredibly corrupted. There is no denying, then, that Herbert is a daytime TV watcher.

  3. Halliwell cuts himself shaving every morning. So Halliwell cuts himself every morning.

  *4. More than 50 percent of sex criminals have watched pornographic movies. Thus, more than 50 percent of those who have watched pornographic movies are sex criminals.

  5. All bats are mammals, and most mammals do not have wings. Clearly, then, bats do not have wings.

  6. All those who guide their lives by the horoscope column in the newspaper are superstitious. And some people who are superstitious will not stay on the thirteenth floor of a hotel. That means that no one who reads the horoscope column in the newspaper will stay on the thirteenth floor of your new hotel.

  *7. Because it is one of the most fundamental principles of physics that it is not possible for any object to move faster than the speed of light, a spacecraft cannot go faster than the speed of light if physics is right.

  8. Ten minutes ago Henrietta ingested a dose of arsenic that is unfailingly lethal within five minutes. Henrietta is quite dead.

  9. All pleasurable things are good, so all good things are pleasurable.

  *10. He hit the ground at 500 mph. At minimum, then, he must have severe bruises and a multitude of broken bones.

  11. I told Jake that if he stayed out late partying the night before the calculus final, he would fail the course. I just heard he failed. I guess that means he did stay out partying.

12. The moon is bigger than the earth, and the earth is bigger than the sun. So the moon is bigger than the sun. VALID

13. The earth is bigger than the sun, and the moon is bigger than the earth. So the sun is bigger than the moon.

14. There is no water at all in the desert. Palm Springs is in the desert. That means that there is not a drop of water in Palm Springs.

15. Tennessee needs 4 yards for a first down. If the penalty on the other team is for roughing the kicker, Tennessee gets 15 yards. If the penalty is for running into the kicker, Tennessee gets 5 yards. So either way Tennessee gets a first down.

16. All flying squirrels are mammals. No birds are mammals. So, no flying squirrels are birds even if they can soar like an eagle and dive like a hawk.

*17. Some students are hard workers, and some students get very good grades. That shows that at least some hard workers get very good grades.

18. If the medicine is the correct one, then if you take it according to directions, you will recover. The medicine is correct. Thus, you are sure to recover.

*19. XLP is a robot.
Robots cannot think.
XLP is a child, not a robot.
Children can think.
_____
XLP cannot think.

*20. XLP is a robot.
Robots cannot think.
XLP is a child, not a robot.
Children can think.
_____
XLP can think.

21. Jumbo the elephant stepped off the end of the platform and then there was nothing between Jumbo and the ground. So Jumbo fell to the ground.

22. All vegetarians are undernourished. Some undernourished people need vitamin supplements. You can't deny then that some vegetarians need vitamin supplements.

23. Since Randy has squash and beans in his refrigerator, he has some vegetables there.

24. I am going to hand out twenty pieces of candy to the students in the class. Because there are exactly nineteen students, at least one will get more than one piece of candy.

B. *Deductive arguments are arguments that are meant to be valid whether or not they succeed in being so. Decide which of the following arguments are deductive and whether they really are valid. Explain your decision in each case.*

*1. I have driven about 80 miles today. There are about .6 miles to a kilometer. Therefore, I have driven about 48 kilometers today.

2. Because a son can have only one mother, a mother can have only one son.

3. Most people who score well on IQ tests earn above-average salaries. So most people who earn above-average salaries are probably quite intelligent.

*4. Because Catholics are Christians, Christians must be Catholics.

5. Everyone takes up space, so you take up space.

6. God exists and believes that you will turn left when you get to the corner in one minute. God cannot believe anything false. This completely guarantees that you will turn left when you get to the corner in one minute.

7. It is totally dark in here, but I know the only things in the drawer are socks, ten black, ten white. I had better take out eleven socks to be sure I get a matched pair.

8. The cost of the car was $9600 and the sales tax was 6 percent. So, the cost of the car plus the sales tax was $10,176.

*9. I think I have been cheated. The cost of the car was $9600 and the sales tax was 6 percent. So, the cost of the car plus the sales tax should have been $10,076. But I paid more than that.

10. Because all birds have wings, it follows with complete certainty that anything that is not a bird does not have wings.

Nondeductive Arguments

As we said at the start of this chapter, a nondeductive argument is not meant to be valid but is meant to make the conclusion likely. In this section, we begin by discussing general features of such arguments and then look at criteria appropriate for evaluating them. Finally, we characterize several types of these arguments. (Here is an odd possibility. Suppose an argument is stated in such a way that clearly the conclusion is meant to be made likely. But in fact the argument is valid. This rarely happens, but if it should we would just note that the argument is valid and go on to ask if the premises are true. The discussion that follows applies to the more normal nondeductive arguments that are not unintentionally valid.)

Characteristics of Nondeductive Arguments

Nondeductive arguments share some basic characteristics. We illustrate three of these with the following nondeductive statistical arguments. (Note, however, that not all nondeductive arguments are statistical.)

> Ninety-six percent of adult Americans watch television more than ten hours per week.
> Davis is an adult American.
> _____
> Davis watches television more than ten hours per week.

> Seventy-eight percent of adult Americans own a VCR.
> Ebert is an adult American.
> _____
> Ebert owns a VCR.

> Fifty-five percent of adult Americans watch cable television.
> Farrell is an adult American.
> _____
> Farrell watches cable television.

These arguments are not valid even though their premises provide some support for their conclusions. The first general characteristic of nondeductive arguments is that they are not meant to be valid, but they are meant to make their conclusions *probable* or *likely*.

Next, notice that in the first argument the premises make the conclusion very probable (96 percent likely); the premises of the second do not support its conclusion nearly as well (making it only 78 percent likely); and in the third case it is barely more probable than not that Farrell watches cable television.

This illustrates the second general characteristic of nondeductive arguments. Whereas validity is not a matter of degree (an argument is either valid or it is not), nondeductive support for a conclusion *is* a matter of degree. We will say that an argument is *nondeductively successful* if it is nondeductive and its premises make its conclusion more likely than not. Of course, this is a minimal criterion for success. We prefer that premises make conclusions more than just "more likely than not."

The third general characteristic of nondeductive arguments is that, whereas valid arguments remain valid no matter what new premises are added, the addition of new information in the premises of a nondeductive argument may radically alter the overall amount of support we had for the conclusion. Suppose we add some new premises to the first of the above arguments:

> Ninety-six percent of adult Americans watch television more than ten hours per week.
> Davis is an adult American.
> *Just 40 percent of adult Americans who work two jobs watch television more than ten hours per week.*
> *Davis works two jobs.*
> _____
> Davis watches television more than ten hours per week.

Since Davis is *both* an adult American *and* works two jobs, the likelihood of the conclusion, given all of these premises, is just 40 percent. That additional premises can make this sort of difference is important in evaluating the conclusion of a piece of nondeductive reasoning. (See "Overall Argument Evaluation" below.)

Some Varieties of Nondeductive Arguments

Nondeductive arguments come in a variety of types. We will distinguish some of these here and briefly consider how to evaluate the degree of support the premises give to the conclusions.

1. Statistical Syllogism A syllogism is a three-line argument. In a **statistical syllogism,** the reasoning is from some proportion of a population having (or not having) a certain attribute to some individual within the population having (or not having) that attribute. Each of the three original "television arguments" above is a statistical syllogism. Here is one that is slightly different in that it argues that an individual does *not* have a certain attribute.

> Only 3 percent of college students know the capital of South Dakota.
> Morris is a college student.
> _____
> Morris does not know the capital of South Dakota.

Evaluating statistical syllogisms is usually simple and straightforward. The conclusion of the last argument is 97 percent probable given the premises. In general, a premise that x percent of a population has a certain attribute makes it likely to degree x that a given individual in the population has that attribute.

In most nontechnical discourse, however, arguments are not put in such precise statistical terms.

> Most people who read *The New Republic* are liberals.
> Freedman reads *The New Republic*.
> _____
>
> Freedman is a liberal.

Phrases such as "almost all of," "the great majority of," or "well over half of" frequently occupy the place of "most" in syllogisms such as the last example.

The lack of precision of phrases such as "most," "almost all of," and the like may make it difficult to evaluate these arguments. "Most," for instance, could mean anything from 51 percent to 99 percent. When such differences are important, we should try to obtain more information so we have, if not some specific percentage, at least a sufficiently precise estimate for whatever the purposes at hand may be.

2. Inductive Generalization   In an **inductive generalization**, the inference is from some sample of a population to all or some percentage of its members.

> Every wolverine so far encountered by humans has been unfriendly and aggressive.
> _____
>
> All wolverines are unfriendly and aggressive.

> In the phone survey, 58 percent of the registered voters intending to vote in the election said they planned to vote for Larson.
> _____
>
> Larson will receive about 58 percent of the votes in the election.

When is evidence adequate to support a generalization? The question has no simple answer, but we can use statistical techniques and standards to avoid gross errors. The aim is to generalize from cases representative of the population being studied (wolverines, voters in the next election). The sample is more likely to be representative if the number of cases is large and if they are selected in a random way to avoid bias. Consider a conclusion about the public attitude toward federal economic policy based on a survey of twenty delegates to the Republican National Convention who arrived by private jet. Such a sample would be neither large nor random and we would have little reason to accept the conclusion.

Finally, it is important to be aware that "induction" (and "inductive") is used in at least two incompatible ways. Often it is used simply in contrast to "deduction," so that any argument that is not deductive is inductive. We use the term *nondeductive* in contrast to *deductive* and reserve *inductive* or *induction* for reasoning that generalizes from particular instances.

3. Causal Arguments   Causal arguments are crucially important in everyday reasoning as well as in specialized fields such as medicine and the natural and social sciences. We care a great deal about reasoning correctly to the causes of our automobile not starting, of lung cancer, or of persistent poverty in our society. Because of the importance and complexity of causal analysis, we will devote Chapter 6 to this topic.

4. Arguments by Analogy   If one reasons that hamsters make good housepets, that gerbils are *like* hamsters in various respects, and so gerbils will make good housepets, then one is reasoning by analogy. Arguments of this form are common in everyday life, particularly in moral reasoning, and in many specialized areas of study. The use of models in science is a form of reasoning by analogy. In Chapter 7, we will discuss analogies in more detail.

5. Plausibility Arguments   Many nondeductive arguments do not neatly fit any particular pattern.

> The First Federated Bank was robbed yesterday.
> Kelly bought a gun two days ago.
> Kelly needed money to pay his bookmaker.
> Kelly was seen near the First Federated Bank earlier in the day.
> The bookmaker's enforcers stopped looking for Kelly today.
> ―――
> It was Kelly who robbed the First Federated Bank yesterday.
>
> Lawrence was widely praised for her acting in two films last year.
> Both of these films were huge box-office hits.
> Lawrence has never won a major award for her work.
> ―――
> Lawrence will win this year's "Hollywood Woman of the Year Award."
>
> "Howl" is superficial and dated.
> "The Second Coming" has profound social significance.
> ―――
> "The Second Coming" is a finer poem than "Howl."

The premises of such arguments are meant to work together to build a case for the conclusions, to make the conclusions *plausible*. And we would all agree that they often are successful in doing so. However, it is very difficult to formulate criteria for evaluating the degree to which the premises support the conclusion in such arguments.

One straightforward requirement for the success of any argument is that *at least some of the premises of the argument must be positively relevant to the conclusion;* that is, some premises must count in favor of the conclusion. The argument "Congressman Smith would be an excellent senator because he was born on Independence Day" fails because of its irrelevant premise. (See Chapter 8 for fallacies of relevance.)

The requirement of positive relevance aside, there are no straight-forward criteria for evaluating how well the given premises support the conclusion in a plausibility argument. We can, however, describe two evaluative procedures that can be used for any nondeductive argument and that are particularly helpful in thinking about plausibility arguments.

a. Conducting Thought Experiments. This procedure is a variation of the informal check for validity discussed earlier. A plausibility argument, like any other nondeductive argument, is meant to make its conclusion at least more likely than not, given the premises. ("His jacket was covered with blood, and he can't explain why. It is a better than fifty-fifty chance he killed her.") It is meant to show that the conclusion is true in the majority of circumstances in which the premises are true. This informal check for likelihood, then, requires one to imagine a variety of circumstances in which the premises of an argument are true and consider whether the conclusion would be true in the majority of these situations.

To see how this procedure works, consider the example of Lawrence and the "Hollywood Woman of the Year Award." Because we do not know what the criteria for the award are, we cannot be sure the premises are even relevant to the conclusion. But even if they are, we can easily imagine that another actress performed better in more films; that other films with another actress made more money; and that other actresses had been more overlooked for many years. We can also imagine other criteria for the award that Lawrence does not fulfill but others do. On the whole, then, we must judge the argument to be unsuccessful because there are so many circumstances under which the premises could be true but the conclusion false.

The argument about the relative merits of "Howl" and "The Second Coming" fares somewhat better when we evaluate it in this way. Surely some circumstances occur in which one poem possesses profound social significance, the other is superficial and dated, but the former is not the finer poem. The superficial one, for instance, could have technical merits entirely independent of its superficial content. But in most cases, a poem receiving high marks for profundity will on the whole be better than one that is rated superficial and dated. These premises do, then, give good nondeductive support for the conclusion.

b. Adding Premises. Frequently, evaluating the truth of a premise is easier than evaluating the degree to which premises support a conclusion. Thus, when it is difficult to determine the degree to which premises support a conclusion, it may be helpful to look for additional premises that *explicitly link* the original premises to the conclusion so that the degree of support is clear, and then to consider whether these premises are acceptable. This approach has the effect of changing questions about degree of support into questions about truth of premises. In following this procedure we should look for linking premises that promise to result in the best argument overall, for our aim is not to catch others in error but to examine the strongest cases that can be made for the truth of claims.

Look once more at the "Howl"–"The Second Coming" argument. If we are puzzled about the degree to which the premises support the conclusion, we can add the premise

> Most poems that possess profound social significance are finer than most poems that are superficial and dated.

Now the premises together very clearly make the conclusion considerably more likely than not. So, any puzzlement that remains must be about the truth of the premises. And we may well find the question about truth to be easier to deal with than the question about degree of support.

The procedure of adding premises is at first not easy to apply to the argument about Kelly and the bank robbery. It is implausible to say that all, or even most, people who needed money, recently purchased a weapon, and so on are bank robbers (much less that they committed that particular robbery). What we can say is that each of these characteristics is one the guilty party may well have, and so having it counts, however slightly, toward guilt. The persuasiveness of the case against Kelly depends on the degree to which he is distinguished from others by having more, or more important, characteristics that count toward guilt.

This, then, would be a reasonable analysis of the argument.

> The First Federated Bank was robbed yesterday.
> Kelly bought a gun two days ago.
> Kelly needed money to pay his bookmaker.
> Kelly was seen near the First Federated Bank earlier in the day.
> The bookmaker's enforcers stopped looking for Kelly today.
> *Each of these characteristics counts toward Kelly being the bank robber.*
> *No one else has this many guilt-making characteristics of comparable overall importance.*
> _____
> It was Kelly who robbed the First Federated Bank yesterday.

This analysis relocates our uncertainties about Kelly's guilt. Our previous questions about the strength of an inference are transformed into a more precisely focused question about the truth of the last premise. The new question should be by far the easiest one to deal with.

Neither the procedure of conducting thought experiments nor the one of adding premises is at all rigorous or foolproof. But they may be very useful in evaluating the degree to which the premises of an argument support the conclusion. And that is an important part of an overall evaluation of any argument. We will come back to overall evaluation in the last section of this chapter.

Complex Arguments

To estimate the degree to which the premises of an argument support its conclusion when they do so through two or more inferences, we (1) assess the strength of each individual inference and then (2) use these assessments to arrive at an evaluation of the support the premises give for the final conclusion. We assess individual inferences just as we would assess a simple argument: consider whether deductive inferences are valid, whether analogies are good enough, and so on.

We carry out the second step according to the following principles.

a. *If each inference in a complex argument is valid, the whole argument is valid.*

Consider the simplest form of a complex argument.

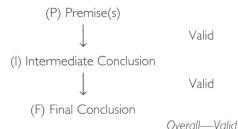

If the truth of *P* would guarantee the truth of *I*, and the truth of *I* would guarantee *F*, then obviously the truth of *P* would guarantee *F*. And that is what this principle tells us.

b. *If any inference in a complex argument is unsuccessful, the whole argument is unsuccessful.*

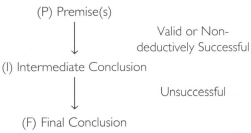

No matter how strong any other inferences are, since the reasoning from *I* to *F* is unsuccessful, the overall reasoning from *P* to *F*, because it includes step *I* to *F*, must be unsuccessful.

c. *If a complex argument is made up of one or more valid inferences and exactly one nondeductively successful inference, the whole argument is nondeductively successful.*

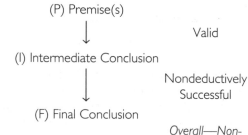

If the truth of *P* would guarantee the truth of *I*, and *I* makes *F* likely to be true, then the truth of *P* would make *F* likely to be true.

d. *If a complex argument is made up of two or more nondeductively successful inferences or of two or more nondeductively successful and some valid inferences, the whole argument may be either nondeductively successful or unsuccessful.*

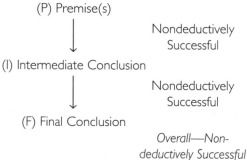

Because the presence of valid inferences can never weaken an argument, what we need to understand is why the combination of two or more nondeductively successful inferences may not result in a nondeductively successful argument. Consider this example:

1. Sixty percent of the volunteers in the arthritis study were given placebos rather than ibuprofen.

2. Cohen was a volunteer in this study.

3.   Cohen was given a placebo. 1, 2

4.   Seventy percent of those given placebos experienced increased stiffening of the joints.

5.   Cohen experienced increased stiffening of the joints. 3, 4

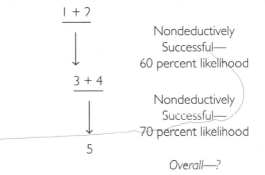

$$1 + 2$$

Nondeductively
Successful—
60 percent likelihood

$$3 + 4$$

Nondeductively
Successful—
70 percent likelihood

$$5$$

Overall—?

Determining the overall likelihood that Cohen experienced increased stiffening of the joints is easy enough. Suppose that there were exactly 100 volunteers. By premise 1, sixty of them would have received placebos. By premise 4, 70 percent *of those sixty*, that is, forty-two (of the 100 volunteers), will have experienced increased stiffening of the joints. Thus, it is just 42 percent likely that Cohen will have experienced increased stiffening of the joints, so, overall, the argument is unsuccessful.

The general point here is that in any nonvalid inference, even those that are nondeductively successful, some loss of certainty occurs, and the loss of certainty accumulates with each additional step in a series of inferences. The result may be an argument that is, overall, unsuccessful. (Of course, it need not be. If the number in premise 1 above was 90 percent, the conclusion would be 63 percent likely, and the argument overall would be nondeductively successful.)

As we have noted before, most everyday arguments are not given in such precise numerical terms, and that makes it difficult to estimate the overall degree of loss of certainty through several inferences. Nonetheless, we often have to carry out these estimations. And we can do it with enough accuracy for practical purposes if we are thoughtful and careful.

Overall Argument Evaluation

Deductive Arguments

Evaluating deductive arguments is fairly straightforward. They aim at validity. If an argument meets this aim and its premises are true, then its conclusion will be true. Thus, we need ask only whether the premises are true and the argument valid. (In some cases, if a deductive argument fails to be valid, we might want to consider whether its premises supply any support at all for its conclusion. If they do, we could go on to evaluate it as if it were a nondeductive argument.)

We evaluate validity by using the thought experiment method described above or, in some cases, by the formal methods discussed in the next two chapters. The truth of the premises might be established by some further arguments, based on experience, self-evidence, or the word of others. Chapter 9, "Reasonable Beliefs," looks at nonargumentative ways of establishing premises.

Nondeductive Arguments

Nondeductive arguments are not meant to demonstrate their conclusions, but to make cases for them, to make them likely. Thus, we must ask whether the given premises do, in themselves, make cases for the conclusions and whether the premises are true.

Evaluating nondeductive arguments is generally more difficult than evaluating deductive ones for two reasons. First, determining how well the given premises support a conclusion is (except in statistical syllogisms) far less "rule-governed" than is determining validity. This is particularly true for the nondeductive arguments we have called plausibility arguments. We have offered useful ways of thinking about degrees of nondeductive support (conducting thought experiments, adding premises), and we will resume discussion of the evaluation of causal and analogical arguments in Chapters 6 and 7. But no one would pretend that these methods have the precision of a demonstration of validity.

Second, we have seen that the introduction of new information in the premises can affect the degree to which nondeductive arguments support their conclusions. And so, when we are dealing with a nondeductive argument, we must consider whether known information that would have an important effect on the acceptability of the conclusion is left out of the premises. We saw that we would reach a false conclusion about how much television Davis watches if we did not take other information into account. Here is a case where we would ignore relevant information at our peril:

> Almost all snakes found in the U.S. are nonpoisonous. So, the little snake in my path ahead is nonpoisonous.

Suppose it is also true that

> The little snake in my path ahead has rattles on its tail.

Given this information, together with what we all know about rattlesnakes, our assessment of the conclusion that the little snake is nonpoisonous is radically altered.

Ideally, of course, we should take *all* relevant information into account in evaluating a nondeductive argument. But we do not know all the relevant information, and we can take into account only what we know. And there are practical constraints on what we can find out in a timely manner. Still, when the issue in question is of great importance, it may be necessary to do all we can to learn more of the relevant information.

We want to make rational decisions about a myriad of difficult matters: Is Kelly really guilty? Should the death penalty be abolished? Is there a god? Could everyone around me actually be a robot? Was Faulkner a better novelist than Hemingway? Will I make more money if I go to business school or law school? To answer such hard questions in a rational way we must consider arguments and counterarguments, taking into account evaluations, practical results, and plain facts. No magic formulas exist for reaching the truth about such questions, but knowledge of the critical tools discussed in this book can help us think clearly and effectively about them.

Exercises

C. *Analyze the arguments and determine whether they are valid, nondeductively successful (the premises make the conclusion more likely than not), or nondeductively unsuccessful. For those that are nondeductively successful, consider whether the premises make the conclusions barely more likely than not, a great deal more likely than not, or close to certain. (We are concerned here with the degree to which the premises support the conclusions. Assume the premises are true for this exercise.)*

  1. Eighty-four percent of regular moviegoers under the age of 30 cannot identify "Rosebud." Orson is 26 and sees lots of movies. So Orson cannot identify "Rosebud."

  *2. Five hundred of the two thousand Cactus County Public Library cardholders were randomly selected and asked whether they prefer fiction or nonfiction. Three hundred thirty-eight said they prefer fiction. Thus, you can bet that most of the Cactus County cardholders prefer fiction.

  *3. Since Xaviera has a proven IQ of 153 and is an experienced test-taker, she will do very well on the law school admissions exams next week.

4. Fewer than 2 percent of people who work in New York City live in Connecticut, so you should infer that Allen, who works in a Times Square bookstore, doesn't live in Connecticut.

*5. It is clearly the will of the people that it should be illegal to sell or rent dirty videos. I know a lot of people, and not one of them thinks this stuff should be available.

*6. Since most birds can fly, the bird over there can fly. And all flying creatures can elude any mammal. So that bird can elude the bear that is sneaking up on it.

7. I asked several other students in my Advanced Algebra class what they thought of Professor Crator's Intro to English Literature last semester. Most of them were really bored with the lit class. So, Professor Crator must be a boring teacher. I'm sure not going to take her course.

8. Dumwaith is an expert on the eighteenth century, and he is a well-regarded teacher. Therefore, he is the person best qualified for the opening in the English department.

9. The great majority of children of Republicans are Republicans. I know Teasdale's parents are devoted Republicans. So surely Teasdale is one too.

10. The Notre Dame football team is stronger, bigger, and quicker than its opponents. So, Notre Dame will win the game.

11. Hundreds of self-styled psychics have been investigated by magicians since the late nineteenth century. Every one that has been investigated has been exposed as a fraud. This gives very good reason to think that all supposed psychics are frauds.

*12. Usually freshmen do better work than seniors in Professor Cohen's course on English literature. Thus, because Harold is a freshman and his brother is a senior, we should expect Harold's work in the course to be better than his brother's.

13. Studies of the lowland gorilla in zoos have revealed virtually no cases of aggressive behavior. We can conclude that the gorilla is generally a nonaggressive beast.

14. An animal has been gnawing at my sleeping bag. Some of my trail mix has been eaten. I was awakened by something scurrying across my face last night. There are no signs of bears or other large mammals around. So, there must be giant rats in our campground.

15. Because Bodwell is a graduate of Upper Western University, and 90 percent of the graduates of UWU become Methodist ministers, Bodwell is surely a minister today. And, in a re-

cent poll, the majority of Methodist ministers reported themselves happy with their work. So, Bodwell's chosen line of work makes him happy.

*16. A popular television "newsmagazine" surveyed viewers on the question, "Should citizens who do not have criminal records be allowed to carry concealed handguns?" Callers dialed one 900 telephone number to vote "yes," another to vote "no." Each call cost 50 cents. Sixty-five percent of the callers voted "yes."

Conclusion 1: "The survey shows that the American people approve of the concealed weapons proposal by a margin of nearly 2 to 1."

Conclusion 2: "The survey shows that viewers of this newsmagazine approve of the concealed weapons proposal by a margin of nearly 2 to 1."

Conclusion 3: "The survey shows that people who chose to call at the cost of 50 cents/call approve of the concealed weapons proposal by a margin of nearly 2 to 1."

*17. A *New York Times*/CBS News poll conducted March 31 to April 2, 1996, concluded that if the presidential election were held at that time, 49 percent of registered voters would back President Clinton and 39 percent would support Republican nominee Robert Dole. The poll was based on telephone interviews with 1,257 adults throughout the United States. The margin of sampling error of the poll is plus or minus three percentage points.—*The New York Times* (April 7, 1996)

We can, then, be quite sure that if the election had been held at that time, Mr. Clinton would have won fairly handily.

18. Many people from all walks of life are energized by our pure, odorless, tasteless garlic tablets. You will be too. Try them today!

*19. CD-ROMs for Christmas? A respected computer magazine sampled 100 randomly chosen computer programs on CD-ROM and found that more than 60 of them were difficult or impossible to install on a typically configured PC. Since most CD-ROMs have installation problems, don't expect to be happily running your new program by breakfast time on Christmas.

*20. A large majority of persons who die of lung cancer have been heavy smokers. So, if you smoke, the odds are that you will die of lung cancer.

* 21. A large majority of heavy smokers develop lung cancer, and most people with lung cancer die within five years. So, since most smokers eventually die of lung cancer, you should never begin smoking.

22. Prosecutor: "This poor, mutilated man was sleeping peacefully at the time of the attack. The DNA evidence makes it overwhelmingly likely that the blood on this woman's knife is the victim's blood. No one saw her drinking at the bar where she says she was at the time of the attack. Everyone had heard her threaten that if she couldn't have him, no other woman would either. Clearly she is guilty."

23. Any cat normally found in the wild is classified as a non-domesticated animal, and cheetahs are normally found in the wild. So cheetahs are classified as nondomesticated animals. Since a permit is required to keep a nondomesticated animal in one's home, Alexander needs a permit to keep his cheetah at home. I know that Alexander does not have a permit. Anyone who needs a permit but does not have one is subject to arrest, so Alexander is subject to arrest. In this town, most people who are subject to arrest for animal violations do get arrested pretty quickly. Chances are, then, that Alexander will be arrested before long.

24. Usually a tax cut makes the people of this state very happy, and taxes are about to be cut. So, at election time next year the people will be happy, and most often that means the incumbent governor is re-elected. This governor has not been very effective in her first term, and more frequently than not a governor who is ineffective in one term is no better in a second one. It looks like we are stuck with an ineffective governor for a while.

D. *An argument may be unconvincing overall because its premises are not true, because the premises are not relevant to the conclusion or (even if relevant) do not give adequate support to the conclusion, or (in the case of nondeductive arguments) because known, relevant information is not taken into account. Explain exactly why each of the following arguments is unconvincing overall.*

1. When the going gets tough, a man can outsmart a woman. So Arnold, a man, can always outsmart his wife Emma when he really needs to.

2. There are times when any of us may need to protect him- or herself from intruders. Thus, we should all keep hand grenades on our bedside tables.

*3. Most intellectuals cannot explain the mathematical supposition called "Goldbach's Conjecture." My calculus professor is an intellectual, so he wouldn't know about the Goldbach thing.

*4. Cats are mammals, and no mammal can fly. Stop telling me your cat can fly!

5. Pierce is the best person to be put in charge of the arrangements for our club's trip to the International Debate Meet next year. After all, he does hold down the number-one position on our team.

*6. James is strong and quick and tall. We should recruit him for our basketball team.

7. It is all right to shoplift that necklace. You like it, and there is almost no chance you will be caught.

8. I was kept up all night by something barking. It must have been a big terrier.

9. All American automobiles are much better than any Japanese one. So buy a Buick, not a Toyota.

10. Arkansas is hardly a breeding ground for national politicians. Don't expect there to be a U.S. president from Arkansas in our lifetimes.

*11. If you believe in God, you will be happier. That shows that God really does exist.

12. If you believe in God, you will be happier. So, you should believe in God.

13. One way of being healthier is to work out at a gym every day. So, since you want to be healthier, you should go to Bailey's Gym every day.

14. Most undergraduate students never take organic chemistry. So, the chances are that Claude, a graduating premed student, did not take it.

*15. What you don't know can't hurt you. You won't even miss this $10 bill I am taking out of your wallet. So, it won't hurt you if I take it.

Chapter 4

SOME VALID ARGUMENT FORMS

In the last chapter we explained an informal thought experiment method for determining whether arguments are valid. In this chapter and the next we'll show how the validity of some arguments can be demonstrated by rigorous and accurate methods.

The methods use argument *forms*. It is sometimes said that formal methods of determining validity have little application outside mathematics and abstruse areas of logic. That is simply not true. The methods we will explain let us recognize immediately the validity of many practical, simple inferences and construct demonstrations showing the validity of certain longer, more complex, important arguments. Acquaintance with valid forms often has the added benefit of helping us analyze arguments, since the forms are likely to be important clues as to how the parts of an argument are meant to fit together.

Valid argument forms are not the arbitrary invention of logicians. Rather, they reflect and clarify the structure of arguments we recognize as valid when our everyday reasoning is at its best.

In this chapter we will be concerned with arguments that are valid because of their *sentential forms*.

Sentential Form

Form and Variables

Consider these arguments:

> If the presence of the anthropologist changed the normal lifestyle of the islanders, then her conclusions are not reliable. Her presence did cause such a change. So her conclusions are not reliable.

> If the spider is a brown recluse, then it is dangerous. The spider is a brown recluse. Therefore, it is dangerous.

The subject matter of these arguments is entirely different, but the arguments have similarities. In each case,

The argument contains two premises and a conclusion.

One premise is a conditional ("If . . . , then . . . ") sentence.

The other premise is the same as the sentence that comes immediately after the "if" in the conditional.

The conclusion is the same as the sentence that follows "then" in the conditional.

The arguments, then, have the same form.

If we use letters to replace the component sentences in either argument, we represent the form in this way:

$$\text{If } P, \text{ then } Q$$
$$P$$
$$\text{Therefore, } Q$$

Since the letters replace the simple sentences that make up the compound sentences of the argument, this is called the **sentential form** of the argument, and the letters (*P, Q,* and so on) are called **sentential variables** (*variables* because they stand for any sentence that might be substituted for them). We can use any letters for variables. Logicians often start with *P* and move on to *Q, R, S,* and so on. We usually choose letters that remind us of the sentences in the original argument. Also, it is customary in sentential form to use either the three-dot pattern ∴ or the line before the conclusion instead of the word *therefore.*

[Connectives]

In addition to using sentential variables, we can simplify the representation of argument forms by using symbols to replace ordinary connective words like "and," "or," and "if . . . , then . . . " that are used to join simple sentences.

Ordinary Words	Symbol	Name
either . . . or	∨	Disjunction
. . . or . . .		
Either it is a cat or it is a dog. $C \vee D$		
and, but, yet	•	Conjunction
It is a dog, and it bites. $D \bullet B$		
if . . . , then . . .	→	Implication
If it bites, then you should be wary. $B \rightarrow W$		

Sentences of the form "if . . . , then . . . " are called **conditionals** or **hypotheticals**. In a conditional, the component immediately following *if* is called the **antecedent**; the component sentence following *then* is the **consequent**. That is, in $P \rightarrow Q$, P is the antecedent, and Q is the consequent. In our example, "it bites" is the antecedent, and "you should be wary" is the consequent.

Negation

There is also a useful symbol for *not*.

not (and other ways of denying)   ~   Negation
It is not a dog.   ~D

Putting the negation symbol ~ before a variable forms its **denial**. It is like putting "It is not the case that" before a sentence. When denied (negated), the sentence "Cats like cream" becomes "It is not the case that cats like cream," or, more idiomatically, "Cats do not like cream." In formalizing arguments, use the negation of a variable for a negative sentence. (For instance, use ~C for "Cats do not like cream.")

Note that a *negative* sentence such as "Cats do not like cream" can also be denied by adding the prefix, "It is not the case that." Similarly, we can deny a negative variable, ~C, by adding another ~. But the resulting double negatives ("It is not the case that cats do not like cream" and ~~C) are clumsy and sometimes hard to understand. In ordinary speech, we recognize that we can deny that cats do *not* like cream by saying, "Cats do like cream." Instead of adding another "not," we remove the one we already have. This commonsense practice is entirely legitimate. We will treat the denial of negative variables in the same way, generally using C (rather than ~~C) to deny ~C. (The formal equivalence of C and ~~C will be discussed on p. 72 below.)

An Example of Symbolizing

This sentence may at first seem difficult to symbolize:

> If cigarette advertising leads teenagers to smoke and advertisers lie about their aims, then either cigarette advertising should not be allowed or it should be strictly regulated.

Actually, such sentences are easy to deal with if we consider their constituent parts one at a time. The antecedent in this case is

> Cigarette advertising leads teenagers to smoke, and advertisers lie about their aims.

$$C \bullet L$$

And the consequent is

> Either cigarette advertising should not be allowed or it should be strictly regulated.
>
> $$\sim A \lor R$$

Once we have analyzed the form of the antecedent and consequent, we see the form of the whole conditional must be

$$(C \cdot L) \rightarrow (\sim A \lor R)$$

Generally, symbolizing complex sentences and even lengthy arguments presents little difficulty if we take them one part at a time.

Before leaving this example, notice how parentheses are used to group simple sentences into units to prevent ambiguity. In the same way that $2 + 5 \times 3$ is ambiguous without parentheses, so too is a formula such as $A \cdot B \rightarrow C$. Does this mean "If A and B, then C" or "A and if B, then C"? Parentheses can resolve the doubt: $(A \cdot B) \rightarrow C$ gives the first reading; $A \cdot (B \rightarrow C)$ gives the second. (Very long sentences might require brackets, braces, and large parentheses to keep the reading straight.)

Exercises

A. *Using sentential variables and symbols for negation, disjunction ("or"), conjunction ("and"), and implication ("if . . . , then . . ."), show the form of each of the following. Be sure to use negative variables to represent negative statements. (We suggest letters that would be convenient to use in each case.)*

1. If the quarterback is healthy and the referees are honest, then either the team will win or the coach will be fired. (Q, R, W, F)

2. If animals are capable of feeling pain, they should not be used in surgical experiments without anesthesia. Animals are quite capable of feeling pain.

   Animals should not be used in surgical experiments without anesthesia. (P, E)

*3. If the book is exciting, then if it is well advertised, it will be a best-seller.
    The book is being well advertised, and it is exciting.

    The book will be a best-seller. (E, A, B)

4. Mick Jagger wrote an excellent new song or the song was an old reggae tune and the arrangement was new.
The song was not an old reggae tune.

Jagger wrote an excellent new song. (N, O, A) $N \lor (O \cdot A)$

*5. If Captain Kirk is brilliant or he is very lucky, then the Starship Enterprise will not be destroyed by the aliens.
Captain Kirk certainly is very lucky.

The Starship Enterprise will not be destroyed by the aliens. (B, L, D)

Valid Argument Forms

The eight argument forms given below are valid forms; that is, any inference having one of these forms will be valid. (There is no possible way for its premises to be true and its conclusion false.) As we have said, acquaintance with the forms is of significant practical value, helping us to analyze, evaluate, and construct convincing arguments in everyday life and specialized disciplines.

We give each form twice. On the left we express it in variables and ordinary connective words; on the right we put it in its most succinct form, using variables and connective symbols. We then give an example of an argument having the form. We also give the standard name attached to each form and its abbreviation.

1. *Modus Ponens* (MP)

antecedent   consequent

If P, then Q $P \to Q$

P   P

Therefore, Q   Q

The anthropologist and spider examples (p. 56 above) are both instances of *modus ponens*. Here is another:

If Smith is healthy, the Cowboys will win.
Smith is healthy.

The Cowboys will win.

Three observations may help avoid some possible confusions. First, complex as well as simple sentences can occupy the places of *P* and *Q*. An argument whose form would be fully expressed as

The fallacy of affirming the consequent → For (MT)
1. $P \to Q$
2. Q
   P

$$(P \cdot Q) \to (R \lor S)$$
$$P \cdot Q$$
$$R \lor S$$

is also a case of *modus ponens* because there is a conditional, a premise that asserts the antecedent of the conditional, and a conclusion that asserts the consequent of the conditional.

Second, the components can be negative sentences. These are also cases of *modus ponens*:

$\sim P \to \sim Q$	$\sim P \to Q$	$P \to \sim Q$
$\sim P$	$\sim P$	P
$\sim Q$	Q	$\sim Q$

Finally, the order in which the premises are given does not matter. This is also *modus ponens*:

$$P$$
$$P \to Q$$
$$Q$$

These observations apply equally to any of the argument forms given below.

2. Modus Tollens (MT)

If P, then Q	$P \to Q$
Not Q	$\sim Q$
Therefore, not P	$\sim P$

If Putnam is guilty, he is lying now.
He is not lying now.

Putnam is not guilty.

Since the second premise in *modus tollens* denies the consequent of the conditional, and P and Q are ways of denying ~P and ~Q, the following, and other obvious variations, are also *modus tollens*:

$$\sim P \to \sim Q$$
$$Q$$
$$P$$

For (MP)

The fallacy of denying the antecedent.
1. P→Q
2. ~P

3. Hypothetical Syllogism (HS)

$$
\begin{array}{ll}
\text{If } P, \text{ then } Q & P \rightarrow Q \\
\text{If } Q, \text{ then } R & Q \rightarrow R \\
\hline
\text{Therefore, if } P, \text{ then } R & P \rightarrow R
\end{array}
$$

If taxes go up, inflation goes down.
If inflation goes down, most people are better off.

If taxes go up, most people are better off.

The forbidding name of this argument is easy to remember if we bear in mind that a syllogism is a three-line argument (p. 42 above) and that this argument form is made up entirely of hypotheticals (conditionals).

4. Disjunctive Syllogism (DS)

$$
\begin{array}{ll}
\text{Either } P \text{ or } Q & P \vee Q \\
\text{Not } Q & \sim Q \\
\hline
\text{Therefore, } P & P
\end{array}
$$

or

$$
\begin{array}{ll}
\text{Either } P \text{ or } Q & P \vee Q \\
\text{Not } P & \sim P \\
\hline
\text{Therefore, } Q & Q
\end{array}
$$

Either Picasso was this century's greatest artist or Klee was.
Klee was not this century's greatest artist.

Picasso was this century's greatest artist.

The name of this argument form derives from its being a three-line argument whose crucial premise is a disjunction, an either/or sentence.

5. Constructive Dilemma (CD)

$$
\begin{array}{ll}
\text{Either } P \text{ or } Q & P \vee Q \\
\text{If } P, \text{ then } R & P \rightarrow R \\
\text{If } Q, \text{ then } S & Q \rightarrow S \\
\hline
\text{Therefore, } R \text{ or } S & R \vee S
\end{array}
$$

Either astrology is a science or it is superstition.
If it is a science, then newspapers shouldn't print horoscopes on the comics page.
If it is superstition, horoscopes shouldn't appear in newspapers at all.

Either newspapers shouldn't print horoscopes on the comics page or horoscopes shouldn't appear in newspapers at all.

A **dilemma** is a set of alternatives. This argument form uses a set of alternatives and a disjunction to allow the inference to another set of alternatives.

6. Conjunction (Conj)

P	P	or	P
Q	Q		Q
Therefore, P and Q	$P \cdot Q$		$Q \cdot P$

The tomato plants are dying.
The squash have rotted.

The tomato plants are dying, and the squash have rotted.

This form just makes explicit the obvious fact that it is valid to join two separate sentences to form a single conjunctive sentence. The following form is equally obvious.

7. Simplification (Simp)

P and Q	$P \cdot Q$	or	$P \cdot Q$
Therefore, P	P		Q

I am a sick man, and I am a spiteful man.

I am a sick man.

8. Addition (Add)

P	P
Therefore, P or Q	$P \vee Q$

Harpo was one of the Marx brothers.

Harpo was one of the Marx brothers or Karl was one of the Marx brothers.

This form may look peculiar, but it is valid. For if P is true, then of course P *or* anything else whatsoever will be true.

Two Invalid Argument Forms

Two invalid argument forms are easily confused with *modus ponens* (in which the antecedent of the conditional is affirmed) or *modus tollens* (in which the consequent of the conditional is denied).

1. Denying the Antecedent—NOT VALID

$$P \rightarrow Q$$
$$\underline{{\sim}P}$$
$${\sim}Q$$

> If Haley shares drug needles with strangers, he is at considerable risk of contracting the AIDS virus.
> Haley does not share drug needles with strangers.
>
> Haley is not at considerable risk of contracting the AIDS virus.

This argument is clearly not valid. (Perhaps Haley does not share drug needles, but for other reasons, such as his sexual practices, he is at considerable risk.) So, the argument form it exemplifies cannot be valid.

2. Affirming the Consequent—NOT VALID

$$P \rightarrow Q$$
$$\underline{Q}$$
$$P$$

> If Petrie is an atheist, she opposes compulsory prayer in public schools.
> She does oppose such compulsory prayer.
>
> Petrie is an atheist.

Again, it should be clear that this argument form is not a valid one. (Many who are not atheists oppose compulsory school prayer.)

At least partially because of their similarities to *modus ponens* and *modus tollens,* it is easy to fall into thinking particular cases of these invalid forms are valid. And, often, mistaken reasoning taking these forms has important or even dangerous consequences. (The examples just given may be cases in point.) This is just one reason why we should be acquainted with valid and invalid argument forms and be able to tell the difference.

(Denying the antecedent and affirming the consequent are often called **formal fallacies.** We will discuss fallacies in Chapter 8.)

Exercises

B. *Identify the inference form (modus ponens, disjunctive syllogism, denying the antecedent, and so on) in each case, and note whether or not it is valid.*

1. $P \to Q$
   P
   ___
   Q *valid (MP)*

2. $P \to Q$
   $\sim Q$
   ___
   $\sim P$ *VALID (MT)*

3. $P \to \sim Q$
   $\sim P$
   ___
   Q

4. $\sim P \to \sim Q$
   $\sim P$
   ___
   $\sim Q$ *commit to confirm fallacy to consequent*

5. $P \to Q$
   Q
   ___
   P *INVALID*

6. $\sim P \to \sim Q$
   Q
   ___
   P *(MT)*

7. $(P \cdot Q) \to R$
   $\sim R$
   ___
   $\sim (P \cdot Q)$

8. $P \to \sim Q$
   $\sim Q$
   ___
   P

9. $(P \cdot Q) \to R$
   $P \cdot Q$
   ___
   R *VALID (MP)*

10. $\sim P \to Q$
    P
    ___
    $\sim Q$ *INVALID*

11. $(P \cdot Q) \to R$
    R
    ___
    $P \cdot Q$

12. $(P \cdot Q) \to R$
    $\sim (P \cdot Q)$
    ___
    $\sim R$

13. $P \to Q$
    $Q \to R$
    ___
    $P \to R$

14. $\sim P \vee \sim Q$
    P
    ___
    $\sim Q$ *(DS) valid*

15. $P \to (R \vee S)$
    P
    ___
    $R \vee S$

16. $\sim Q \to R$
    $P \to \sim Q$
    ___
    $P \to R$ *valid (DS)*

17. $R \to \sim (P \cdot Q)$
    $\sim (P \cdot Q) \to S$
    ___
    $R \to S$

18. $(P \cdot Q) \vee (R \vee S)$
    $\sim (R \vee S)$
    ___
    $P \cdot Q$

19. P
    ___
    $P \vee Q$

20. $P \vee Q$
    $P \to R$
    $Q \to S$
    ___
    $R \vee S$

21. P
    $\sim Q$
    ___
    $P \cdot \sim Q$

22. $\sim P \cdot Q$
    ___
    $\sim P$

23. $\sim P \vee \sim Q$
    $\sim Q \to R$
    $\sim P \to \sim S$
    ___
    $R \vee \sim S$

24. $(P \cdot Q) \to (R \vee S)$
    $\sim (R \vee S)$
    ___
    $\sim (P \cdot Q)$

25. $(P \cdot Q) \to (R \vee S)$
    $(R \vee S)$
    ___
    $(P \cdot Q)$

C. *Using sentential variables and symbols, show the form of each of the following. Also identify the inference form (modus ponens, disjunctive syllogism, denying the antecedent, and so on) in each case, and note whether or not it is valid.*

*1. If sharks are not fish, then they do not have gills.
Sharks do have gills.
——————————————
Sharks are fish. (F, G)

2. If recent census figures are accurate, Malthus was right.
If Malthus was wrong, there will not be famine.
If Malthus was right, there will soon be world famine.
——————————————
If recent census figures are accurate, there will soon be world famine. (C, M, F)

*3. I am a sick man.
——————————————
I am a sick man or I am a spiteful man. (S, P)

4. If Hoyle's theory of why the universe is expanding was correct, then the universe had no beginning in time.
Hoyle's theory turned out not to be correct.
——————————————
The universe did have a beginning in time. (H, B)

5. Bill Gates is a fraud or he is a genius.
He is not a fraud.
——————————————
Bill Gates is a genius. (F, G)

6. Mix either killed all the people he said he killed or he is totally out of touch with reality.
If he killed them all, he should be locked up in the state penitentiary at Raiford.
If he is totally out of touch with reality, he should be locked up in the state hospital at Macclenny.
——————————————
Mix should be locked up in the state facility at Raiford or he should be locked up in its facility at Macclenny. (K, O, R, M)

7. If Aristotle was a more profound thinker than Wittgenstein, then there has not been progress in philosophy.
Aristotle was the more profound thinker.
——————————————
There has not been progress in philosophy. (A, P)

8. There are clouds.
   It is very cold.

   There are clouds and it is very cold. (C, V)

*9. If she was involved in the bombing, she won't testify at the trial of her lover.
    She won't testify at the trial.

    She was involved in the bombing. (B, T)

10. If capital punishment deters murder, then the murder rate should increase when capital punishment is abolished.
    The murder rate does not increase when capital punishment is abolished.

    Capital punishment does not deter murder. (D, I)

Showing the Validity of Complex Arguments

Here is an argument made up of two inferences, each of which is an instance of a valid argument form. We have identified and numbered each claim in the example, and after each claim we have given its sentential form in brackets. (Notice that each different sentence is represented by a different variable, each repetition of a sentence by the same variable, and the negation of any sentence by a negated variable.)

(1) If life imprisonment is as effective as capital punishment in deterring murder, then capital punishment is not necessary. [E → ~N] (2) If it is not necessary, then it should be abolished altogether. [~N → A] So (3) if life imprisonment is as effective as capital punishment in deterring murder, capital punishment should be abolished altogether. [E → A] And all the evidence indicates that (4) life imprisonment is just as effective in deterring murder. [E] Thus, (5) capital punishment should be abolished altogether. [A]

To show the argument is valid, we arrange the sentential forms into *standard form* (pp. 17–18 above). (We will again give two versions, one without and one with the symbolic connectives.)

1.	If E, then not N		1.	$E \rightarrow \sim N$	
2.	If not N, then A		2.	$\sim N \rightarrow A$	
3.	If E, then A	1, 2 HS	3.	$E \rightarrow A$	1, 2 HS
4.	E		4.	E	
5.	A	3, 4 MP	5.	A	3, 4 MP

As when we used standard form before, on the right of each conclusion we write the line(s) from which it follows. We also give the *justification* for each valid inference; that is, we give the name of the form of the inference, a form we know to be valid. It is natural, now, to think of the valid forms, *modus ponens* and so on, as **inference rules,** rules that enable us to move from one step to another in a valid way. When we have justified each inference in an argument, we have **demonstrated** that the argument as a whole is valid.

Each inference in the above argument was explicitly given to begin with. Often that is not the case. Consider this argument that might be given in reaction to rising college grades.

(1) Either students are learning more than in the past or professors are becoming more lax in their grading standards. [$S \vee P$] But (2) if students are actually learning more, their scores on standardized tests would be higher than they used to be. [$S \rightarrow H$] The sad fact is that (3) scores on standardized tests are not higher than they were in the past. [$\sim H$] The conclusion is inescapable: (4) Professors are becoming more lax in their grading standards. [P]

The argument, as given, has this form:

1.	Either S or P		1.	$S \vee P$	
2.	If S, then H		2.	$S \rightarrow H$	
3.	Not H		3.	$\sim H$	
4.	P	1, 2, 3 ?	4.	P	1, 2, 3 ?

If this is all we have, there is no justification we can offer for the conclusion. Premises 1, 2, 3, and Conclusion 4 do not conform to any of our valid argument patterns. But if we are clever we can *deduce* 4 from the premises. That is, *we can devise a set of valid inferences leading from the premises to the conclusion. And if the conclusion follows from the premises by valid inferences, then the argument is valid, whether or not those inferences are explicit in the argument to begin with.*

Here is the complete deduction for the grading argument. (The conclusion, *P*, of course, has a different number because there are now more lines before it.)

1.	Either S or P		1.	$S \vee P$	
2.	If S, then H		2.	$S \rightarrow H$	
3.	Not H		3.	$\sim H$	
4.	$\sim S$	2, 3 MT	4.	$\sim S$	2, 3 MT
5.	P	1, 4 DS	5.	P	1, 4 DS

How do we know which inferences will get us to the desired conclusion? If it isn't obvious to begin with—which it probably won't be if the argument is at all long or complicated—the best strategy is to *try something* and see if it is promising. In the grading argument, the only valid form we can use at the outset is MT with 2 and 3, and so we try it. Then the valid step to the conclusion should be obvious. (Failing to find a valid deduction does not necessarily mean there is not one; it may be we just failed to find it.)

Exercises

D. *Using sentential variables and symbols, put the following arguments in standard form. Be sure to cite the lines from which each conclusion follows and give its* justification. *(The capital punishment argument above can serve as a model for the form in which these arguments should be expressed.)*

*1. (1) If Harvey did not win the croquet tournament, then either his mallet was broken or Mary has been taking lessons. (2) Harvey did not win the competition. So, (3) either Harvey's mallet was broken or Mary has been taking lessons. But (4) Mary has not taken any lessons. Thus, (5) Harvey's mallet was broken. (H, B, L)

2. (1) If the private industrial sector had been willing and able to install effective scrubbers in smokestacks, harmful emissions would not now be a problem. Further, (2) if these emissions were not now a problem, there would not be ongoing damage to the environment. And so, (3) if the private sector had been willing and able to install the scrubbers, there would not be ongoing damage to the environment. But it is entirely clear that (4) there is ongoing damage to the environment. (5) The private sector, then, has just not been willing and able to install effective scrubbers. (6) If it has not been willing and able to install these devices up until now, it will not change its ways in the future regarding the control of pollution. Thus, (7) it will not change its ways in this regard. But there are really only two possibilities: (8) Either the private industrial sector will change its ways in the future or there must be strict governmental regulation of industry when the environment is at issue. As regrettable as some may find it, (9) there must be strict governmental regulation of industry when the environment is at issue. (P, E, D, C, G)

E. *Using sentential variables and symbols, show that the conclusions follow from the premises by a series of valid inferences. Be sure to cite the lines from which each conclusion follows and give its* justification. *(The grading argument on p. 68 above can serve as a model for these exercises.)*

Find two different ways of reaching the conclusions in #3, #5, #6, and #13.

We will start with two arguments you have already symbolized (pp. 59–60 above).

*1. If the book is exciting, then if it is well advertised, it will be a best-seller.
The book is being well advertised, and it is exciting.
____
The book will be a best-seller. (E, A, B)

2. If Captain Kirk is brilliant or he is very lucky, then the Starship Enterprise will not be destroyed by the aliens.
Captain Kirk certainly is very lucky.
____
The Starship Enterprise will not be destroyed by the aliens. (B, L, D)

3. If *Moby Dick* is an important novel, then you should study it.
If you should study *Moby Dick,* it would be smart for you to sign up for English 433.
Moby Dick is an important novel.
____
It would be smart to sign up for English 433. (M, S, E)

4. If my grass won't grow, either the soil contains too much acid or I am using the wrong fertilizer.
The soil tests out OK, but the grass doesn't grow.
____
I am using the wrong fertilizer. (G, S, F)

*5. If killing is always wrong, then war is always wrong.
If war is always wrong, then we should have allowed Hitler to rule the world.
We should not have allowed Hitler to rule the world.
____
Killing is not always wrong. (K, W, H)

Constructive dilemma

*6. Either we have been put here for some special purpose or life has no meaning.
If we have been put here for a special purpose, we know what the purpose is.
If life has no meaning, most of us live in quiet despair.
We do not know what the purpose of life is.
____
Most of us live in quiet despair. (P, M, K, D)

$P \lor \sim M$
$P \to K$
$\sim M \to D$
$\sim K$
____
D

7. Either there will soon be a vaccine to prevent AIDS or a massive "safe sex" educational campaign is required. If the medical establishment is correct, there will not be a vaccine in the immediate future. Unfortunately, there is little doubt that the doctors are correct this time. But if a large-scale educational campaign is required, the prospects are not bright due to the costs involved. The prospects, then, are not at all bright. (V, E, M, P)

8. $\sim P \rightarrow \sim Q$
Q
$P \rightarrow S$
—————
S

*9. $P \rightarrow Q$
$P \vee R$
S
$S \rightarrow \sim Q$
—————
R

10. $P \rightarrow Q$
$\sim Q \vee R$
$\sim R$
—————
$\sim P$

11. $P \rightarrow (Q \vee R)$
$\sim Q \cdot P$
—————
R

12. $P \rightarrow \sim Q$
$P \vee S$
$\sim Q \rightarrow R$
$S \rightarrow T$
—————
$R \vee T$

13. Q
$Q \rightarrow \sim R$
P
$\sim R \rightarrow S$
—————
$P \cdot S$

⌈ Conditionals ⌉

Since several of the valid argument forms involve the use of conditionals, we must be able to recognize and deal with conditional sentences even when they're not stated precisely in the "If *P*, then *Q*" form. Clearly

Q if P means $P \rightarrow Q$.

More surprising, in the "only if" locution, the word *if* immediately precedes the *consequent* of the conditional.

P only if Q means $P \rightarrow Q$.

For instance, in

Tom is a cat only if Tom is a mammal

"Tom is a mammal" is the consequent, and the meaning of the sentence is the same as the meaning of "If Tom is a cat, then Tom is a mammal." This equivalence makes sense. Since being a mammal is a *requirement* for being a cat, then Tom is a cat *only if* Tom is a mammal. And, *if* Tom is a cat, he *must* be a mammal.

It is easy to become confused when dealing with sentences using "only if," but we can avoid the confusion by remembering that

P only if Q means $P \rightarrow Q$.

Ordinary English contains yet other ways of expressing conditionals.

P provided that Q means $Q \rightarrow P$.

She will win the election provided that she debates well.

means

If she debates well, then she will win the election.

P unless Q means $\sim Q \rightarrow P$.

The grass will die unless there is rain soon.

means

If there is not rain soon, the grass will die.

Equivalent Forms

We observed before that it is seldom necessary in arguments to use clumsy sentences such as "It is not the case that cats do not like cream," because the clearer "Cats like cream" has the same meaning. We can rephrase this idea now by saying that the sentences are *equivalent,* for neither one can be true unless the other is. That is,

$C \rightarrow \sim\sim C$ and $\sim\sim C \rightarrow C$.

If we take it that the arrow can go either way, we can express the equivalence relationship most succinctly as

$C \leftrightarrow \sim\sim C$.

(The double arrow is usually read as "if and only if," often abbreviated as "iff.")

When two forms are equivalent, we can infer either one from the other. Thus, knowing equivalent forms puts another supply of valid inferences at our disposal and increases our ability to evaluate and construct arguments. Like *modus ponens* and the other valid forms discussed above, equivalences can be thought of as inference *rules* because they justify valid argument steps. Here are six equivalent forms. (Symbols should be familiar enough now so that we can dispense with ordinary language connectives and negations.)

1. Double Negation (DN)

$P \leftrightarrow \sim\sim P$

This just makes explicit the equivalence discussed before.

2. Commutation (Com)

$(P \cdot Q) \leftrightarrow (Q \cdot P)$
The chairman is a convicted felon, and he is a moral pervert.

>   is equivalent to

The chairman is a moral pervert, and he is a convicted felon.

Also, $(P \vee Q) \leftrightarrow (Q \vee P)$
Either April is the cruelest month or December is.

>   is equivalent to

Either December is the cruelest month or April is.

3. Contraposition (Contra)

$(P \rightarrow Q) \leftrightarrow (\sim Q \rightarrow \sim P)$
If the Biblical account of creation is correct, then the scientific account is wrong.

>   is equivalent to

If the scientific account of creation is not wrong, then the Biblical account is *incorrect*.

Both contraposition and *modus tollens* involve a conditional and the negation of its consequent. To avoid confusing them, remember that in *modus tollens* we infer to the negation of the antecedent. In contraposition, we *contrapose* the component sentences of a conditional and end with another conditional.

4. Definition of Implication (Imp)

$(P \vee Q) \leftrightarrow (\sim P \rightarrow Q)$
Either judges are being too lenient in their sentencing or parole boards are behaving irresponsibly.

>   is equivalent to

If judges are not being too lenient in their sentencing, then parole boards are behaving irresponsibly.

To see that these forms are equivalent, consider that $(P \lor Q)$ says that either P is true or Q is true. So, if P is not true, then Q is. And that is what $(\sim P \to Q)$ says.

5. Exportation (Exp)

$[(P \cdot Q) \to R] \leftrightarrow [P \to (Q \to R)]$

If the tire is flat, and the spare is missing, then you must walk.

is equivalent to

If the tire is flat, then if the spare is missing, then you must walk.

To export something is to send it out. This rule tells us we can send out one of the sentences in a conjunction that appears in the antecedent of a conditional.

6. De Morgan's Rules (DM)

There are two of them. The first is:

$\sim(P \cdot Q) \leftrightarrow (\sim P \lor \sim Q)$

Oh, come now. It can't be *both* that Darwell works for the CIA *and* that he is employed by the FBI.

is equivalent to

Either Darwell does not work for the CIA or he does not work for the FBI.

This form is not nearly as mysterious as it may first appear. It says that *not both* P *and* Q *are true* is equivalent to *either* P *is not true or* Q *is not true.*

The second De Morgan equivalence is

$\sim(P \lor Q) \leftrightarrow (\sim P \cdot \sim Q)$

It just isn't true either that Ellis will have a competent attorney appointed by the court or that he will be able to defend himself.

is equivalent to

Ellis will not have a competent attorney appointed by the court, and Ellis will not be able to defend himself.

This form says that *it is not the case that either* P *or* Q *is true* (neither is true) is equivalent to *both* P *and* Q *are false.*

If we should become confused about a De Morgan equivalence, there is a simple mechanical way to proceed. Change everything! For instance, starting with $\sim(P \lor \sim Q)$, drop the negation sign outside the parentheses, getting $(P \lor \sim Q)$. Change the signs of the component sentences, getting $(\sim P \lor Q)$. And change the disjunction to a conjunction, getting $(\sim P \bullet Q)$. Thus, we see that $\sim(P \lor \sim Q)$ is equivalent to $(\sim P \bullet Q)$.

Following these simple steps will infallibly result in producing a De Morgan equivalent of any conjunctive or disjunctive sentence.

Using Inference and Equivalence Rules

Finally, consider this argument:

> (1) If women are paid less than men, and sexism is not the reason, it must be that women are not as good at their jobs as men are. $[(L \bullet \sim S) \to \sim G]$ (2) Women are paid less, but there is not a shred of truth to the charge that they are not as good at their jobs as men. $[L \bullet \sim\sim G]$ So, (3) there is clearly sexism at work here. $[S]$

That is,

1. $(L \bullet \sim S) \to \sim G$
2. $L \bullet \sim\sim G$
   _____
3. S

Let's see if we can deduce the conclusion from these premises.

Looking for a starting point, we see we can easily develop a step of *modus tollens*. We will try this and see if it proves useful. (If it doesn't work out, at worst we will have wasted a little time.)

1. $(L \bullet \sim S) \to \sim G$
2. $L \bullet \sim\sim G$
3. $\sim\sim G$ 2 Simp
4. $\sim(L \bullet \sim S)$ 1, 3 MT

What might we do now? Since the first negation sign in line 4 goes with everything inside the parentheses *as a unit*, we cannot deal with L or $\sim S$ as individual variables as long as they appear within the parentheses. It would be a promising strategy then to change line 4 in such a way that we could deal independently with the individual variables. Fortunately, we now have a way to make a change of this sort.

5. $\sim L \lor S$ 4 DM

Since L was part of premise 2, another step of simplification leads to L, and L combined with 5 gives the conclusion we were after.

The entire deduction, then, is as follows:

1. $(L \cdot \sim S) \to \sim G$
2. $L \cdot \sim\sim G$
3. $\sim\sim G$ 2 Simp
4. $\sim(L \cdot \sim S)$ 1, 3 MT
5. $\sim L \lor S$ 4 DM
6. L 2 Simp
7. S 5, 6 DS

As we have said, being able to construct and recognize valid arguments is a skill, and developing it requires practice. Honing the skill and applying it in the everyday world also requires a certain turn of mind, a habit of looking at arguments with a constantly careful and critical eye. The more we do this, the better we will be able to construct our own valid arguments, to recognize whether the arguments of others are valid, and to avoid being taken in by arguments that appear to be valid but are not.

Exercises

F. *Identify alternate ways of expressing the conditionals.*

1. Which of the following are ways of expressing the conditional, "If she is telling the truth, then she is innocent"?
   a. She is innocent if she is telling the truth.
   b. If she is innocent, then she is telling the truth.
   c. She is innocent only if she is telling the truth.
   d. She is telling the truth only if she is innocent.
   e. Only if she is innocent is she telling the truth.

*2. Which of the following are ways of expressing the conditional, "If the knots are secure, escape is impossible"?
   a. The knots are secure, and escape is impossible.
   b. Escape is impossible provided that the knots are secure.
   c. The knots are secure unless escape is impossible.
   d. Escape is impossible unless the knots are not secure.
   e. The knots are secure provided that escape is impossible.

G. *Using sentential variables and symbols, show the form of each of the following. Also identify the inference form (modus ponens, contraposition, definition of implication, and so on) in each case and note whether or not it is valid.*

1. There will be peace in our time only if the great nations conclude that peace is in their self-interests. And they will reach this conclusion only if they sit down and talk to one another. So there will be peace in our time only if the great nations sit down and talk to one another. (P, N, T)

*2. If the earthquake was not severe, life will go on as usual.

   If life will not go on as usual, the earthquake was severe. (E, L)

3. If we have to know what an artist was thinking in order to understand the work of art, then its meaning cannot be known. Thus, if the meaning of the work can be known, we do not have to know what the artist was thinking in order to understand it. (T, K)

*4. It just isn't true that capital punishment will be abolished and also the murder rate will go down. So, either capital punishment will not be abolished or the murder rate will not go down. (A, D)

5. If you have no cash, then, if your credit card has expired, you will have to sleep in the park.

   If you have no cash and your credit card has expired, you will have to sleep in the park. (C, E, S)

*6. If you don't shape up, you will ship out.

   Either you will shape up or ship out. (S, O)

7. Watson: I tried to tell them that it is a vampire or it is a werewolf. But they deny that.

   Holmes: They deny that either it is a vampire or a werewolf? Interesting. So, they think it is not a vampire and not a werewolf. I wonder what they think it is. (V, W)

8. If we have to know what an artist was thinking in order to understand a work of art, then the meaning of a work can never be known. But obviously we often do know the meaning of works of art. So, we do not have to know what an artist was thinking to understand works of art. (U, K)

9. What she used in the casino was either a $1000 bill or it was an incredibly good imitation. So, if it wasn't a $1000 bill, it must have been an incredibly good imitation. (B, I)

10. Many people have looked at the suffering in the world and have concluded that either God is not good or God is not powerful. So, they think, God is not both powerful and good. (G, P)

H. *Using sentential variables and symbols, show that the conclusions follow from the premises by a series of valid inferences. Be sure to cite the lines from which each conclusion follows and give its justification.*

   Find two different ways of reaching the conclusions in #5, #6, and #7.

*1. The AIDS panel will be perceived as balanced only if it includes leaders of the gay community. And it will include leaders of the gay community only if pressure is brought to bear on politicians. Thus, the panel will be perceived as balanced only if the pressure is brought to bear. Because no one will be able to bring about pressure on politicians, the panel will not be perceived as balanced. Clearly, the AIDS panic will continue to increase if this panel is not perceived as balanced. And so, sadly, the AIDS panic will continue to increase. (B, L, P, I)

2. If Blakely is the thief, then either the jewels are hidden in his bureau drawer or they are hidden in his old sneakers. The jewels are not hidden in Blakely's old sneakers. And they are not hidden in his bureau drawer. So Blakely is not the thief. (T, B, S)

*3. If today is Friday, then if it is the thirteenth, it is not a lucky day.
   Actually, it is a lucky day.

   Either today is not Friday or it is not the thirteenth. (F, T, L)

4. If it is not true that a strike by the teachers will both harm their image among the local members of the Steelworkers' Union and cause them to lose the support of white-collar workers in the community, then the teachers should strike. But either a strike by the teachers will not harm their image among the steelworkers or it will not cause them to lose the support of the local white-collar workers. Therefore, the teachers should strike. (H, L, S)

5. If William Bligh is made Captain of the *Bounty,* then he will be unhappy if Fletcher Christian is not made First Mate. He will be made Captain, and Christian will not be made First Mate. So, Captain Bligh will be unhappy. (B, U, F)

*6. If the prosecution did a good job of presenting the evidence, and the jury gave due deliberation, the defendant would have been found guilty of murder. The prosecution did do a good job, but the defendant was acquitted on all counts. Thus, the jury did not give due deliberation. (P, J, D)

7. If the governor is going to wear a monkey costume when he objects to the teaching of evolution in schools, then if the legislators listen to him, they are all manifest fools. He is going to wear the monkey suit, but many of the legislators aren't fools at all. So, the legislators will not listen to the governor. (G, L, F)

8. If we should seek only the good, and happiness is the only good, then we should seek only happiness. It is surely not true that we should seek only happiness. So, if we should seek only the good, then it is false that happiness is the only good. (G, H, S)

9. $(\sim P \vee Q) \to \sim(R \bullet \sim S)$
   R
   $\sim P$
   ———————————
   S

10. $\sim(P \bullet Q) \to (R \to S)$
    $\sim P \vee \sim Q$
    $\sim S$
    ———————————
    $\sim R$

*11. $Q \vee (R \bullet S)$
    $\sim Q$
    $S \to (T \vee U)$
    ———————————
    $\sim T \to U$

12. $\sim(P \bullet Q) \to R$
    $\sim Q \to S$
    $\sim R \bullet \sim P$
    ———————————
    $S \vee T$

13. $\sim(\sim P \bullet \sim Q) \to R$
    P
    ———————————
    R

Atomic sentences or simple sentences
compound sentences

Chapter 5

MORE VALID ARGUMENT FORMS: CATEGORICAL REASONING AND VENN DIAGRAMS

In the previous chapter we saw how some arguments are valid because of their sentential form—that is, because of formal relationships between whole sentences. For instance, *modus ponens,*

If *P*, then *Q*
P
———
Q

is valid because the complete sentences represented by *P* and *Q* occur in the way they do in the premises and the conclusion. Now we will show that arguments can be valid because of the *relationships between the terms within the sentences* of arguments.

Categorical Statements

Many everyday sorts of statements put things into **categories** or **classes.** "All trout are fish" says that anything included in the category (class) *trout* is also included in the category (class) *fish*. "Some numbers are even" says that some of the members of the category *numbers* are also members of the category *even numbers*. "Moby Dick is a whale" says this individual is a member of the class *whales*. Other familiar sorts of statements *exclude* things from classes or categories. "No dogs are reptiles" excludes every member of the class *dogs* from the class *reptiles*. *Categorical statements* such as these enter into some reasoning patterns whose validity or invalidity we can conclusively demonstrate. (Often we use adjectives just as a sort of shorthand to put things into categories. "All dogs are lovable" can mean "All dogs are lovable animals.")

The easiest and perhaps most commonsensical way of showing validity or invalidity in categorical reasoning is to construct intersecting circles to form Venn diagrams (named for the nineteenth–twentieth century logician John Venn, who devised the method). Let's begin with a diagram of the single statement "All trout are fish." We need one circle to represent the category *trout*

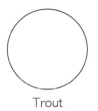

Trout

and another circle to represent the category *fish*.

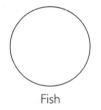

Fish

Anything within the first circle is a trout, and anything within the second circle is a fish.

Since we want to represent the relationship between the trout and the fish categories, we must connect the circles so they overlap.

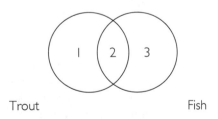

Trout   Fish

The section called "1" here (Venn diagrams do not really contain such numbers) is within the trout circle but not within the fish circle, so it contains everything that is a trout but not a fish. Section 3, being within the fish circle only, includes all things that are fish but not trout. The intersection, "2," is within both circles, so it contains all and only things that are *both* trout and fish.

Now it is easy to use the diagram to represent "All trout are fish." Since section 1 would contain things that are trout but not fish, section 1 is *empty;* it has no members. We show that a section of a diagram is empty by shading it. So, we shade out section 1 and have

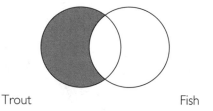

Trout   Fish

This shows that all the trout there are within the fish circle—that is, "All trout are fish."

To this point all we have is a picture. It is not a particularly pretty picture, but it is a very useful one. Suppose we wonder whether "All trout are fish" means the same thing as (in logic terms, is *equivalent to,* p. 72 above) "No trout are not fish." A quick look back at the last diagram shows that it does mean just that. Since in that diagram of "All trout are fish" we have shaded out just the trout-not-fish area, "All trout are fish" must mean just what "No trout are not fish" means.

Suppose instead that somehow we are not sure if

All trout are fish.
———————————————
All fish are trout.

is valid. Inspecting the "All trout are fish" Venn diagram again shows clearly that it is not. Section 3, the fish-not-trout section of the diagram, is not shaded out. So, given the premises, there can be fish that are not trout. The premises can be true while the conclusion is false, which means the inference is not valid.

No one is likely to make the "Trout are fish so fish are trout" mistake, but mistakes like it are too frequent. We often hear "All users of hard drugs started with marijuana" cited to show that all users of marijuana become users of hard drugs. Or that "All sex criminals use pornography" proves that all users of pornography become sex criminals. The Venn diagrams for the premises in these cases are exactly like the diagram for "All trout are fish," and the inferences are not valid for the same reason: section 3, the one on the right, is not shaded out. The diagram for "All sex criminals use pornography" is

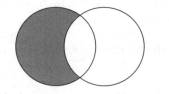

Sex Criminals   Pornography Users

which clearly does not validly imply "All pornography users are sex criminals," since there is an unshaded portion of pornography users who are not sex criminals. And the Venn diagram for "All hard drug users use marijuana" does not show "All users of marijuana are hard drug users."

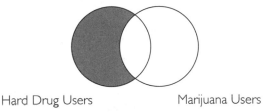

Hard Drug Users   Marijuana Users

The popular inferences about drugs and pornography may be appealing, but the most basic use of Venn diagrams shows that they are *just wrong.*

Categorical statements that *exclude* members of one class from another class are easily understood. Statements like "No snakes are mammals" say that anything that is a snake is *not* a mammal. This means that in the Venn diagram the part of the snake circle that intersects the mammal circle must be shaded out. (From now on we will label the circles with convenient letters rather than whole words.)

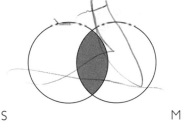

S   M

What would the Venn diagram for "No mammals are snakes" look like? We shade out any part of the mammal circle that intersects the snake circle.

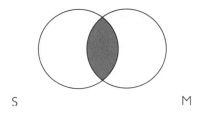

S   M

Since the diagrams are identical, "No snakes are mammals" and "No mammals are snakes" are saying the same thing (are *equivalent*).

Categorical statements may not be about *all* Xs or *no* Xs but rather about *some* Xs. "Some students are females" and "Some politicians are not honest" are examples. To understand statements like these, first we need to know that in logic "some" means "at least one." In everyday talk, "some" may mean "several but not all." An announcement that some students passed the test would likely not be taken to mean that just one student out of 500 passed nor that all 500 passed. But in logic, the statement is true if one student, several students, or all students passed. It is false only if no student passed. (As long as we know this, it causes no problems.)

In Venn diagrams, we show that some (at least one) *S* is or is not *F* by putting a mark (for instance, an asterisk) in the relevant section of the diagram. The diagram for "Some students are female" would be

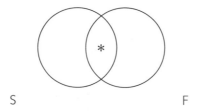

The diagram for "Some females are students" would be just the same, and so they are equivalent and we can infer either one from the other. The diagram for "Some politicians are not honest," on the other hand, would be

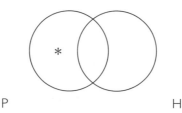

(It may seem that we never need to use the asterisk, since a diagram like the one for "All trout are fish"

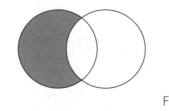

already shows that some [*all* in this case] trout are fish and some fish are trout. But according to modern logic the diagram shows no such thing. "All trout are fish" says that anything that is a trout is a fish. It does not say that there exists anything that actually is either a trout or a fish. This makes good sense. "All unicorns have one horn" says that anything that is a unicorn is a one-horned creature. It does *not* say there really are any such things as unicorns or one-horned animals. On the other hand, "*Some* trout are fish" and "*Some* unicorns have one horn" do say that *there exist* trout that are fish and unicorns that have one horn. And that is what the asterisk means in the Venn diagrams. Of course a segment of a diagram cannot both be shaded and contain an asterisk.)

Exercises

A. *Draw a Venn diagram for each of the following. Determine which of the statements are equivalent.*

* 1. All snakes are reptiles.
* 2. No snakes are not reptiles.
* 3. All reptiles are snakes.
  4. Some snakes are reptiles.
  5. Some reptiles are not snakes.
* 6. A few reptiles are snakes.
  7. No snakes are reptiles.
  8. All snakes are not reptiles.
  9. Some reptiles are snakes.
* 10. Only reptiles are snakes.
  11. No reptiles are not snakes.
  12. Some snakes are not reptiles.
  13. No reptiles are snakes.
  14. All reptiles are not snakes.
  15. Some things that are not reptiles are snakes.
  16. Snakes are the only reptiles.
  17. All nonsnakes are nonreptiles.

Categorical Syllogisms

Categorical syllogisms are syllogisms (p. 42 above) that have two premises and a conclusion, all of which are categorical statements.

> All lawyers are educated people.
> All educated people are clever people.
> _____
> All lawyers are clever people.

> All bankers are wealthy.
> No wealthy people are happy.
> _____
> No bankers are happy.

> Some novelists are astute observers.
> All astute observers are reliable witnesses.
> _____
> Some novelists are reliable witnesses.

In order to evaluate such arguments, we diagram the premises together and then see whether the result shows the truth of the conclusion. The basics of Venn diagrams that we have already seen give us what we need to construct the diagrams.

We will take each of the above arguments in turn.

> All lawyers are educated people.
> All educated people are clever people.
> _____
> All lawyers are clever people.

We must have three interlocking circles to represent the relationships between the categories in the three statements. Putting the circles for the conclusion at the bottom (this is not necessary but it is usual and helpful), first we have

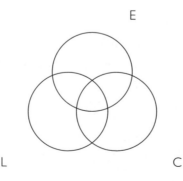

Ignore the *C* circle for the moment and shade the lawyer-not-educated area to represent the information given in the first premise.

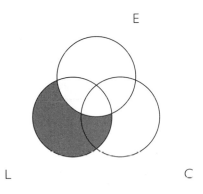

Look just at the *E* and *C* circles and do the same for the second premise, "All educated people are clever people."

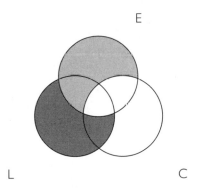

The diagram now represents all of the information given in the premises. What does this tell us about the conclusion? The *L* and *C* circles represent the conclusion, "All lawyers are clever." The only nonshaded, that is, nonempty, area of the *L* circle is within part of the *C* circle, so all lawyers are clever. We might say that, after taking into account all the information in the premises, "the only lawyers left" are the clever ones. So the truth of the premises guarantees the truth of the conclusion. The argument is shown to be *valid*.

Turning to the second of the examples above:

All bankers are wealthy.
No wealthy people are happy.

No bankers are happy.

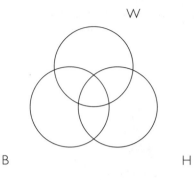

The first premise gives

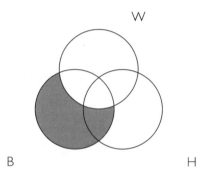

Now we shade in accordance with the second premise.

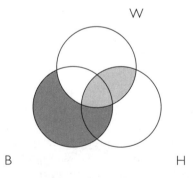

Since the entire overlap between the B and H circles now is shaded out, the premises do show that no bankers are happy, and the argument is *valid*.

The third example is

Some novelists are astute observers.
All astute observers are reliable witnesses.

Some novelists are reliable witnesses.

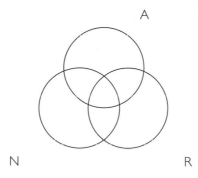

We will use the asterisk to indicate "Some novelists are astute observers." But since the overlap between *novelists* and *astute observers* is divided into two parts, we do not know just where to put the asterisk. (Look carefully at the blank diagram above to see that this is so.) This brings out the general rule that we should *begin with any premise of universal form.* Here we start with "All astute observers are reliable witnesses."

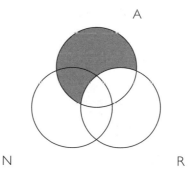

Now we have only one possible place to put the asterisk, in the one unshaded area of the *N* and *A* intersection.

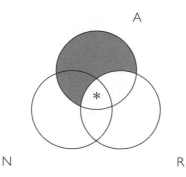

Since the asterisk is within the intersection of *N* and *R,* the premises show that at least one member of *N* is a member of *R.* So, the truth of "Some novelists are reliable witnesses" is dictated by the premises, and the argument is *valid.*

Of course not all categorical syllogisms are valid. When they are not, Venn diagrams tell us that too.

All works of art are profound.
No cartoons are works of art.
──────────────────────────
No cartoons are profound.

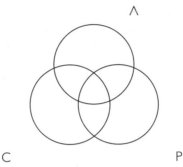

Shading each premise in turn we get

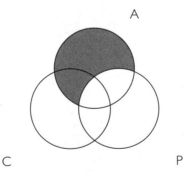

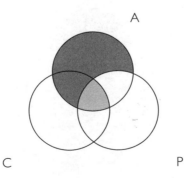

Does this show that "No cartoons are profound"? Not at all. Part of the intersection between the *C* and *P* circles is unshaded, so the argument does not rule out there being cartoons that are profound. The argument is *not valid*.

A final case:

All vegetarians are very thin.
Some very thin people are undernourished.
_____

Some vegetarians are undernourished.

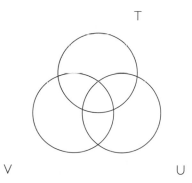

Again, we first represent the universal premise.

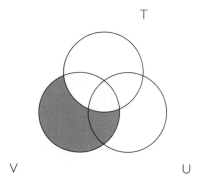

But where do we put the asterisk to represent the second premise? It has to be in the overlap of the *T* and *U* circles, but that overlap is divided into two parts, and we have no warrant for choosing one or the other of these. A convenient way of showing this is to put it on the line between the sections.

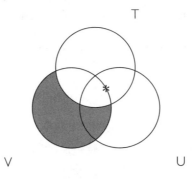

Since we do not know whether the asterisk is inside the intersection of V and U (the very center section of this diagram), the argument is *not valid*.

Exercises

B. *Draw a Venn diagram for each of the categorical syllogisms below. Using your diagram and the section numbering in the "Dummy Diagram," explain why each argument is or is not valid. The given answers to #1 and #2 serve as models for the sorts of explanations you can give.*

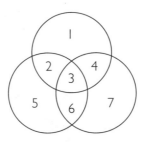

*1. All computers are machines.
    No machines can think.
    _____
    No computers can think.

*2. All pro basketball players are fine athletes.
    No professor of mathematics is a pro basketball player.
    _____
    No professor of mathematics is a fine athlete.

 3. All fallacies are dangerous.
    All dangerous things are things to be avoided.
    _____
    All fallacies are things to be avoided.

4. Some snakes are poisonous.
   Anything that is poisonous should be destroyed.
   _____
   Some snakes should be destroyed.

5. All slow learners require extra attention in school.
   Some who require extra attention in school need to
   be in specialized classrooms.
   _____
   Some slow learners need to be in specialized classrooms.

6. All flying squirrels are mammals.
   No birds are mammals.
   _____
   No flying squirrels are birds.

7. All flying squirrels are mammals.
   No birds are mammals.
   _____
   No birds are flying squirrels.

8. All tortoises are terrestrial.
   Some turtles are not terrestrial.
   _____
   Some turtles are not tortoises.

*9. All tortoises are terrestrial.
   Some turtles are not tortoises.
   _____
   Some turtles are not terrestrial.

10. No Martians speak English.
    All officers on the Starship do not speak English.
    _____
    All officers on the Starship are Martians.

*11. No officers on the Starship do not speak English.
    No Martians speak English.
    _____
    No officers on the Starship are Martians.

12. No spiders are insects.
    No insects are lizards.
    _____
    No spiders are lizards.

13. All religious fundamentalists are conservative.
    All Republicans are conservative.
    _____
    All religious fundamentalists are Republicans.

*14. Some students are hard workers, and some students get very
    good grades. So, some hard workers get very good grades.

15. No poor person who is willing to work deserves to be hun-
    gry. And every poor person who does not deserve to be hun-
    gry should get government aid. Thus, every poor person who
    is willing to work should get government aid.

16. Some murderers were molested as children. Everyone molested as a child deserves pity. So, some murderers deserve pity.

17. All alligators do not enjoy cold weather. Some carnivores do not enjoy cold weather. Thus, some carnivores must be alligators.

Chapter 6

CAUSAL ANALYSIS

Identifying causes is important in ordinary life, as well as in business, law, medicine, and the sciences. Our interest in causes reflects a variety of concerns. These four are among the most important:

1. *Explanation.* We wish to explain why an event occurred, so we attempt to discover its cause. (What caused the explosion of the *Challenger?*)

2. *Responsibility.* We want to know whether we can hold anyone responsible for an event (who deserves praise? who blame?), so we ask what someone did to cause it. (Did Franklin's speech incite the crowd to riot? Did Bennett's AIDS brochure save lives?)

3. *Control.* If we know the causal factors that produce an event, we may be able to control them and obtain results we want. (What causes coronary artery disease? Why do some families remain on welfare for generations?)

4. *Prediction.* We want to know if we can expect a certain kind of event to happen, so we attempt to discover what causes such events. (When will a major earthquake strike California? What are the consequences of escalating interest rates?)

We start by considering what we may mean in saying one event is the cause of another. We then discuss what leads us to designate a factor as "the cause" of an event even though other factors are also involved. We next describe the nature of causal explanation, and finally we examine four standard experimental methods to test for causal relationships.

Basic Causal Relationships

The term *cause* is used in several distinct but related ways. Hence, it is not possible to give the word a single definition without being arbitrary. Instead, we must review several prominent uses of the term.

1. Cause as Sufficient Condition

The eighteenth-century British philosopher David Hume formulated the basic analysis of a causal relationship that is still generally accepted. According to Hume, by "cause" we mean nothing more than that a "constant conjunction" holds between events. We notice that events of kind *A* are always followed by events of kind *B*, and we say "*A* causes *B*." Thus, to claim a causal relationship between events of types *A* and *B* is to say: Whenever *A* occurs, then *B* occurs. (To say all causal relations are regular in this way is not to say all regular relations are causal. See "Testing Causal Claims" on p. 103.)

Consider this example. You are driving and notice the red warning light glowing on your dashboard—the engine has overheated. You pull over, raise the hood, and see a long tear in a radiator hose. The hose has burst and all the coolant has run out. We can say the engine overheated because there was no coolant in the radiator. The lack of coolant *caused* the engine to overheat. Hence, we are asserting that "Whenever a car engine is running and no coolant is in its radiator, the engine will overheat."

In this construal of "cause," the lack of coolant is also said to constitute a **sufficient condition** for the engine's overheating. A factor is a sufficient condition for the occurrence of an event if whenever the factor occurs, then the event occurs: Whenever *A*, then *B*. We regard factual generalizations of this form, if true, as **causal laws**.

We have named one factor sufficient for the occurrence of the event "overheated engine." Yet other factors can also make an engine overheat. That is, other conditions are also sufficient for overheating:

> The water pump breaks, so coolant no longer circulates through the engine.
>
> The fan belt breaks, so the fan no longer blows on the radiator and carries off the heat from the liquid circulating inside.
>
> The small tubes inside the radiator become clogged, so coolant no longer circulates in them.

Any one of these three factors is a sufficient condition for the occurrence of the event, and it is in this sense we may say that an overheated engine can have several possible causes. If your engine overheats, even if you know the possible causes, you have no way of knowing the actual cause without investigating the matter. (This list of sufficient conditions is not complete. We might mention a faulty thermostat, a defective oil pump, an oil leak, or a number of others.)

We may want to know more about the overheated engine than the sufficient condition responsible for it. For example, we may want to know how the coolant came to be absent; that is, we may want a sufficient condition for that event. The radiator may have rusted through, the drain valve may have broken off, or (as in our example) the radiator hose may have burst—any of these would be sufficient for a loss of coolant.

By such inquiries, we establish causal chains leading to the occurrence of an event that interests us. In principle, we can extend the chain as far into the past as we wish or are able to. (We may ask what caused the radiator to rust, the drain valve to break off, the hose to burst.) In practice, we usually end causal inquiry at the point where our actions can affect the outcome. We can do little about the chemistry of metals and their interaction with coolant and water, so we are not likely to ask what caused the metal of our radiator to become rusty. We are most likely to stop when we learn why the coolant drained out of the radiator. (Replacing a radiator or checking it for leaks is something we can do.) By contrast, a radiator designer would push the inquiry further backward and want to know why the radiator rusted. In a new design, he might use different metal alloys or coatings.

The lack of coolant cannot genuinely be a sufficient condition for an overheated engine, although we have talked as if it were so. The engine is not going to overheat if it has been running for only a minute or so or if the outside temperature is very low. And of course we did not specify that we were talking about an internal combustion engine, not an electric or atomic one. We accept the lack of coolant as a sufficient condition because we have taken for granted that we are talking about an ordinary car being driven down the street under normal operating conditions for some typical period of time. If we had any reason to do so, we could specify just what additional factors should be added to the lack of coolant so that the sum of the factors would constitute a sufficient condition for an engine's overheating.

Thus, the *A* in the scheme "Whenever *A,* then *B*" must actually be understood to represent a set of conditions, not a single factor. To take another familiar example, we know room lights do not go on just because you flip the switch. Other factors must be present: The points of the switch must come into contact with the power source; electricity must be flowing through the wires; a working lightbulb has to be properly screwed into the socket; and the socket has to be connected to the power source through the switch. You may flip the switch all you wish, but if all these conditions are not satisfied, the light will not come on. Strictly, then, the whole set of conditions constitutes a sufficient condition for the event. The whole set is "the cause" of the event. To recognize this, we can elaborate our scheme:

Whenever $A [= C_1, C_2, \ldots C_n]$, then B.

We may not be able to fill in the whole set of conditions (C_1, C_2, C_3, and so on). Often we know some of them, but not all of them. If an event is important, we may try to reduce our ignorance by causal investigation. Thus, we try to determine more completely the factors that lead to suicide, cancer, and heart disease. Similarly, we try to discover what causes children to fail at school and what turns some people into serial killers.

What about effects? Just as the cause of an event is not a single factor, the effect of a cause is not a single event. The leaking radiator does more than make the car engine overheat—it leaves puddles on the ground, releases vapors into the atmosphere, and deposits chemicals in the soil. To be accurate, we should amend our causal scheme in the following way:

Whenever A [= C_1, C_2, ... C_n], then B [= E_1, E_2, ... E_n].

As we have seen, we often choose one factor from a set of factors and call it "the" cause of an event. The same holds for the set of outcomes. The one we call "the" effect is the one with which we are most concerned for some reason or other. An interest in highway safety might lead us to focus on the puddle of liquid left on the road as the effect, whereas a concern with the environment might lead us to focus on the chemical coolant that soaks into the soil.

2. Cause as Necessary Condition

Poliomyelitis—polio—is a disease of the central nervous system caused by a specific virus. Yet not everyone infected with the virus gets polio. Thus, infection with the polio virus is not a sufficient condition for getting the disease. But we do not know what other factors have to be present for someone to contract it.

Does this mean we don't know the cause of polio? Not according to one legitimate use of the term *cause*. What we know about the cause of polio is that anyone who has the disease has been infected by the virus. The virus, we can say, is a **necessary condition** for the disease.

A factor is a necessary condition for an event if the event does not occur in the absence of the factor. Everyone who gets polio has been infected with the polio virus, but not everyone infected with the polio virus gets polio. Thus, the polio virus is a necessary, but not sufficient, condition for the disease.

We can represent the relationship of a necessary condition to the occurrence of an event more formally. Let A stand for the causal factor and B for the event.

1. If *B*, then *A*. (If polio occurs, then the virus is present.)
2. If not-*A*, then not-*B*. (If the virus is not present, then polio does not occur.)

Both schemes express the meaning of sentences of the form "*A* is a necessary condition for *B*."

We usually do not speak of just any necessary condition as a cause. The presence of oxygen in the air was a necessary condition for World War II; yet we would consider it absurd to mention oxygen as the cause of the war. We regard such conditions as trivial with respect to explanation because they constitute relatively constant background conditions. Unusual factors or those varying from case to case (the presence of the polio virus, for example) are the necessary conditions we identify as causes.

3. Cause as Necessary and Sufficient Condition

The most rigorous interpretation of a causal relationship consists in construing "cause" as a condition both necessary and sufficient for the occurrence of an event. If factor *A* is *necessary and sufficient* for the occurrence of event *B*, then: Whenever *A* occurs, *B* occurs; and whenever *A* does not occur, then *B* does not occur. In an abstract scheme:

If *A*, then *B*; and if not-*A*, then not-*B*.

For illustration, assume diamonds are produced only when carbon is subjected to great pressure and in no other way. Carbon and great pressure are each a necessary condition for diamonds, and both together constitute a sufficient condition. Thus, if you know something is a diamond, you know great pressure acting on carbon caused it. Also, you know how to produce (cause) diamonds—subject carbon to great pressure.

This construing of cause is so rigorous that very few (if any) actual relationships in ordinary experience can satisfy it. A technique for producing diamonds without employing pressure has recently been developed, so even the standard example used here is no longer a genuine case.

Some philosophers hold that this construing of cause represents the kind of invariant relationship scientific laws ought to express. Laws of physics provide examples. For instance, according to Newton's second law, objects attract one another with a force equal to the inverse of the square of the distance between them. Thus, if we know the force of attraction between two bodies, we can calculate the distance between them; and if we know the distance between them, we can calculate the force of attraction. The values assigned to one set of factors determine the values assigned to the others, and the relationship can be understood in terms of necessary and sufficient conditions.

Causal generalizations in the social and biological sciences are rarely offered as expressions of necessary and sufficient conditions. Many consider the demand that laws be of this sort to be unrealistic and inappropriate. Further, some philosophers have denied that laws like Newton's are causal ones. This would make them inappropriate as models.

Designating Factors as Causes

The factor we mention as the cause of an event is rarely one we consider sufficient or even necessary for such events. We frequently select one factor from a set and say it is the cause of the event. Our aims and interests, as well as our knowledge, affect that choice. Thus, practical, moral, or legal considerations may influence our selection. Here we discuss only three considerations that may lead us to designate a single factor as "the cause" of an event, but others are easily imagined.

1. Triggering Factor

The factor that triggers an event is often designated the cause of the event. Usually this factor is the one occurring last, and it completes the causal chain (the set of sufficient conditions) producing the event.

We might say, "Turning on the light caused the explosion." Turning on the light was the last event to occur before the explosion, but flipping the switch was a successful trigger only because the room was filled with methane gas. In addition, oxygen was also present, and the light switch was not sealed, so a spark arced across the poles when the switch was thrown. These factors are ingredients that go toward making up a sufficient condition for an explosion, and they constitute the **standing conditions** that allow the event to be triggered by the switch. Throwing the switch was the factor that completed a set of sufficient conditions for the explosion. *Proximate* means "nearest," so the triggering factor of an event is often called the event's **proximate cause.**

2. Unusual Factor

Sometimes we say "the cause" of an event is the unusual factor in a set of sufficient conditions. We might say, "The explosion was caused by an accumulation of gas." The "whole cause" of the explosion was the accumulated gas, the presence of oxygen, and the arc from the light switch. But oxygen is usually in the air, and people ordinarily turn on lights. What is unusual is the accumulation of methane.

If we are concerned with fixing moral or legal responsibility for the explosion, we are likely to focus on the person who left the gas on, not the one who turned on the light.

3. Controllable Factor

Sometimes we emphasize the possibility of controlling occurrences of a certain kind of event by calling attention to a factor instrumental in producing the event and pointing out that since the factor can be controlled, so can the event.

We may construe "Cholesterol causes heart disease" as saying that eating foods high in saturated fats increases the chances of developing heart disease. Hence, to avoid heart disease, avoid eating such foods. We might with equal truth say "Heredity causes heart disease," but since heredity is not a controllable factor, we rarely call it the cause of heart disease.

Causal Explanations

To explain an event is often to say what caused it to occur. Thus, we say "The explosion occurred *because* somebody left the gas on," or "The chicks ran for cover *because* the hawk-shape is a releasing mechanism." Such an explanation apparently involves no laws, and we explain the event merely by mentioning its cause. The causal sentence has the form "*A* caused *B*" and seems to be about individual events and circumstances.

Despite appearances, such explanations are really incomplete versions of explanations that rely upon causal laws. The explanatory force of sentences with the form "*A* caused *B*" (about particular events) depends upon an implicit reference to a generalization asserting an invariant or constant connection between occurrences of events of the two kinds. Thus, we can express the claim of a causal relationship between events of type *A* and type *B* by the scheme

When *A* occurs (under conditions *C*), then *B* occurs.

Generalizations of this form, if true, are causal laws. (We will limit discussion to laws expressing a causally sufficient condition.) In terms of this analysis, a causal sentence such as "A bacterial infection is the cause of Mr. Wu's bronchitis" gains its power to explain from the implicit assumption that a bacterial infection, under the appropriate conditions, is a sufficient condition for bronchitis. That is, the sentence acquires its power to explain from a causal law.

If we make the causal law explicit and describe the circumstances Mr. Wu is in, we can see how the explanation consists of showing that this particular event is an instance of a general pattern:

> Whenever a bacterial infection occurs in the lungs, bronchitis results.
> Mr. Wu has a bacterial infection in his lungs.
> _____
> Mr. Wu has bronchitis.

Causal explanation thus consists in bringing a case under a law—in showing that a particular case is an instance of a connection that always holds between events of two kinds.

In philosophy of science we refer to such explanations as **deductive nomological explanations**. The word "nomological" means "containing a law," and "deductive" refers to the fact that the explanation involves deducing a description of the event requiring explanation from the law or laws. A deductive nomological explanation has this form:

$$\frac{L_1 \ldots L_n}{C_1 \ldots C_n}$$
$$E$$

The abbreviations in the first line stand for laws or generalizations. Those in the second line stand for what are called **initial conditions**—the circumstances under which an event took place. (They typically include the condition we identify as "the cause" of the event.) In the sciences, these conditions are usually called **experimental variables**, and they include such factors as temperature, years of education, coefficient of expansion, and so on. The letter E stands for a description of the event that is explained.

The following criteria are generally accepted as adequate for determining that a deductive nomological explanation is worthy of acceptance:

1. The explanation contains at least one law established by evidence and accepted as true.
2. The law (or laws) is actually employed in explaining the event. (This condition rules out pseudoscientific explanations that mention laws but do not actually use them.)

3. The sentences describing the initial conditions are true. (That is, the experimental conditions and the values assigned to the variables are correctly stated.)

4. The description of the event is true. (If the event did not occur as described, the laws are irrelevant to explaining it.)

5. The sentence describing the event is a deductive consequence of the laws and initial conditions. (This condition shows that the event fits into the pattern expressed by the laws and that, in this circumstance, the laws are properly applied.)

Testing Causal Claims

Two kinds of events can be regularly related without being causally related. "Whenever the maple leaves in Canada change color, the geese fly south" may be true; yet the change in leaf color does not *cause* the geese to fly south. We recognize the two events are independent and are related the way they are only because both are triggered by a third event—the onset of winter, with the lowering of the average daily temperature and fewer hours of daylight.

We need ways to separate causal relationships from regular but accidental relationships. That is, we need ways to identify causal factors and distinguish them from merely associated conditions.

The following four experimental methods help us make such distinctions. First formally stated in the nineteenth century by the philosopher John Stuart Mill, they are often called "Mill's methods." (Mill actually proposed five methods, but the fifth is essentially equivalent to one of the others and is omitted here.) Although science has now become more complicated, Mill's methods continue to express the underlying logic of many experimental investigations. The methods themselves are relatively straightforward, but often unknown or uncontrollable factors complicate actual cases. Hence, there is no automatic way of applying the methods that will guarantee a solution to any causal question.

1. The Method of Difference

The **method of difference** involves comparing situations in which an event of interest occurs with similar situations in which it does not. If the presence of a certain factor is the only difference between the two kinds of situations, it may be said to be "the cause" of the event.

Suppose we are comparing two situations, S_1 and S_2, and we represent them as sets of conditions or variables. We find through inquiry that event E occurs only in S_1 and never in S_2. (That is, when the conditions of S_1 are present, E occurs, but it does not when the conditions of S_2 are present.) Next we list the conditions we believe constitute S_1 and S_2 and look for differences between them:

S_1: p, q, r, s

S_2: p, q, r

The two sets are exactly alike except that S_1 contains condition (variable) s and S_2 does not. The factor s marks the difference between S_1 and S_2. Hence, s is the cause of E.

The identification of s as the cause of E doesn't mean s has to be (although it may be) either a sufficient or a necessary condition for E. It may be a standing or triggering condition. (See the discussion above.) We may need to investigate further to determine just what sort of causal role s plays.

The method of difference is frequently employed in clinical trials of experimental drugs. If we construct two situations that resemble each other in every respect and if a drug is employed in one but not the other, then we can ascribe to the drug any change in one situation not matched by a change in the other.

Suppose you are a researcher interested in determining whether the chemical compound THC is effective in lowering blood pressure. You begin your research with animal studies. You identify a large population of laboratory rats with high blood pressure. Then you divide the rats into a control group and an experimental group, taking care that the two groups resemble one another in all respects you consider relevant.

The rats must all come from the same genetic line to reduce or eliminate the influence of potential genetic variables. Further, the distribution of blood-pressure readings should be the same for each group. (That the groups have the same average is not enough because they might have different ranges of readings, making any results potentially misleading.) Also, the groups should be equally distributed for sex, age, physical condition, and weight. Both groups should also be treated in exactly the same way: fed the same diet, housed in the same kind of cages, kept at the same temperature, and so on. The control group and the experimental group should resemble one another as much as possible in all respects.

The only way you treat the groups differently is that you administer the drug THC to the rats in the experimental group and withhold it from those in the control group. Of course, giving an injection in itself may cause a difference between the two groups. To keep this from affecting the results, you also inject the rats in the control group, only instead of using the drug you use an inactive substance, such as distilled water.

At the end of some predetermined course of treatment, you measure the blood pressure of the rats in each of the groups and compare the results. If the blood pressure of the rats in the experimental group is lower than the blood pressure of those in the control group, you have grounds for concluding that THC was the cause. After all, the injection of THC is the only relevant difference between the two groups.

The method of difference seems obvious and its results unquestionable. Yet even in a relatively simple experimental setup like this one, we may easily find grounds for doubting that the causal claim has been adequately established. For example, the possibility of **experimental bias** has not be eliminated. If the experimenters know which rats are getting THC, they might unintentionally treat them differently. They might spend more time with them, be more gentle in handling them, and so on. Thus, these differences, not THC, may be the factors causally responsible for lowering the blood pressure in that group. Or the experimenters might make unconscious errors in recording blood pressures. Without meaning to, their measurements might favor the hypothesis that the drug can lower blood pressure.

To prevent possibilities like these, so-called **blind experiments** have been devised. Those conducting the experiment are kept in ignorance about which animals are in the control group and which are in the experimental group. Experimenters do not know whether they are injecting distilled water or the actual drug. Whatever errors the experimenters make tend to cancel out one another, and the possibility of a systematic error is minimized.

Also notice that even this simple experiment assumes the experimenter can identify the factors likely to affect the outcome of the test and will set up the groups accordingly. Control and experimental groups, because they cannot be identical, must be made similar in relevant ways. If we are interested in testing the effects of a drug on blood pressure, we assume it does not matter if the experimental group contains more rats with black spots on their fur. As far as we know, the presence or absence of spotted fur has no connection with blood pressure. Age and weight are known to be relevant, but coat color is not.

We may be wrong in such assumptions. We may ignore variables that do affect blood pressure, either because we are ignorant of their existence or we wrongly consider them irrelevant. Thus, we may fail to keep constant in both groups a variable affecting the results and end up identifying a factor as the cause of a result when it is not.

For these and similar reasons, causal inquiry is usually not a matter of conducting a *single* experiment. Often we cannot even control for all relevant factors at the same time, and once an experiment is concluded, doubts about other factors may crop up. A series of experiments in which different factors are kept constant, while others are varied, is always preferable.

The complications connected with using the method of difference are basically the same as those connected with the other methods. We will not repeat this discussion in connection with them, but it should be kept in mind.

2. Method of Agreement

The **method of agreement** involves comparing situations in which the same kind of event occurs. If the presence of a certain factor is the only respect in which the situations are the same (that is, agree), then this factor may be identified as the cause of the event.

We represent two situations as two sets of conditions or variables, and we assume each set is associated with an occurrence of an event of type E:

S_1: p, q, r, s

S_2: t, u, v, s

The two sets differ in every respect but one—S_1 and S_2 share factor s. Hence, s is the cause of the event E.

Of course, the world never presents us with two situations wholly unlike except for one shared factor. When we use the method of agreement, as with the other methods, we must use our knowledge and judgment in designing experiments to fit the requirements of the method and in determining when the method may be appropriately employed in any given nonexperimental situation.

Suppose three people share a dish of moo shu pork at a Chinese restaurant. Afterwards, they have different desserts: the first has pie; the second, ice cream; the third, almond cookies. Later, all three develop headaches, mild sweating, and a feeling of tension around the temples. What is the cause of these symptoms? The method of agreement identifies the moo shu pork as the cause because it is the only factor common to all three people.

Notice that in reaching this conclusion, we rely on unstated assumptions about what is relevant to consider and what is not. We do not compare the people's age, gender, race, shampoo, politics, and so on. We assume, quite naturally, that the symptoms are the result of something the three of them ate. We might be wrong, but additional evidence would be necessary to determine if we are.

Ordinary experience (common sense) also tells us we need to look further at the circumstances in which the symptoms occurred. Did other people develop the same symptoms? What did they eat? Did they also eat moo shu pork? We might decide to test the particular dish the initial three ate from for the presence of bacteria or chemicals that might cause such symptoms; or to check the ingredients that went into all dishes associated with the symptoms. Indeed, we now know from empirical studies that the presence of monosodium glutamate (MSG), a flavor enhancer commonly used in Chinese cooking, is the cause of so-called Chinese restaurant syndrome.

3. Joint Method of Agreement and Difference

The **joint method of agreement and difference** involves the simultaneous application of the two methods discussed above. We compare cases in which an event of interest occurs with ones in which it does not occur. The cause of the event will be the only factor *present* in each case in which the event occurs and *absent* in each case in which the event does not occur.

Suppose Sikes, Miller, and Kline have lunch at the same restaurant, and later Sikes and Miller become ill with something resembling food poisoning (nausea, vomiting, and so on). Since all three dined at the same place, it is reasonable to suspect that something Sikes and Miller ate caused their illness.

Accordingly, we interview all three, and they provide a list of what they ate:

Sikes: chicken salad, onion soup, chocolate pie

Miller: chicken salad, arugula, sliced oranges

Kline: steak tartare, arugula, chocolate pie

Since Sikes and Miller both became ill and Kline did not, we want to find a dish Sikes and Miller consumed (agreement) but Kline did not (difference). Looking at the list, it is immediately obvious that chicken salad meets this description. Thus, we can identify it as the cause of the illness.

We could not have identified the chicken salad as the causal factor had we been limited to comparing Sikes and Kline or Miller and Kline. Neither of these comparisons meets the conditions for the method of agreement or the method of difference. (Though both Sikes and Kline have chocolate pie, only Sikes gets sick. Though both Miller and Kline have arugula, only Miller gets sick.)

4. Method of Concomitant Variation

Concomitant means occurring at the same time. The **method of concomitant variation** involves varying a factor and determining whether a change in it is accompanied by variation in some other factor that interests us. If the two factors vary together, this is a reason to consider the first factor causally related to the second.

For example, if the more beer a group of people drink, the drunker they get, then it is reasonable to believe drinking the beer is causing the drunkenness. To verify this connection, we might seek more exact information. We might use criteria that allow us to determine in a more precise fashion particular states or stages of drunkenness. Too, we would want to measure the quantity of beer consumed and the time it took. We could then collect data allowing us to plot curves relating beer consumption over time to drunkenness. Presumably we could show, in a more definitive way, a connection between the amount of beer consumed and stages of drunkenness. (At a certain point, we probably could not formulate criteria to distinguish stages reliably.)

The problem with this method is that it is no more than a technique for establishing correlations, even when used in conjunction with sophisticated statistical techniques. Yet many correlations are not causal connections. Suppose that as the number of maple leaves turning brown increases, the number of geese flying south increases. The method of concomitant variation would assure us the change in leaf color is causally responsible for the departure of the geese. Once again, though, what is actually happening is that as the weather gets colder and the days shorter, the number of leaves changing color increases and the number of geese flying south increases—both for the same reason.

While establishing a correlation between two factors does not demonstrate a causal connection between them, finding a correlation is often an important step in uncovering a causal relationship. Correlations suggest what factors might be causal ones and so directs additional investigation.

Further, when correlations are expressed statistically, they may serve as a basis for prediction or as a guide to action. A statistically significant correlation between the amount of animal fats consumed and the incidence of coronary artery disease may lead the prudent person to eat less animal fat. The connection may be only fortuitous and not causal; yet that possibility might not be the one to bet on.

Much experimental thinking in ordinary life and the sciences involves these methods. The methods of agreement and difference express the underlying logic of the controlled experiment, and the method of concomitant variation is the basis of statistical correlation.

Exercises

A. *Explain and illustrate the following causal concepts.*

1. Necessary condition
2. Sufficient condition
3. Necessary and sufficient condition
*4. Controllable condition
5. Standing condition
*6. Triggering condition (or event)

B. *Explain the apparent meaning of the causal identifications made in the cases below. Is "the cause" a necessary condition, sufficient, triggering, or what?*

1. Decapitation causes instantaneous death.
*2. "In societies that are not free, art dies." —Ronald Reagan
3. "Marriage is the chief cause of divorce." —Groucho Marx
*4. On June 28, 1914, a member of a Serbian secret society called the Black Hand assassinated Archduke Ferdinand, heir to the Hapsburg Empire, in the streets of Sarajevo. It was this event that led warring alliances into World War I. —Based on R. R. Palmer, *A History of the Modern World*
5. The crash of Flight 701 was due to wind shear.
6. Christopher Columbus was able to make a voyage to the New World only because he received financing from Queen Isabella of Spain.
*7. Bacterial infection is one of the causes of fever.
8. A high level of dietary fat is now recognized as a significant risk factor in the occurrence of colon cancer.
*9. Adolf Hitler's deliberate weakening of the German officer corps by replacing professional soldiers with loyal, hand-picked amateurs was partly responsible for the atrocities committed by the German army during the Second World War.
10. Scientists now agree that the cause of AIDS is the Human Immunodeficiency Virus.
*11. Earthquakes are caused by the shifting of tectonic plates. When the margins of two plates moving in opposite directions come together, get stuck, then suddenly break loose and slide past one another, the result is an earthquake.

12. Oxygen and water corroded the steel support structures and caused the bridge to collapse when a tank truck filled with milk attempted to cross it.

C. *Explain how you might go about constructing deductive nomological explanations for the occurrence of the events described below, given the circumstances mentioned. A sketch of an explanation would be adequate.*

*1. The salt sprinkled on the snow covering the sidewalk turned the snow to slush.

2. Baby *A* was born with congenital syphilis. This caused a condition called interstitial karatitis. His symptoms included eye pain, excessive watering, sensitivity to light, and severely diminished vision. After treatment with antibiotics, his symptoms disappeared and normal vision returned.

*3. A straight stick partially submerged in a pool of water with a smooth surface looks bent.

4. Your car fails to start when you turn the key.

D. *Discuss the use of Mill's methods in identifying the (possible) cause in each of the following schemes and examples.*

1. $(A, B, C) \rightarrow$ Event
   $(A, D, F) \rightarrow$ Event

2. $(A, B, C) \rightarrow$ No event
   $(A, B, D) \rightarrow$ Event

3. $(A, B, C) \rightarrow$ Event
   $(A, D, E) \rightarrow$ Event
   $(B, C, D) \rightarrow$ No event

*4. You have two battery-operated flashlights. One works, the other doesn't. You switch batteries. The flashlight that worked no longer does, and the one that didn't now does.

5. Same as above, except when you switch batteries, the flashlight that didn't work still doesn't. What else might be wrong?

6. Same as initially described, except when you switch batteries, neither flashlight works. How could this be possible?

E. *Discuss the methods of experimental investigation illustrated in the cases below. (The investigation need not have led to a conclusion we now accept as true.)*

*1. Joseph Goldberger conducted the classic investigation into the cause of pellagra, which we now know to be a disease caused by nutritional deficiency. Goldberger was convinced that pellagra was not, as many claimed, an infectious disease. To demonstrate his belief, he conducted experiments in which he and his assistants injected themselves with blood drawn from people with the disease. To rule out another source of transmission, he and his assistants also swallowed capsules filled with excrement taken from pellagra sufferers. Neither Goldberger nor any of his assistants developed pellagra.

2. Interest rates (the cost of borrowing money) and the real estate market appear to be closely connected. When interest rates go down, the sales of new and existing houses rise.

3. Blaise Pascal provided evidence for Torricelli's hypothesis that the earth is surrounded by a "sea of air" by sending his brother-in-law to the top of a mountain with a barometer. The barometer consisted of a tube of mercury upended in an open dish. Torricelli had claimed that the mercury in a full tube falls until it reaches the level at which the force it exerts balances the weight of air pressing on the surface of the dish. Pascal reasoned that as altitude increases, air grows thinner. Hence, the weight of the air pressing on the dish should progressively diminish. This is exactly what his brother-in-law reported.

*4. Pasteur tested the claim that living organisms can arise by spontaneous generation by performing an experiment in which he allowed a sample of meat broth to stand in an uncovered flask, while he placed another sample in a sealed flask from which the air had been evacuated. Within days, the uncovered broth was teeming with microorganisms, while the broth in the sealed container was sterile.

5. In the circumstances just described, when the sterile broth was allowed to come into contact with the air, microorganisms developed in the broth.

6. Considerable evidence exists to support the claim that the AIDS virus cannot be spread by casual contact. Most important, families living with children who test positive for the virus have not developed any new cases during a five-year period.

*7. Dr. Dorothy O. Lewis in a 1986 study found that each of the thirteen men and two women convicted of murder and awaiting execution had suffered severe head injuries earlier in life. Yet this fact was not known prior to her study. Lewis believes her findings show the inadequacy of psychiatric screening procedures. Many condemned criminals probably suffer from unrecognized neurological and psychiatric disorders that, properly considered, might have mitigated their sentences. —Reported in *The New York Times* (July 7, 1987)

8. Research reported in 1987 and since has shown that as people become more depressed, they become more realistic about themselves. Dr. Richard Lazarus claims, "As you become depressed, you become more aware of your defenses and start to feel hopeless. People who function well strive against odds because they hold on to hope." Also, a little self-deception makes accomplishment more likely. As Daniel Goleman summarized the research, "People with a positive sense of themselves will work harder and longer and . . . their perseverance allows them to do better." —Reported in *The New York Times* (November 26, 1987)

Chapter 7

ARGUMENT BY ANALOGY AND MODELS

To draw an **analogy** is to call attention to specific similarities between two distinct subject matters. In an argument by analogy, the similarities are offered as a basis for the conclusion. **Models,** as employed in the sciences, are special kinds of analogies. We begin by characterizing analogical arguments and distinguishing factual from moral ones. Next we consider the use of models, then end by presenting criteria for evaluating conclusions based on analogies.

Analogical Arguments

An **analogical argument** (argument by analogy) is one to the effect that because two distinct subjects have certain features in common and one subject possesses an additional feature, then the other subject probably possesses that feature as well. Thus, analogical arguments have the form

> A is similar to B in possessing features 1, 2, 3, . . .
>
> A also possesses feature N.
>
> Thus, B possesses feature N.

(Moral analogical arguments claim that B *ought* to possess the additional feature.) Arguments by analogy are a special kind of nondeductive argument. The premises support, but do not guarantee, the conclusion.

Factual Arguments

A factual analogical argument uses an analogy to establish a claim about some (nonmoral) state of affairs. The two subject matters may be different people, policies, countries, ceremonies, styles of dress, or whatever. This example compares a different historical period with the present one:

> This country is headed for an economic depression. Just compare the way things are getting to be now with the way they were before

the depression of the 1930s. We've had a major stock market crash, and investors are increasingly unwilling to put their money in the market. A large number of banks and savings and loans have failed. Manufacturing is not growing, and jobs are getting scarcer daily. People who want to work can't because our productivity is falling. These conditions parallel those of the '30s in every respect, so it is just a matter of time before massive unemployment puts such a strain on our economic systems that they collapse—just the way they did in the '30s.

The premises spell out resemblances between the present economy and that of the 1930s and offer them as evidence for the conclusion that we are headed for economic collapse.

Not all analogical arguments deal with such ordinary matters of fact. John Stuart Mill originally formulated an argument that addresses the problem of other minds: How can we know whether the subjective experiences of others are like our own? Mill reasoned as follows about the experience of pain:

Other people have the same sensory equipment as I have—eyes, nose, ears, and so on.
The physiological mode of operation of this equipment seems the same for other people as for me.
When I accidentally cut myself or drop a heavy weight on my foot, I feel pain.
In my own case, such circumstances are usually accompanied by such behavior as jumping around, contorting my face, cursing, and so on.

Anyone else who cuts himself or drops a heavy weight on his foot and exhibits the same sort of behavior as I do is also feeling pain.

Arguments from analogy are often not as explicit as our examples. "I don't see why Tom didn't get accepted into the program. He writes as well as Jill" is just as much an analogical argument as the ones we have considered.

Moral Analogical Arguments

Analogical arguments are used in the moral context to argue that cases similar in relevant respects should be treated in similar ways. (Some arguments try to show the cases *may* be treated similarly, that the treatment is permissible but not morally required.) Since fairness demands we apply moral rules, as well as social policies and laws, in a uniform fashion, the arguments may be seen as arguments for equal treatment. We can distinguish two types of arguments of this sort.

One form of moral analogical argument is to the effect that because two cases are similar, we should extend the treatment *already given* to one to the other. Such arguments often have the following structure:

A and B both have characteristics 1, 2, 3, 4,
A received treatment T.
B did not receive treatment T.
_____

B *ought* to receive treatment T.
(Or we ought to compensate B for not receiving T.)

The following argument has this form:

Because migrant farmworkers are hired on a part-time basis, employers are legally exempt from paying them the minimum wage they must pay workers classified as full-time. However, during peak harvesting periods, migrants labor at least as many hours as workers classified as full-time. Thus, migrants ought to be paid minimum wage for work done during peak periods.

A variation on arguments like these holds that *if* a treatment is going to be accorded to one case, then it *ought* to be accorded to a similar case as well:

A and B both have characteristics 1, 2, 3, 4.
_____

If A receives treatment T, then B should receive it too.

The treatment includes penalties as well as benefits. This example illustrates the above form:

The evidence shows that both Ling and Hawkins worked together to plan and execute the theft of the documents, and both profited from their sale to a foreign government. So, if Ling receives a prison term for his role in the crime, then Hawkins should receive a similar sentence. It would be unfair to treat Hawkins in a different way.

A second form of moral analogical argument involves attempting to show that an instance in which an action's legitimacy is in doubt resembles an instance in which the action would be justified:

Action A is not obviously justified in case C.
A is obviously justified in case D.
C resembles D in respects 1, 2, 3, . . .
_____

Action A is justified in case D.

Here is a sketch of this kind of reasoning in an argument for the right of a woman to have an abortion:

> We know it is generally wrong to kill an innocent person. But we also know that in some unusual cases it is morally permissible to do so.
>
> For instance, suppose a mad scientist invents a brain-driver machine that can take over the brain of an individual, blank out his consciousness, and control his body like a robot's. The mad scientist takes over your neighbor's brain, and as you arrive home, your neighbor grabs you, holds a knife to your throat, and in a toneless voice says, "I'm going to kill you." You have an autosyringe with a poison that will cause instant paralysis and death to anyone injected. Is it morally permissible to kill this brain-controlled but innocent person?
>
> It is obviously permissible, although unfortunate. The same is true of abortion. The fetus is innocent but poses a threat to the pregnant woman. Just as she would be warranted in defending herself from the brain-controlled assassin, she would be warranted in defending herself from the fetus.

Moral analogical arguments involve an implicit premise to the effect that "Similar cases should be treated in similar ways." This is a *formal* principle of justice or equality. The formal principle does not say what makes two cases similar or how they should be treated. "It is wrong to kill an innocent person, except in self-defense" is a material principle. What should count as a person, as innocent, and as self-defense must be spelled out and established by argument.

We can regard moral analogical arguments as enthymemes, where the formal principle of equality is the implicit premise. When the principle is added, such arguments may become valid. But as we discuss below, this does not necessarily mean they are good arguments. (See p. 9 on enthymemes and pp. 29–31 on validity in general.)

Models

Analogical reasoning in the natural and social sciences often takes the form of using models to reach conclusions. A **model** involves using a familiar and well-understood system to represent a system not as well understood. We assume that features of the model are similar to those of the unfamiliar system, and we extend conclusions about the model to it. Two important kinds of models in science are formal and material ones.

Formal Models

A **formal model** is a set of concepts and principles belonging to one system employed to develop an understanding of another system. The kinetic theory of gases may be modeled as a room filled with Ping-Pong balls. We assume that an ideal gas is made up of small spheres, represented by Ping-Pong balls, and the room represents its container. The room and balls are assigned certain characteristics—for example, the walls of the room are perfectly elastic and the diameter of the balls is negligible compared to the distance between them. Heating the gas is like making the balls bounce faster, and increasing the pressure is like moving the walls closer, which increases the number of balls within a unit of space. Thinking in these terms lets us apply concepts and laws holding for a familiar type of physical system to an unfamiliar one.

Other examples of formal models are equally familiar. Galileo modeled free-falling bodies by rolling marbles down a slanted board, and Charles Darwin modeled his theory of natural selection on the behavior of animal breeders in making artificial selections. Aspects of Sigmund Freud's psychodynamical theory were developed in terms of analogies with hydraulic forces. Repressed rage, for instance, is like built-up pressure inside a pipe.

Material Models

No one believes gas molecules are literally Ping-Pong balls or that rage flows through pipes in the body. In formal models, we consider only certain abstract properties of the model to hold for the system modeled. The case is different with **material models**, in which a physical system is taken to represent parts of another physical system. The representation rests on the assumption that the systems share enough features to allow us to extend discoveries about the model to the system it models.

The most familiar material models are laboratory animals. We use rats, mice, monkeys, dogs, cats, rabbits, and other organisms to study the causes and treatments of human diseases and the effects of drugs and other chemicals on human health. No scientist claims these animals and humans are biologically the same. However, sometimes we can assume animals and humans share enough relevant features to permit us to test hypotheses that, because of time or moral constraints, cannot be tested directly on people.

For example, we often use rhesus monkeys as biological models for humans in nutrition experiments. If monkeys fed a diet deficient in folic acid develop anemia, we may extend this finding to humans; we may conclude that humans eating a folic-acid deficient diet will also develop anemia. Animal models are sometimes essential to biological and medical research. Some scientists claim that research into the causes of mental illness is severely hampered by the lack of animal models for disorders like schizophrenia.

Material models are also used in other areas of science. Tanks filled with a mixture of water and sand represent quicksand, and hydraulic presses represent the weight of a rock mass on top of a stratum. Archaeologists employ modern garbage dumps to represent middens, and construction techniques used in parts of contemporary Peru are taken as models for ancient ones. In all such cases, reasoning from a material model to the system modeled involves making a claim about this system on the basis of similarities between it and the model. Hence, reasoning from models is a kind of analogical argument.

Evaluating Analogical Reasoning

We have no rules that let us decide automatically whether an analogical argument is a good one. Yet two criteria are helpful in deciding whether a conclusion is worthy of belief.

1. The Degree of Analogy Must Be High

Common experience tells us that as the number of similarities between the two subjects in an analogy increases, the more likely it is that if one has an additional feature, the other will have it also. If the number of resemblances is 100, it is more probable that an additional resemblance will be found than it would be if the number were only ten. However, the number of points of resemblance must be balanced against the number of points of dissimilarity between the two subjects. That two subjects share 100 features may mean little if the subjects differ in a thousand other ways.

The ways subjects resemble one another constitute the **positive analogy** and the ways they differ constitute the **negative analogy**. If the points of resemblance and difference are taken together, then the degree of analogy is the ratio of the positive and negative analogies. When the positive analogy is proportionately larger than the negative analogy, then the degree of analogy is high.

The **limiting case** of a high degree of analogy occurs when two cases are virtually identical in every respect except for the space they occupy. Two hydrogen atoms or two water molecules are examples of limiting cases. Larger, more familiar objects begin to diverge from one another in specific ways. Glass marbles produced one after another from the same batch of glass and by the same machine come to resemble the limiting cases, but dogs, people, historical events, conversations, paintings, and political situations, even when they are of the same kind, may differ radically from one another. Biologists, psychologists, sociologists, anthropologists, and political scientists often point out that this lack of exact similarity among the objects they study makes getting reliable results more difficult than is the case in physics and chemistry.

We have no mechanical procedure to determine when the degree of analogy between two cases is adequate to justify a conclusion. Whether a conclusion should be accepted requires acquiring and weighing relevant facts. Ultimately, though, the decision is a matter of judgment.

For instance, without violating copyrights, can individuals use videotape recorders to copy television programs to watch later or to form a library for their personal use? A court decision held this was fair use. It decided that the degree of analogy between videotaping and audiotaping was sufficiently high that past rulings about the "fair use" doctrine and audiotaping applied to video. Another court might have decided otherwise, for where degree of analogy is the issue, reasonable people can differ.

Criticism of moral analogical arguments often consists of pointing out that whereas similarities may exist between two individuals or groups, their dissimilarities are more important. A man previously convicted of child molesting, for example, can hardly claim he is being unfairly treated when a day-care center denies him employment and hires others who are otherwise comparable. In such cases, the number of similarities or dissimilarities does not count so much as their *relative importance*. We have no way, then, merely to count similarities and differences, get a numerical ratio, decide on a number at which we will accept a conclusion, then use the ratio to make the decision for us. We cannot avoid exercising judgment.

2. The Analogy Should Be Relevant to the Conclusion

Confidence in a conclusion is also increased when the shared characteristics are closely connected with the additional characteristic possessed by the first subject and attributed to the second.

Suppose we want to predict whether the residents of a recently incorporated district are likely to support a proposition to increase the school tax. When we compare the district with another with a known voting record, we find we get a good match for average income, distribution of occupation, age, and gender. In addition, the older district has always supported a school tax. We determine also that the degree of analogy is high; little difference seems to exist between this election and previous ones and between the two districts.

Can we now conclude that the new district will support the tax increase? Perhaps. Our confidence would be greater if we knew that the proportion of residents with school-age children in both districts was roughly the same, since parents of school-age children are known to be more likely to support school taxes than are others. Thus, while the information we have about the similarities and voting records of the two districts is relevant to the conclusion, important relevant information is missing, casting doubt on the truth of the conclusion. In this sort of case, relevance (that is, average number and distribution of school-age children) can be statistically determined if we have the right kind of data.

For moral analogical arguments, the similarities between cases must be relevant if the similarities are to support a contention of unfairness or a demand for equality of treatment. To award an A to Gomez, who scores a ninety on a calculus exam, and an F to Whitley, who scores a ten, is prima facie fair. The numerical score on the exam is relevant to the letter grade a student deserves. If Whitley were to argue that the grades are unfair because she and Gomez studied the same amount for the exam and have similar overall grade point averages, we would reject her claim. These similarities are not relevant to the grade she received on the calculus exam.

Critics of the use of mice as models to determine the effects of saccharin claimed that mice were bad models, that the way in which they metabolized the substance is different from the way humans metabolize it. Accordingly, the discovery that saccharin produced bladder cancer in mice cannot be extended to humans. The physiological process of metabolism is relevant to bladder cancer, so the differences in physiology make the animal model an inappropriate one. Other scientists disputed the relevance of the differences and defended the use of mice as the proper model.

We have no rules for determining relevance. Even when we agree to the facts and share the same principles, disagreements about relevance may still divide people. This is particularly so in areas like criminal justice and moral and social decision making where analogical arguments play a common and important role.

Exercises

A. *Identify the following arguments by analogy as* factual *or* moral. *Specify the points of comparison between the two different subjects in each case, then evaluate the argument.*

*1. I read with great interest the recent proposal by the American Medical Association . . . that doctors would be forbidden to conduct death-by-injection executions of convicted murderers because "a physician, as a member of a profession dedicated to preserving life where there is hope of doing so, should not be an active participant in a legally authorized execution, but should be excluded." I find this view highly incongruous considering the fact that hundreds and possibly thousands of doctors are today involved in destroying human life at its very beginning by their participation in and encouragement of abortions throughout this country. —Virginia Banner, *Dallas Morning News* (June 26, 1980)

2. Imagine someone placing your head in a stock. As you stare helplessly ahead, unable to defend yourself, your head is pulled back. Your lower eyelid is pulled away from your eyeball. Then chemicals are poured into the eye. There is pain. You scream and writhe hopelessly. There is no escape. This is the Draize Test. The test which measures the harmfulness of chemicals by the damage inflicted on the unprotected eyes of conscious rabbits. The test that . . . cosmetic firms force on thousands of rabbits to test their products. . . . A healthy society does not inflict violence on the powerless; does not pursue "glamour" at the expense of innocent animals. — *The Millennium Guild* (advertisement), *The New York Times* (April 15, 1980)

3. The laws of this country are unfair to the users and sellers of heroin, cocaine, and other so-called dangerous drugs. Such drugs pose a health risk to individuals who use them, but the same is true of such common drugs as nicotine and alcohol. We rely on social pressure and public education and rehabilitation programs to discourage individuals from smoking and drinking. We don't throw smokers and drinkers into jail just for smoking and drinking, and we don't put grocery and liquor store owners into prison for selling dangerous drugs. We allow people to smoke and drink because we believe people have a right to do whatever they want to do so long as it affects no one but themselves. It's time this nation started thinking clearly and applied this principle consistently. When it does, then most of the laws that attach criminal penalties to using and selling drugs will deservedly be thrown out.

4. Revenue must cover expenditures by one means or another. Any government, like any family, can for a year spend a little more than it earns. But you and I know that a continuation of that habit means the poorhouse. —Franklin D. Roosevelt, Presidential Nomination Acceptance Speech, 1932

*5. The planet Mars possesses an atmosphere with clouds and mists resembling our own; it has seas distinguished from the land by a greenish colour, and polar regions covered with snow. The red colour of the planet seems to be due to the atmosphere, like the red colour of our sunrises and sunsets. So much is similar in the surface of Mars and the surface of the Earth that we readily agree that there must be inhabitants there as here. —W. S. Jevons, *Elementary Lessons in Logic*

*6. Saunders should not be admitted to the Whitman College Honors Program. Her grade point average is a half point lower than that of anyone already in the program. While it is true that the University of Washington, where Saunders earned her transfer credits, gives proportionally fewer As and Bs than Whitman does, this does not alter the fact that Saunders's GPA is lower than the GPAs of the honor students.

7. A full-grown cat is capable of much more than a human infant. The cat has a sense of its own interest and is capable of receiving and displaying affection. Further, it engages in play and activities like hunting that show that its level of intelligence is as great as, if not greater than, that of the infant. Hence, if we consider painful, destructive experiments performed on cats to be morally legitimate, we must also accept the legitimacy of similar experiments on human infants.

8. Travel agents don't force people to take trips, but they can make a city or country sound so appealing that customers will want to take a trip. Once customers have taken an enjoyable trip, they'll be more likely to take another. Teachers should be more like travel agents. They should make a book so appealing to children that the children will want to read it. Once they have had an enjoyable reading experience, they will be eager to have another.

B. *In the cases below, (i) distinguish between the model and the subject modeled, and (ii) discuss the ways in which the model may fail to serve as a reliable basis for conclusions about the subject modeled.*

*1. A major problem in the study of mental illness is that it is not clear that there can be animal models for the most serious of the psychiatric disorders. Schizophrenia, for example, does not have an animal model.

Discuss some of the difficulties that stand in the way of getting appropriate animal models for studying mental illness.

2. Adolescent male hamsters were each placed in the cage of a mature adult male hamster for an hour a day for a week, and the older hamsters threatened and attacked the younger ones.

The adolescents were given their own cages at maturity, and other male hamsters (interlopers) were placed in with them. If (a) the interloper was the same size or larger, the hamsters tended to cower or run (become cowards). If (b) the interloper was smaller and weaker, the hamsters tended to attack far more aggressively (become bullies) than hamsters never subjected to the threats of territorial males during their adolescence.

The study suggests that humans who are treated violently or threatened with violence during their developing years will later (a) behave in a cowardly way if they feel threatened by their peers; and (b) react violently (be bullies) when in conflict with someone smaller and weaker.

3. In a study of high blood pressure, Derek Denton examined twenty-six adult chimpanzees at a research center and found that none had high blood pressure. Measurements of systolic and diastolic blood pressures (in millimeters of mercury) fell into the range of 110/70 to 120/80.

    Denton selected half the chimpanzees (the experimental group) and fed them a daily diet in which the salt was progressively increased from five grams to fifteen grams. The diet of the others (the control group) was unchanged. After twenty months, the blood pressure in the chimpanzees in the experimental group rose as high as 150/90. Six months after the feeding of extra salt was discontinued, all the animals in the experimental group had blood pressure falling in the normal range.

    The similarities between humans and chimpanzees are quite close. Hence, Denton's study suggests that a high level of salt in the human diet is one of the major factors responsible for high blood pressure. Those wishing to prevent or reverse high blood pressure are well advised to decrease the amount of salt they consume.

4. Discuss whether spilling a bag of marbles would be a good abstract model for the behavior of people in a parking lot. Would it be a good model for the behavior of a crowd leaving an office building during a fire?

Chapter 8

ERRORS IN REASONING: FALLACIES

Any error in reasoning may be called a **fallacy**. Traditionally, though, only common errors with a strong psychological appeal have been described, named, and referred to as *fallacies*.

You will see that many of the fallacies below have Latin names. This is an indication that philosophers since antiquity have tried to identify and describe failures of reasoning. The aim of those philosophers, and our aim, is to make it less likely that any of us will be taken in by fallacious appeals.

We divide fallacies into two groups. The first consists of errors in making a case for a claim. The second consists of errors committed in criticizing arguments for a claim or in responding to such criticism. The categories and their subdivisions are not exclusive, and we might easily place some fallacies in more than one. (Other fallacies are discussed on p. 64.)

Fallacies in Supporting a Claim

Some of the traditional fallacious arguments in this category have premises that fail to be *relevant* to the conclusion. Others have relevant premises but fall far short of making an *adequate* case for the conclusion. A third subdivision consists of fallacies that depend on some *mistaken assumptions*.

Five Fallacies of Relevance

Fallacies in this group involve premises not relevant to the conclusions they are meant to support.

1. Appeal to Ignorance (*Ad Ignorantiam*) The **appeal to ignorance** consists in arguing that because a claim has not been demonstrated to be false, the claim is true. Or, because a claim has not been demonstrated to be true, then it is false. To see how very mistaken such inferences are, suppose you are flipping a coin that appears to be a regular fair nickel, and I have to bet on the outcome of the next flip.

"The next flip will come up heads," I say with confidence. "It has not been demonstrated that it will not come up heads, so it will."

I obviously have made an error. Not having a demonstration that the coin will *not* come up heads gives no reason at all to think that it *will* come up heads.

Furthermore, from the same information we can reason in the *ad ignorantiam* way for exactly the opposite conclusion. "We have no demonstration that the next flip *will* be heads, so it will *not* be heads." Since we can "support" either side equally, it is even more clear that lack of demonstration of one side of an issue does nothing to indicate the correctness of the other side.

The reasoning in the coin case is clearly mistaken. Unfortunately, the mistake is not always so obvious, and appeals to ignorance occur often.

> Of course there is a god. No one has ever shown there isn't.
>
> Neither you nor anyone else can give me one good reason why we should legalize marijuana. Obviously, then, we should do no such thing.
>
> I firmly believe in astrology since it has never been shown to be mistaken.

Consider this recent case of legislative reasoning:

> The legislature has passed a law requiring public school teachers to swear an oath of loyalty to the United States. The House Speaker summed up the thinking of the legislature. "There didn't seem to be any reason we shouldn't have such a law," he said. "No one showed us anything wrong with it, so we concluded it was all right."

In sum, to establish a claim by argument, we must present reasons *for* it. Not having a case against a claim is different from having reasons for it.

Sometimes good reasoning can resemble *ad ignorantiam* reasoning. For instance, we look in the living room, do not see an elephant, and conclude no elephant is there. Taken at face value, this looks like just another appeal to ignorance.

> It has not been shown that there is an elephant in the living room.
> _____
> There is not an elephant in the living room.

Really, though, the argument is entirely acceptable if we elaborate and add the commonsense unstated premise.

It has not been shown that there is an elephant in the living room;
that is, I did not see one there.
If there were an elephant in the living room, I would have seen it
there.

There is no elephant in the living room.

Sympathetically interpreted in this way, the argument is valid (an instance of *modus tollens*) and the premises are nearly certainly true. So, despite its superficial similarity to an appeal to ignorance, the argument gives strong ground for accepting its conclusion.

Further, some arguments may look like appeals to ignorance only because we are ignoring information we already have (our background beliefs, see pp. 157–160) that relates to the argument. Suppose that you profess your odd beliefs about big cockroaches in jungles. I reply,

No one has given any good reason to think there are 10-foot-long
cockroaches hiding out in the darkest jungles of the earth.

There are not any such giant cockroaches.

On the surface this looks like the *ad ignorantiam* fallacy. But in practice we are surely relying on our experience that insects just do not get nearly that big. If we are sophisticated in biology we also know that huge insects could not live because their lungs could not take in enough oxygen relative to body size. With the unstated premise that reflects this other knowledge, the argument is

Everyday experience and principles of biology tell us that insects
are mostly under 6 inches in length.
No one has given any good reason to think there are 10-foot-long
cockroaches hiding out in the darkest jungles of the earth.

There are not any such giant cockroaches.

The argument now gives good support for its conclusion.

In short, both the elephant and the cockroach arguments look like cases of appeals to ignorance, but both can be understood to assume unstated premises. Without the unstated premises they really are fallacious appeals to ignorance. With the unstated premises they are good arguments. We never want to be convinced by arguments that amount to nothing but appeals to ignorance. But we also want to be sensitive to interpretations that would show any underlying merit an argument may have.

Finally here we should note that legal decisions of "not guilty" in the United States may seem to commit the *ad ignorantiam* fallacy.

> It has not been proven that the defendant is guilty.
> _____
> The defendant is not guilty.

Issues of legal guilt are enormously complicated, but no fallacy is committed here. For in the U.S. system, a person is presumed innocent until proven guilty, so to be "not guilty" just *means* not to have been found guilty. The argument about guilt should be understood as

> It has not been legally proven that the defendant is guilty.
> Anyone not proven to be legally guilty is not legally guilty.
> _____
> The defendant is not legally guilty.

This is faultless reasoning.

2. Appeal to Inappropriate Authority (*Ad Verecundiam*) We base much of what we believe on the evidence of authority, and citing an authority is a legitimate way of justifying a belief. The rationale is that the authority is in a position to provide compelling evidence, even though we are not. A fallacy, however, is committed when the authority cited is not an authority in the proper area. The expertise of the authority is thus irrelevant to the claim and provides no support for it.

Aldous Huxley, the author of *Brave New World,* was convinced that nearsightedness can be corrected by eye exercises (the Bates method) and that glasses are unnecessary. He wrote a book advocating this position, and because of his eminence as a novelist, other writers frequently cited him to establish the claim that the Bates method could cure nearsightedness. Those who appealed to Huxley's authority in support of the claim were committing the fallacy of **appealing to inappropriate authority**.

The fallacy is one committed, usually implicitly, by those who base their political views on the claims of physicians, their economic views on the pronouncements of psychologists, or their nutritional views on the assertions of hairstylists. (See pp. 152–156 for more discussion.)

3. Appeal to Belief (*Ad Populum*) This fallacy consists in asserting that a claim is correct just because people generally believe it is. Such an inference is in error because we have no reason to take what most people believe as a reliable indicator of what is true.

Probably the most common appeal to this fallacious argument type is this one: "People the world over have always believed God exists. It has to be true." (Notice that the premise is false as well as being irrelevant to the conclusion.)

Sometimes an appeal to popular belief is incorporated into a larger argument:

> We all know most people on welfare are just too lazy to work. So, we should start a program requiring those on welfare to provide community service to earn their money.

Here popular opinion is used as the authority for accepting an asserted claim, so this is a form of appealing to authority. But since it is difficult to think of any case in which "most people" should be regarded as a genuine authority, it is a particular case of the fallacy of appeal to *inappropriate* authority.

4. Appeal to Popular Attitudes and Emotions (also called *Ad Populum*) Popular attitudes and the emotions associated with them can be manipulated to incline people to accept claims that have not been demonstrated. Racial fears and prejudices, patriotic impulses, and the wish to be associated with a special social group are some sources of such sentiments and attitudes. This fallacy is committed by appealing to these rather than to relevant reasons and evidence.

Here is an unsubtle appeal to patriotism: "I'll tell you why I still believe we were right to fight in Vietnam. It's because I love my country. If you love it, you'll agree." In the following appeal, a presumed wish to be associated with a special social group is used. "Now look, Sally. You know that Marxism isn't right. What would your friends at the club think if they heard you talking this way?" Obviously such purely emotional appeals offer no relevant support for the issues in question.

5. The Gambler's Fallacy A classic and very tempting case of the **gambler's fallacy** goes this way:

> According to the law of averages, if I flip a fair coin it should come up *heads* about 50 percent of the time and come up *tails* about 50 percent of the time. The last ten flips have been *tails*. So, it is well past time for *heads* to come up. We'd better bet all we have on *heads*.

This is tempting reasoning. There should be an equal number of *heads* and *tails*. Overall they should be equal. So, we think, in this case it is time for *heads* to be catching up. *Expect the next flip to be heads.*

Tempting as it is, this reasoning is badly mistaken. Each flip of the coin is independent of the others. If the coin is fair, even 100 previous flips of either *heads* or *tails* have nothing to do with the likelihood that the next flip will or will not be *heads*. In the very long run, *heads* and *tails* can be expected to even out, but that has nothing to do with what we should expect on the next or any particular coin flip.

The idea that some things are "due" usually plays a role in the gambler's fallacy. Ten flips and no *heads,* so *heads* is due; fifty years and Jacksonville, right there on the coast, has not had a major hurricane, so a hurricane is due; the best hitter in baseball has not had a hit in twenty at bats, so he is due. All of these understandable and tempting claims are instances of the gambler's fallacy, and they all need to be resisted.

Two Fallacies of Inadequate Evidence

Fallacies in this group are arguments with premises that present relevant but inadequate evidence.

1. False Cause (*Post Hoc*) The *post hoc* fallacy involves concluding that because one event occurred before another, the first was the cause of the second. Suppose, for example, that Templeton eats a candy bar, then commits a murder. It would be fallacious to conclude, on this ground alone, that eating the candy bar caused Templeton to commit the murder.

Legitimate causal explanations invoke a causal law that connects events of one type with those of another. Such laws must be based on data from a number of cases and established by an empirical investigation that rules out the possibility of a merely accidental correlation between the two types of events. (See pp. 103–108.)

We have no law connecting candy bars and murder. (We do not even have laws connecting murder with physiological changes that occur when particular kinds of people eat candy bars.) That one event occurs before another is relevant to identifying the first as the cause of the second. However, we cannot regard everything that happens before a particular event as causing it.

2. Hasty Generalization The fallacy of **hasty generalization** consists of generalizing on the basis of an inadequate set of cases. As a sample from a larger population, the cases are too few or too unrepresentative to constitute adequate evidence. Suppose you are a psychotherapist and your first two clients lie to you about crucial aspects of their lives. If you conclude from this experience, "All clients lie to their therapists" or even "Most clients lie to their therapists," then you are open to the charge of hasty generalization. Even if your generalization is true, your evidence is inadequate because your sample is very small, and we have no reason to think it is representative of the entire group. (See p. 43.)

Errors in reasoning are always difficult to avoid and often hard to detect. Knowing the names of a few prominent kinds of fallacies may be helpful, but it is no substitute for constant vigilance and ready skepticism.

Exercises

A. *Identify the fallacies of relevance and inadequate evidence in the passages below. Use the standard names where possible, but if a fallacy does not seem to fall easily into a category, then simply explain what is wrong with the argument.*

*1. Radio ad: "What is the best reason to call Carpetmasters? There is no good reason not to."

 2. The Dallas group held a rain dance at the Turtle Creek fountain Sunday night, and the group leader Debra Denton claimed it got results. "It rained, didn't it?" she asked Monday. —*Dallas Morning News* (July 22, 1980)

*3. "You are going to stay in the library and study this afternoon? And not go to the first big football game of the year? You sure are going to be popular!"

 4. Just going on through red lights at 3 o'clock in the morning when there are no other cars in sight is the right thing to do. You can't show there is anything wrong with it.

 5. I have been sitting at this bridge table for three hours and haven't gotten a decent hand yet. I am bound to get a really good one before long.

 6. A talk show host was fired by ABC Radio shortly after the company merged with the Walt Disney Company. The host claimed he was fired because he had often been very critical of Disney. In support of this claim, he said that his employers' attitude toward him "changed right after the merger was announced. Within six weeks, I was toast."

*7. R. J. Palmer, D.D.S., one of this community's leading dental practitioners, says that because evolution theory requires saying that a species of reptile changed into a birdlike creature, he thinks the whole theory is mistaken. Dr. Palmer's scientific assessment of the situation is sufficient proof that no reasonable person can be an evolutionist.

 8. Don't try to fool me. A family that lives down the street gets food stamps, and I know what they do with them. That's enough to show me. Just about everybody who gets food stamps uses them for expensive frozen stuff and candy. And the taxpayers foot the bill.

 9. That couple was romping naked on the beach. Of course they should have been arrested. Look at history! Where do you find a society that approved of nudity in public?

10. Your neighbors won't be shoveling snow this winter. Do you want to be the only one on your block with a shovel? You had better buy a Smith Brothers Snow Blower before it is too late.

Four Fallacies of Illegitimate Assumption

Fallacies in this group are tied together by the fact that each invokes some illegitimate assumption.

1. False Dilemma (False Alternatives) A dilemma is a situation in which we are faced with choosing between alternatives. In the most strict case, the dilemma has exactly two alternatives that are both exhaustive and exclusive. "You must either marry or remain single" offers exactly two possible choices. These alternatives exhaust all the possibilities. (Nothing exists outside the alternatives of married or single.) And they are exclusive in that it is not possible to be both married and single.

We usually take a less strict view and think of a dilemma as involving two or more alternatives, and this view is the one we adopt here. Hence, "The government of Ruritania must either dissolve itself, replace its prime minister, or turn over power to the opposition leader" presents three alternatives facing the government.

Furthermore, we typically do not require the alternatives to be exhaustive and exclusive in a strict way (marry or not marry, for example), but only in a practical way. For instance, having fish or steak for dinner does not constitute an exhaustive and exclusive set of alternatives in the strict way. But in a practical context, they could be exhaustive and exclusive (if, for instance, they are both on the menu, nothing else is, and you can't have both).

The **false dilemma fallacy** consists of giving arguments that present alternatives as exhaustive and exclusive when they are not. The classic case of this is

> Either you're for us or you're against us. It is obvious you aren't for us. So, you're against us.

The alternatives in the first premise pretend to be exhaustive, but they are neither strictly nor practically so. They leave out the possibility of a person's being carefully neutral or just having no knowledge of the issues.

"Either we cut spending or increase the deficit" is a false dilemma that ignores such possibilities as raising taxes. "Either we have much more capital punishment or keep putting murderers back out on the street" ignores possibilities like mandatory life imprisonment for murderers.

Such false dilemmas are aimed at convincing us to accept certain conclusions (cut spending; have a lot more capital punishment). Generally, false dilemmas are used to make us choose between given alternatives when other choices really exist or we could accept both given alternatives.

2. Loaded Question (Complex Question) The **loaded question fallacy** consists of attempting to get an answer to a question that assumes the truth of an unproved assumption. It "assumes a conclusion." The classic example is "Have you stopped beating your wife?" Whether someone answers yes or no to this question, he is committing himself to the truth of the implicit assumption that he has beaten his wife in the past.

The error is also called the fallacy of the **complex question** because we can analyze the question into a statement and a question: "You used to beat your wife. Do you still do so?"

A "question that assumes a conclusion" is not permitted in courts of law during the examination of witnesses—unless the conclusion at issue has already been established to lay the groundwork for the question that assumes its truth. The fallacy is an attempt to get the truth of the assumed conclusion tacitly acknowledged without presenting any reasons or evidence to support it.

Strictly speaking, loaded questions are not really arguments. But since they are attempts to get claims (the hidden assumptions) accepted without presenting any adequate or legitimate grounds for them, loaded questions resemble fallacious arguments. The important thing is that they are dangerous and misleading and should be recognized and guarded against.

3. Begging the Question (*Petitio Principii*) The "question" is the issue at hand, and the question is "begged," not really addressed, when some reason offered for some conclusion is not really different from the conclusion itself. The ways this may be done differ, but each involves stating as a conclusion something that also serves as a premise.

In one familiar way, the conclusion restates part or all of the meaning of a premise: "James is a murderer because he wrongfully killed someone." To call James a murderer is to say he killed someone wrongfully, so the argument is valid. The premise offered to justify the conclusion logically implies it, but *no independent evidence for the premise is offered.* Yet what we expect from the argument are reasons for believing James killed someone and was wrong to do so. We expect independent evidence for the claim made in both the conclusion and the premise. This evidence is just what is lacking in a question-begging argument.

A question is begged in a second way when a premise is used to support a conclusion while the conclusion is at least implicitly appealed to in support of the premise. This is known as **circular reasoning** or **arguing in a circle**: *A* because *B*, *B* because *C*, *C* because *A*. Such an argument is flawed because the premise purporting to provide independent support for the conclusion is itself taken to be supported by the conclusion.

Consider one interpretation of a famous argument by the seventeenth-century French philosopher René Descartes. Descartes considered the possibility that

> A. There is an evil demon deceiving him about any reasoning process that depends on memory.

Insofar as *A* is possible, Descartes cannot rely on any complex reasoning at all.

Descartes then constructs a fairly complicated proof that

> B. God exists, is himself no deceiver, and would not allow there to be a deceiver.

But how can Descartes know his proof of *B* is correct? To know it is, he must first know no demon is deceiving him about it. And to know that, he must know that God exists and would not allow deception. That is, he must know that *B* is true. So, the proof of *B* tacitly assumes *B*—treats *B* as a premise—which means the reasoning is circular and proves nothing. The more complex an argument, the easier it becomes not to notice that the argument amounts to nothing more than an unsupported assertion.

4. Slippery Slope The mistaken idea behind the **slippery slope fallacy** is that when there is little or no significant difference between adjacent points on a continuum, then there is no important difference between even widely separated points on the continuum.

> A lot of people think a 70-mile-per-hour speed limit on interstate highways is too high. Actually it is too low. Look, everybody admits that 55 is a limit that is as safe as can be. But if 55 is safe, 56 or 57 must be also. For a mile or two can't matter. So 58 or 59 will also be safe. And you have to be crazy to think 60 would be a less safe limit than 59. Similarly, there can't be a significant difference between 60 and 62 . . . between 62 and 64 . . . 64 and 66 . . . 66 and 68. . . . Maybe there should be no speed limit at all on good roads!

Slippery slope arguments look plausible because it does seem arbitrary to draw a line between any particular adjacent points on the continuum. Nonetheless, the arguments are clearly mistaken, since many small and "insignificant" differences can add up to a very large difference.

The slippery slope fallacy often results in claiming that the most extreme and indefensible form of action is not significantly different from the simplest and most defensible form. This is the case in the following example:

> A newborn baby is obviously a person whom it would be wrong to kill. Since there is little difference between a newborn baby and a baby just prior to birth, the latter is also a person whom it would be wrong to kill. And there is little difference between the baby just prior to birth and the fetus at eight-and a half months, between the fetus at eight-and-a-half months and a few days before that. So, the fetus at any of these stages is also a person. But in the same way there is almost no difference between the fetus at eight months and just before that . . . and before that. . . . We must face the fact that there is no stopping place. So the newly fertilized ovum is a person whom it would be wrong to kill. Abortion is murder.

Whatever one's views on abortion, this is not a good argument. Although it may be difficult to draw a line at any particular point along the continuum from a newborn baby to a just-fertilized ovum, this does not mean they are exactly the same in all respects. Consequently, treatment that is morally legitimate in one case is not necessarily legitimate in the other.

Related to slippery slope arguments are those that say a practice should not be initiated because it would lead to, or at least encourage, the adoption of a similar but more extreme practice. For instance, some people oppose any legal regulation of even very late term abortions on the ground that such regulations would be just a first step toward outlawing abortion entirely. Or, consider a law allowing physicians to administer a lethal injection to a terminally ill patient at the patient's request. This could be the first in a step-by-step progression toward a eugenics program involving killing without consent the old, the sick, the handicapped, or those who don't satisfy some social ideal. Arguments like these tell us that we must be careful of "letting the camel get its nose under the tent," for, if we allow this much, soon we will find ourselves sleeping with the beast. "Camel's nose" arguments are not pure slippery slope arguments, since they have to do with similar practices *causing* one another. A camel's nose argument may or may not be a good argument, depending on whether it makes a persuasive case that one practice is likely to lead to another more extreme and undesirable one.

Exercises

B. *Identify the fallacies of illegitimate assumption in the passages below.*

*1. Query to *Tennis Magazine* (March 1995): "In a singles match, after serving, I went to the net to volley the return. My volley went through the net instead of over it. Is the point replayed or do I win the point?"

2. Despite what some modern freethinkers claim, adultery can never be justified. For it is never acceptable to have sex with a person when one is married to another.

3. Pet dogs are thought to be entitled to medical care because of their special place in the hearts of many people. But cats are almost as special to a great number of people. Even hamsters and goldfish are greatly loved by some people. So, all of these would have to be given care. Indeed, so must domestic animals like horses, pigs, cattle, chickens, and so on, for some people come to love them. Yet the amount of money it would take to provide care for chickens alone would virtually bankrupt the country. We can't afford medical care for dogs.

4. All right, Senator, it's either support a constitutional amendment prohibiting burning the flag or support the burners. You are against the amendment. I guess we know whose side you are on.

5. Student to professor: "I missed the exam last week. When can I make it up?"

*6. Smith: Everything the Bible says is true.

Jones: I certainly think so too, but how can we be sure?

Smith: Because it is the word of God, and God would never lie.

Jones: How can we be so sure it is the word of God?

Smith: Because it says so in the Bible, and what the Bible says can't be wrong.

*7. Around 1989–90, factions on many college campuses declared "Gay Jeans Day." On this particular day, students were supposed to wear jeans to indicate their support of gay rights or not wear jeans to indicate their opposition.

8. You say that you should not be convicted. Do you mean that you acted in self-defense when you stabbed your lover?

Fallacies of Criticism and Response

A number of errors in reasoning are commonly committed either in criticizing a supported claim or in responding to such criticisms. Hence, the errors we discuss here are most frequently found in the dialectical context of challenge and reply. We will limit our concern to this context, even though some of the fallacies also occur in nondialectical situations.

Five Fallacies of Criticism

1. Against the Person (*Ad Hominem*) The **ad hominem fallacy** consists in rejecting a claim or an argument by offering as grounds some personal characteristics of the person supporting it. Suppose Barton has argued that David Byrne is a more creative musician than David Bowie. Someone who then argues "Barton is pretty much of a jerk, you know. I am sure he is wrong" is committing the *ad hominem* fallacy.

Strictly, the personal characteristics of individuals offering claims are irrelevant to the truth of those claims. Even if Barton is a jerk, he can still be correct. Similarly, some claims of bleeding-heart liberals, ultraconservatives, doctrinaire communists, and plain fools are right. If we wish to be fair and rational, we must recognize that even a claim presented by a fool can be true and that even the jerk's arguments could be good ones. We must not reject out of hand either claims or arguments because of their source.

However, personal characteristics can be relevant if we are trying to decide whether to accept a claim just on the word of the person making it. Although chronic liars, the demented, and practical jokers sometimes speak the truth, we should place little reliance on the word of such people. If a person is known to be a mentally unstable alcoholic who often has trouble distinguishing his fantasies from reality, something he tells us could be true, but we have no right to expect it to be true on the ground of his saying it.

A special sort of argument against the person is called the **circumstantial *ad hominem***. Here the charge is not against the general character of the person (she is a drunk, a paranoid, and so on); it is against the reliability of the person in a particular set of *circumstances*. The basically sound idea behind this sort of argument against the person is that those with reasons to lie may do so and those with a vested interest are likely to be biased so as not to acknowledge the truth even to themselves. Thus, a chemical company's representative may assure us his company's pesticide is harmless, a manufacturer may claim her product is safe to use, and a bureaucrat may assert his department is underfunded. All may be held suspect because even trustworthy and reasonable people can be affected by their circumstances. We should, then, suspect claims made by some sorts of people in some circumstances. But we commit a fallacy if we assume the claims presented must be false or that we have no need to examine the worth of any argument given.

2. You Too (*Tu Quoque*) This is a special kind of *ad hominem* argument.

> Cook: Your argument for legalizing prostitution is ridiculous. You commit every fallacy in the book.
>
> Gordon: So? You're a fine one to talk. You can never open your mouth without committing a fallacy.
>
> Bledsoe: You are a cheat. You left half your income off your tax return last year.
>
> Manning: Big deal. You lied about deductions and had the nerve to claim your dog as a dependent.

The responses by Gordon and Manning—in effect, "you do it too"— are *ad hominem* and have no relevance to the truth or accuracy of the original claims. Cook and Bledsoe may be hypocritical in preaching what they do not practice, but that does not have any bearing at all on the truth of what they say.

3. Pooh-Pooh To **pooh-pooh** an argument is to dismiss it with ridicule as not worthy of serious consideration.

> We don't have to waste time dealing with Ms. Thompson's claims about women not being promoted to executive positions. She's just giving us more of the usual feminist claptrap.

> Hong once again brings up that old liberal chestnut that minorities are being exploited by businesses out to keep their labor cost low, a view that's worth more of a groan than a laugh.

Pooh-poohing is a refusal to examine an argument seriously and evaluate it fairly. As such, the fallacy is an attempt to obtain by guile what should be earned by work. It is a case of misdirection.

4. Straw Man A straw man is one that is easy to knock over. The **straw man fallacy** consists of misrepresenting an opponent's claim or argument so that it is easier to criticize or so obviously implausible that no criticism is needed. Although the misrepresented version is a caricature (a straw man), the critic treats it as equivalent to the original.

An example is columnist James Kilpatrick's statement of former Supreme Court Justice William Brennan's and Professor Laurence

Tribe's position on interpreting the Constitution. According to Brennan and Tribe, we cannot be sure of the intention of legislators who ratified a constitutional amendment, so the question of how an amendment should be interpreted cannot be answered by appealing to their intention. Kilpatrick represents the view in this way:

> In [Brennan's and Tribe's] view, original intention is often unfathomable and generally irrelevant. What counts is not what a word may have meant "then." It is what the word means "now." Theirs is the school of semantics that says words should mean exactly what they choose them to mean. —*St. Louis Post-Dispatch*, January 16, 1988

Kilpatrick's version of the position suggests that Brennan and Tribe hold that the meaning of a phrase like "equal protection under the law" can arbitrarily be assigned a meaning. This position is absurd and only a straw man version of the actual one.

One common way of creating a straw man is to reduce a complex argument to a caricatured, simplistic claim. For example, instead of presenting the fundamental concepts and principles that make up contemporary evolutionary theory, an opponent might represent the theory in this way:

> The theory of evolution boils down to the idea that human beings are descended from apes.

This statement presents no theory that any serious scientist holds. Yet the opponent who criticizes this position may convince some people that he has refuted evolutionary theory.

5. Loaded Words Some years ago a newspaper columnist questioned the sexual and financial behavior of several senators who opposed a nominee to the Supreme Court. The columnist went on to ask us to consider, by way of contrast to the nominee's record, the records of "the four senatorial *sleazeballs* who are leading the Judiciary Committee's attack on him."

When we apply judgmental words like *sleazeball, incompetent, idiot, morally corrupt, venal, avaricious,* and *decadent* to people, policies, or practices, we must justify the application. (The same is also true of positive words like *competent, genius, intelligent, generous.*) We must give reasons and evidence to demonstrate that, for example, an official or a government is morally corrupt. In effect, an argument has to be presented to establish the conclusion that the word may be legitimately applied.

The use of loaded language in arguments frequently results in begging the question.

> Medical research on animals simply must be stopped at once. This torture of innocent creatures is morally indecent. Those who perpetrate such crimes against feeling creatures are without feelings themselves. It is time to put a stop to these pointless atrocities.

Here it is *assumed* that medical research involves torture of innocents, crimes against feeling creatures, pointless atrocities, and more. With these loaded phrases built into the premises, it is just a short question-begging step to the conclusion that such research should be halted.

In short, to apply judgmental terms without providing reasons is another way of trying to get something for nothing. Such words are also called "loaded" because they assume the truth of a conclusion that has not been established.

Two Fallacies of Defense

A legitimate response to criticism requires addressing the criticism directly. If it cannot be answered, then we may have to withdraw or modify the position taken. **Fallacies of defense** are ways of skirting a criticism to avoid facing it and its consequences.

1. Definitional Dodge The **definitional dodge** consists of redefining a crucial term in a claim to avoid acknowledging a counterexample that would falsify the claim.

Consider an example in which Smith claims "All pornography demeans women," and Hopkins responds by asking, "What about John Cleland's *Fanny Hill*? It's generally considered pornographic, but it doesn't demean women." Hopkins has offered a case apparently inconsistent with Smith's claim. Smith might respond legitimately by trying to show that *Fanny Hill* does demean women and so is not a counterexample at all.

However, if Smith responds by saying something like, "Then *Fanny Hill* is not pornography, because pornography always involves demeaning women," Smith is pulling a definitional dodge. He is ruling out an apparent counterexample to his claim by altering the ordinary meaning of the word to make "demeans women" a necessary feature of pornography. Hence, it becomes logically impossible ever to mention a case of pornography that does not demean women.

If Smith wishes to make "demeans women" part of an arbitrary stipulative definition, he may. (See p. 166–167.) However, the claim is no longer about the character of what is generally considered pornography. The claim becomes nothing more than an implication of Smith's resolution about using the word *pornography*.

Words like *employment, crime, middle class, educated, war,* and *peace* figure often in disputes in which an ordinary meaning is altered for the purpose of escaping from the crushing blows of counterexamples. Yet almost any key term in a claim can be redefined in a way that, in the context of a rational disagreement, is illicit.

2. The Exception That Proves the Rule The word *prove* has the meanings: (1) establish as true, and (2) test or try out. The sentence "The mathematician *proved* an important theorem, but also he *proved* to be a terrible teacher" illustrates both uses. In some contexts, the word is ambiguous, and this is dramatically the case in the traditional expression "the exception that proves the rule." The saying is often mistakenly taken to mean "an exception to a rule establishes its truth," whereas it actually means "an exception to a rule is a test of the rule."

This confusion allows someone defending a claim to commit a fallacy by dismissing apparent counterexamples as no challenge. Consider this exchange:

> Wexford: Women novelists have been nothing more than entertainers. None has been truly outstanding.
>
> Chang: Aren't you forgetting about Jane Austen and Mary Ann Evans?
>
> Wexford: They're just exceptions that prove the rule. We look to women writers for amusement, not literature.

If Wexford is prepared to admit that the cases mentioned by Chang are outstanding novelists, then Wexford's claim simply cannot be true. The counterexamples test it and prove it false.

Exercises

C. *Identify the fallacies of criticism and response in the passages below.*

1. What Ms. Grag says about nuclear disarmament is surely incorrect. Is she a political scientist? No. A politician with experience in foreign policy matters? No. I'll tell you what she is, she's a commercial baker. That's right, a cookie maker!

*2. According to William Buckley, former vice president Dan Quayle gave a speech citing legal costs as a part of the overhead of doing business in America. The head of the American Bar Association responded, "Anyone who believes a better day dawns when lawyers are eliminated bears the burden of explaining who will take their place." —*St. Louis Post-Dispatch* (August 21, 1991)

3. My opponent says that we should spend more on education and less on weapons. Just another tired cliché without any substance.

4. Smith: You know, Robert Frost is my favorite poet. I particularly like his poetry because it all rhymes.

   Jones: Don't be ridiculous. Robert Frost wrote the poem "Mending Wall," and it doesn't rhyme.

   Smith: If it doesn't rhyme, it's not poetry. As I said, all of Frost's poetry rhymes. "Mending Wall" is OK, but it isn't a poem.

*5. An association of teachers interested in critical thinking suggested the following exercise: Listen to radio talk shows—one in particular was mentioned—and look for instances of *ad hominem* arguments, guilt by association, distortion, and so on. The talk show host singled out for scrutiny indignantly denied the charge and replied in this way:

   "Who are these people [the ones in the association]? They talk to maybe 30 people [students] at a time. I talk to five million people every day. They could not begin to do what I do. They are just gnats flying around getting in the way."

*6. It is curious how smut like *Playboy* and *Penthouse* have been whitewashed to the point that decent citizens hardly notice their nasty presence. The notion that we should allow propaganda to be perpetrated on society is a bastardization of free speech. Our nation stands for liberty, not license; expression within the bounds of morality, not incitements to unbridled destructive sexuality. We urge your awareness and action.

7. Abbot: I'm sorry, but I really don't like your haircut. You should get a new barber.

   Blutz: You are a fine one to talk. You always look like you had your hair cut with a lawn mower.

8. Smith: You know, Robert Frost is my favorite poet. I particularly like his poetry because it all rhymes.

   Jones: Don't be ridiculous. Robert Frost wrote the poem "Mending Wall," and it doesn't rhyme.

   Smith: See? I'm right. That is just the exception that proves it.

9. According to Ronald Reagan, "Jimmy Carter says we should sign the SALT II treaty, because nobody will like us if we don't." But in fact, Mr. Carter has said the survival of the world depends on ending the cycle of nuclear arms development. —Robert Lindsey, *The New York Times Magazine* (July 29, 1980)

*10.   Orson swore to me that he saw my boyfriend out with another woman, but I am not sure I should believe him. After all, Orson is known to lie a lot. Besides, I think he has a crush on me himself.

D.   *Identify any fallacies in the passages below.*

1.   The liberal pervents who oppose an all-out ban on pornography must be stopped. They want to let the sort of sick, degrading, violent filth that Ted Bundy says turned him into a serial killer be sold in your city and in your neighborhood and to your teenager. We must all declare ourselves on the side of decency and support federal legislation that makes it a crime to produce, possess, or purvey pornography of any sort.

*2.   Psychologist Brenda Hunter says that increasing numbers of children feel adrift and homeless, feel rejected by their mothers. For this, she indicts feminist leaders like Gloria Steinem, Germaine Greer, and Betty Friedan, who, she says, are products of dysfunctional families and who are rebelling against the poor nurturing she says they experienced as children. Because of their own inadequate childhood experiences, Hunter says, they have led women to make wrong choices that adversely affected their lives as well as the lives of their children.

"Betty Friedan . . . grew up in a household short on mother love." —Cal Thomas, *St. Louis Post-Dispatch* (July 16, 1991)

3.   You don't have to be of noble birth to appreciate Cutty Sark Scots Whisky. All that is required is noble taste.

4.   I am tired of the inconsistencies of anti-abortionists. They claim to think human life is sacred. So, why do they approve of capital punishment and of waging war against the non-white people of the world?

5.   Sports column: "When Dolphins safety Louis Oliver questioned the manhood of Jets quarterback Ken O'Brien on Sunday—after O'Brien didn't plow into traffic on a run toward the end zone—he struck a raw nerve with the Jets.

'It was a stupid statement by a stupid person.' Jets quarterback Pat Ryan said. 'He's a stiff, noplaying free safety. . . . I didn't hear him talking trash when we threw all over him in the first game.'" —*St. Louis Post-Dispatch* (November 19, 1989)

6.   There is absolutely no justification for ever granting parole to convicted murderers. Anyone will tell you that!

7. Promo for TV program: "Is violence in the NHL all that bad, or is it the main reason people come to the games?"

8. Letter to the editor: "Leon Panetta has been seen repeatedly on TV this past weekend lamenting Newt Gingrich's behaving like some 'out-of-control radio talk show host.'

    "How much control would Panetta or, more importantly, the Clinton administration desire to exercise over the constitutional right of free speech?" —*Florida Times-Union* (December 14, 1994)

*9. I know lots of people, and not one of them thinks our senior senator should be re-elected. For sure we will have somebody new next year.

*10. According to Goldbach's Conjecture, every even number greater than 2 is the sum of two prime numbers. I know that is what Goldbach's Conjecture is because my chemistry professor told me so.

*11. Columnist Cal Thomas objects to Hillary Clinton's distinguishing between forced abortions and elective abortions. "If all human life is not valuable, then no human life has value." —Cal Thomas, *St. Louis Post-Dispatch* (July 11, 1993)

12. a. Henry Hudson, chairman of the 1986 Meese Pornography Commission, asked one witness, a therapist, "Could you give us your explanation of what the causal link is between pornography and incest?"

    b. To another witness, "How many sex offenders, Sergeant, have you interviewed who have told you that the reading of pornography had a direct relationship to the crime they committed?" —*Hearings for The Report of the Commission on Obscenity and Pornography*, 1970

*13. "World's tallest tree? Big deal. Cut it down, and you've got the world's tallest tree somewhere else." —A California logger, on being told that the tallest tree grew nearby

*14. Harvey, Herbert, Joanne, and Carol were all bitten by mosquitoes several times in the last year. Now the four all test positive for the AIDS virus. I don't care what the authorities tell us. Mosquito bites can spread AIDS.

15. In support of his belief that covers of detective magazines play a part in serial murders, a member of the Meese Commission asked a witness, "Is there any reason to doubt that such [bad] effects occur?"

*16. In 1993, popular newspaper columnist Lewis Grizzard underwent what was supposed to be "fairly routine heart valve replacement surgery." According to Grizzard's account in his first column after the surgery, complications arose and his life was in very serious danger for days. Later the doctors and nurses involved told him, "We did everything that we knew to do for you, and it probably wouldn't have been enough. What saved you was prayer." One doctor explained, "Everywhere I went during your worst time, I ran into people who said they were praying for you." A friend said, "Everybody I saw said they were praying for you. You had a lot of people asking God to spare you." —*Florida Times-Union* (May 23, 1993)

17. Newspaper editorial objecting to President Clinton's "defense of the drug czar's office" said, "The president who didn't inhale was incensed when a Senate committee voted to eliminate the office." —*Florida Times-Union* (August 11, 1995)

*18. Dissent to the Meese Commission Report: "Pornography cannot effect good, so it must effect evil." —Charles H. Keating, Jr., A Dissent to the *Report of the Meese Commission*

19. For centuries theologians have been devising complicated and tedious arguments for the existence of the god of the Christians and Jews. In spite of all this work by some of the best minds in the history of the world, not one of these arguments comes close to being successful. A rational person has to conclude there is no god.

20. Jerry's business failed, his wife left him, and he lost all his belongings in the fire. But I told him, "With all that bad luck, something good is sure to happen for you soon."

21. Then-President Bush supported building new weapons such as missiles on rails and on road vehicles. In response to the suggestion that these new weapons were not needed, a spokesman for the president said, "This is not a time to lay down our arms." —Anthony Lewis, *St. Louis Post-Dispatch* (February 9, 1990)

22. No one thinks there is anything so great about being a virgin anymore. It's OK to do it if you really want to.

23. Bill: Only foolish people believe that the Loch Ness monster or the Abominable Snowman or the supposed preserved body from the crash of an alien spaceship in the desert are real. So, you should not believe such nonsense.

    Cindy: How do you know all the believers are foolish?

    Bill: They are the only ones who believe in these things, aren't they?

*24. Syndicated columnist Mike Royko argues that cultural trash must be bad for us: "See, you can't have it both ways. Beethoven's *Ninth Symphony* is supposed to lift our spirits, enrich our souls. So is Mozart's music, great literature, and other powerful and lasting works of art. Well, if great art is good for us, then real junk has to be bad for us. You can't say that Shakespeare elevates us, but Madonna has no impact." —*Florida Times-Union* (June 18, 1993)

25. Sports item: "When told that Dodger pitcher Orel Hershiser said this season that Mike Scott of the Houston Astros might scuff baseballs, Oakland manager Tony La Russa said: 'Hershiser should be ashamed of himself for saying that. We had our doubts about him last year during the World Series.'" —*St. Louis Post-Dispatch* (October 24, 1989)

26. Smith: The world is so unjust. Millions of worthy people are poor and homeless while every professional athlete makes thousands of dollars a month.

    Jones: That is the most absurd thing I have ever heard. Snively plays soccer for a living, and he makes only $800 a month.

    Smith: Well, then, if that is all he makes, I would hardly call Snively a professional athlete.

*27. A Texas rehabilitation hospital brought in pets periodically to cheer up the patients and give them a break from the rigors of treatment. One day a German shepherd muzzled and licked the face of a boy who had been in a coma from an accident for several weeks. One week later the boy awoke from the coma. The boy's family and the hospital staff generally credited the attention of the shepherd with the awakening.

28. When I was six years old, I wanted a dog very badly. My parents were nice, so they got me a cocker spaniel. That dog turned out to be mean and ugly, and he ran away every time he could get out the door. I have never forgotten that lesson: Cocker spaniels really are horrible dogs. Don't get one.

29. Only an idiot would think that smoking one cigarette could harm me. And this next one can't make a difference either. The third wouldn't be any more important than the others. I am beginning to wonder if I shouldn't just smoke as much as I want.

30. You don't have to learn how to surf the Internet. I don't really care if everybody thinks you are very backward and not in tune with the electronic universe.

31. Donald Trump dismissed *The New York Times* critic Paul Goldenberger's negative views of Trump's buildings. "Goldenberger," said Trump, "is unqualified to judge my buildings because he wears cheap suits." —*Time Magazine* (July 16, 1989)

32. If you can't come up with something besides the old feminist cliché that our ad demeans women, I don't see any reason to answer you.

*33. My opponent wants to allow people of the same sex to marry one another. That is ridiculous. If people always married others of the same sex, there wouldn't be any children, and pretty soon there wouldn't be any people left in the whole world.

34. In this season, Richy Rushdahl has completed 70 percent of his passes. In the first half of today's game he is only 3 for 17. So, he is sure to have a big half coming up.

35. Americans are decidedly against all forms of gun control. We did a survey at the National Hunting and Fishing Show, and we discovered that fully 71 percent of the 50 people we interviewed are opposed to controls.

36. Nobody wants to say so in public, but we're all aware that immigrants don't have as strong a commitment to this country as those of us who were born here.

37. Do people think your older sister looks younger than you do? You probably never felt you would catch up to a woman who was a few years older than yourself. But, unfortunately, maybe you have. Many women around the world share your concern, and many who do also share the secret of a mysterious beauty fluid that helps them look younger. Here in the United States, that secret is known as Beautiful Body Oil.

38. The illegal actions of the anti-abortion protesters are inexcusable. For what they are doing is against the law in a way for which there is no excuse.

39. Dempsey: I really have to question the objectivity of your report on the effects of pesticides on humans. You do work for a chemical company that manufactures pesticides, after all.

    Elbert: Correct me if I am wrong, but I believe you are the principal author of your oil company's report on the harmlessness of oil spills to the environment.

40. My opponent favors a law that would allow public school teachers to lead students in voluntary prayer every morning. I hardly need to tell you how absurd that is. The establish-

ment of an official state religion would destroy one of the most important freedoms on which our country is founded.

41. In support of her belief that pornography is harmful, Catherine MacKinnon says, "There is no evidence that pornography does no harm." —*Only Words* (Harvard University Press, 1993, p. 37)

42. According to my literature teacher, evolution is only a theory and so it should not be taught as fact in our schools. That is why I joined the protest against the evolution textbook used in my nephew's high school biology class.

43. Member of a House of Representatives committee investigating the tobacco industry: "Why don't you admit you're adding nicotine to your product in order to make it more addictive?" —Columnist William Raspberry, *St. Louis Post-Dispatch* (April 27, 1995)

44. In 1988 Pat Robertson claimed that there were still Soviet missiles in Cuba. "I am not going to back off from that," he reiterated in response to criticism from political opponents, and he challenged his critics to "prove me wrong" on the missile issue. —*St. Louis Post-Dispatch* (February 16, 1988)

45. Columnist Mona Charen says that in Great Britain "the first half of the 19th century was marked by high levels of public drunkenness, theft, violence, and illegitimacy, all of which dropped to remarkably low levels in the late 19th and early 20th centuries.

    "What changed an entire nation's national character? Attendance at Sunday schools rose steadily throughout the latter half of the 19th century. In 1988, 75 percent of children in England and Wales attended religious schools. When attendance fell off in the 20th century, crime, dishonesty, illegitimacy, and disorder increased dramatically." Charen offers this as an explanation of the United States now having a "decaying social fabric in which criminal behavior is rampant, family structure is fragmented, and drug abuse, suicide, and sexually transmitted disease is epidemic." —*St. Louis Post-Dispatch* (April 22, 1993)

Chapter 9

REASONABLE BELIEFS

When we justify claims by giving arguments for them, we take some claims as premises and use them to argue for the truth of conclusions. Obviously, if *every* claim had to be justified by some preceding argument, we would have no place to begin and our reasoning could never get under way. Thus, we must have some starting points, some claims not based on prior arguments. What are the sources of these claims?

We first show that the question can be understood in two ways and so requires two answers. One answer is straightforward, but the second leads us into examining three sources of our beliefs. In discussing these sources, we also consider some ways (bias, for example) we can fall into error in grounding our beliefs.

Granted Claims and Accepted Beliefs

We can interpret the question about the sources of claims in two ways. If we are wondering why some claims are taken as premises in a particular discussion, the answer is simple:

> Claims are taken as premises insofar as all parties in the discussion agree to them.

Imagine you and I agree to go to a movie together. As we discuss which one to see, we discover we agree we want a comedy. With this agreement as a premise, you might argue persuasively that the best comedy showing is Tom Hanks' latest film, and that would settle the issue.

Now imagine that in the same situation I have murder on my mind and want to see something at a 1940s *film noir* festival. In this case, I do not accept the claim that we should choose a comedy, and so you cannot use that as a starting point in your arguments to me about what film we should see. Similarly, in 1955 a southern politician might have taken it as a premise in speeches to his white constituents that school integration ought to be resisted. By 1980 this viewpoint could no longer be assumed.

What claims one may take as premises in a particular discussion does not depend on what is true or even plausible. The southern politician's view was neither, yet he would not have had to argue for it in 1955. In practice, it is not necessary to give reasons for a point people already accept. We can call the premises agreed to in a particular argument **granted claims**.

Now consider the second way of understanding our question. Suppose that instead of looking at premises in particular discussions, we consider the set of claims a person accepts at any given time—the person's entire set of *beliefs*. We all think (or at least hope) our beliefs are reasonable ones. What makes them reasonable? Some are reasonable because they are supported by argument. But as we said, not all our beliefs can be based on arguments because we must have some beliefs as starting points for any chain of arguments. (We must justify eventually even granted claims for a particular argument, assuming we believe them to be true.) We can call our beliefs not based on arguments **accepted beliefs**.

We can identify at least three sorts of accepted beliefs: those that are *self-evident;* those *based on our own experiences;* and those *based on the authority of others.* We will discuss and illustrate each of these separately.

Accepted Beliefs 1: Self-Evident (Necessary) Truths

Most philosophers think some claims are self-evident. We do not need to support such claims by argument, testimony, or experience because their truth is simply obvious to anyone who thinks clearly about them. Just thinking about them makes it evident that they *must* be true, so claims of this sort are often called **necessary truths**.

1. Analytic Statements The best examples of self-evident claims are **analytic statements**. Analytic statements are ones that are true or false because of their form or because of the meanings of the words that make them up. Those analytically true are **tautologies**, and those analytically false are **contradictions**.

These statements are analytically true because of their forms:

A rose is a rose.

If this is hemlock, then it is hemlock.

Either Jane is alive or she is not.

These are analytically true because of the meanings of the terms employed:

> All squares have four sides.
>
> A rose is a flower.
>
> You never get a second chance to make a first impression.
>
> $4 + 7 = 11$.

The following statements are analytically false:

> That girl is male. (meaning)
>
> It is both raining and not raining. (form)
>
> Triangles have four angles. (meaning)

These statements *must* be false because either their forms or the meanings of their terms make them self-contradictory. A *male girl* and *four-sided triangles* are self-contradictory descriptions. And one contradicts oneself in both asserting and denying that it is raining. So, it is *not possible* for any of these statements to be true. They are *necessarily* false.

Besides telling us about analytically false statements, this provides a way of thinking about whether a statement is analytically *true*. If the denial of a statement is a contradiction, that denial cannot be true. Hence, the statement itself must be true. Thus, if we consider a statement and find that denying it produces a contradiction, we know the statement must be true. It is analytically true, a necessary truth.

Recognizing that some statements cannot be true—are analytically false—while others must be true—are analytically true—can prevent us from being uncertain about statements and from raising some foolish questions and inquiries. We do not need to search the world for a living corpse or measure one triangle after another to see if the sum of two right angles is ever less than 180 degrees. We do not need to take polls to determine that dissatisfied voters are not contented voters; there is no point in counting many things to be sure that $73 + 94 = 167$; and we don't even need legal research to know that in the United States a citizen cannot marry his widow's sister.

2. Nonanalytic Necessary Truths? Some philosophers claim there are necessary truths that are not analytic. Here are some candidates:

> Red things take up space.
>
> Every event has a cause.
>
> Every meaningful claim is either true or false.

Perhaps (some have suggested) even truths of arithmetic and geometry, while necessary, are not really analytic.

Still, it is not obvious that any of the examples are actually necessary but nonanalytic. "Every event has a cause" does not appear to be necessary at all. "Red things take up space" seems necessary (how could it be false?), but it may be analytic because part of the meaning of *red* is having a color, and part of the meaning of *color* is being something in space. "Every meaningful claim is either true or false" and mathematical truths are even harder to be sure about. So, the debate goes on.

Fortunately, we do not have to decide about all of these issues. We need only say that a true claim is self-evident if anyone who understands it can see that it *must* be true. (A false claim is self-evident if anyone who understands it can see that it must be false.) We may include any self-evidently true claim in our set of rational beliefs and use it as a starting point for arguments. Further, a self-evident claim has a privileged status within our set of rational beliefs. Since it *must* be true, it is not subject to the possibility of doubt attached to even the best-founded of non-self-evident beliefs.

Finally, we must be careful about what we consider self-evident truths. Most of us find it obvious that fire is a source of warmth, humans are smarter than cows, killing other people for money is wrong, and the Atlantic Ocean contains more creatures than does a wading pool. Yet not one of these is a *self-evident* truth because any of them could conceivably be false. They are all true, but not *necessarily* true. ("Clover is a cow that is smarter than any human" can be conceived to be true, even though we know perfectly well it really isn't.) Failing to keep in mind the difference between "obvious" and self-evident truths could lead to thinking that everything from our well-founded convictions to our most firmly held prejudices deserves to be in the special category of self-evident truths.

Accepted Beliefs 2: Experience

Our senses can be important sources of beliefs:

> This is burgundy. I tasted it.
>
> I can tell by the odor that there is a gas leak.
>
> Judging by the feel, the fabric cannot be all wool.
>
> Don't tell me there isn't a horse nearby. I heard it whinny.

Usually we rely most on our sense of sight. We hold there are clouds in the sky because we look up and see them. We believe a mouse is in the house because we spied the creature running by. Many people are in prison because eyewitnesses identified them as perpetrators of crimes. Our reliance on our senses, particularly vision, is reflected in the common sayings "Seeing is believing" and "I'll believe it when I see it."

Not all our experiences are equally reliable. Dim light, nearsightedness, distance, and a multitude of other factors can make even vision unreliable. A cold can interfere with taste or smell, and an airplane ride can temporarily impair hearing. When conditions like these are present, we cannot completely rely on our senses. With a stuffy nose, we may mistake an onion for an apple.

A less obvious way of falling into error results from a lack of knowledge necessary to experience some things in a correct or useful way. Someone who believes all creatures living in the sea are fish can look at cavorting dolphins and not be aware of observing mammalian behavior. Similarly, someone knowing little about astronomy can gaze through a telescope and not realize he is looking at light that has been traveling for millions of years from distant galaxies.

Too, we typically do not take notice of everything we see, even when we possess the required knowledge to interpret it correctly. If we need a place to sit and read, we are likely to notice a comfortable chair in a room. Yet we are less likely to notice whether the chair has a high back or a low one. We tend to observe in terms of *categories* in which we have interests or needs: chair—good-for-reading; automobile—blocking-my-driveway. Beyond the categories, the details often escape our attention.

Thus, while our experiences are an indispensable source of rational beliefs, they are neither as simple nor as foolproof a source as we may think. We must be careful that conditions are right to enable us to see, hear, smell, taste, and touch accurately. We must have the knowledge that lets us experience certain things in an informed way, and we must be sure we were paying attention to the important features of what we experienced. Under these conditions, our experiences will generally be a reliable source of rational beliefs.

Accepted Beliefs 3: Reliance on Others

A great number of our rational beliefs are based on the words of others. We believe traffic is tied up on the thruway because we heard a radio rush-hour report; that concert tickets for Pearl Jam are sold out because a friend said she was turned away at the box office; that meteors were responsible for the extinction of the dinosaurs because a paleontologist announced it. If we try to trace the source of every belief we think is true, we soon find that many, probably most, are based in some way on the words of others.

The world is too vast and complex for us to attempt to ground all our beliefs on our own experiences or on arguments we constructed personally or even on ones we are aware of. Nothing is wrong with this situation. If we are careful in our assessments, the words of others can be a reliable source of rational beliefs.

However, we should rely on the words of another only if we are sure that person is *in a position to know the truth* about the topic of discussion and is *not biased* on the issue. Together these conditions make it likely that the person (in fact) *knows the truth* about the topic. Also, someone may know the truth about something but lie about it. Hence, before we take someone's word as the basis for our own beliefs, we should be sure the person is not making a deliberate effort to deceive us. We now consider what it is to be in a position to know and how we should evaluate the possibilities of bias and lying.

1. Being in a Position to Know We would not take the word of a child about how it feels to be elderly or the word of an illiterate about the use of images in James Joyce's *Ulysses*. Neither the child nor the illiterate is in a position to know the truth about those particular subjects. In general, we do not want to take the word of another about a claim unless that person can reasonably be expected to know the truth about the claim, and we do not expect a person to know the truth without being in a *position to know* about the claim. What is it to be in a position to know?

a. General Depending upon the topic, many sorts of people are in a position to know. Eyewitnesses are in a position to know about the events they witness, and baseball fans are in a position to know what teams won the World Series the past three years. We may get information directly from such people, but usually we must also rely on less direct information.

Newspapers, magazines, television reports, encyclopedias, atlases, and books of all sorts (including fiction) are important sources of information. We trust such sources because we believe they are the work of researchers, writers, and editors who are collectively in a position to know about their subjects.

Not all sources are equally reliable, and we must exercise judgment as we read or listen. We accept *The New York Times* as more reliable than the *National Enquirer* and a new atlas as more accurate than one fifty years old. We must evaluate many factors to determine the reliability of a source. In most cases our experience with the nature of the source and its public reputation enables us to evaluate its reliability adequately.

b. Experts Some people are in a position to know because they have specialized knowledge of a given subject. They are **experts**. That they have this specialized knowledge usually makes it reasonable for others to rely on them in forming beliefs and making claims.

A person becomes an expert by a combination of education and experience. Years of advanced study in chemistry can turn someone into an expert on chemistry, and years of experience in business might make someone an expert on entrepreneurial matters. Extensive study and hospital experience may make a physician an expert diagnostician. Thus, when those of us who are not experts on a subject must decide who is, we should look for those having the relevant education and experience.

Reputation and position can also indicate expertise. Having a prestigious appointment at a major university or corporation and being known and respected by others in the same field add to the likelihood that an educated and experienced person really is a knowledgeable source.

In many cases it is clear that someone has the requisite education and experience to make her an expert on a given matter. A professor of English specializing in the eighteenth century should be an authority on the early novels *Pamela* and *Joseph Andrews*. A basketball writer of twenty years' experience with a major newspaper is correctly relied on as an expert on the recent history of the game.

By contrast, it would be an obvious mistake to take the word of the newspaper writer about *Pamela* and *Joseph Andrews* because of his experience in basketball or to presume that the person holding a Ph.D. in English is a reliable source about basketball.

Unfortunately, such obvious mistakes are common. Persons known and respected in one field are often treated as if they were experts in quite another one. Advertising actually encourages this error by frequently presenting athletes, actors, and other celebrities as if they were experts on toothpaste, electronics, or automobiles. If we give the matter any thought, we are not likely to take the word of an actor about cold medication or transportation.

In other cases we are more likely to be misled by false representations of expertise. We often encounter claims such as "Scientists say evolution is impossible." But when we look carefully, we find the "scientists" are a few mechanical engineers, a physicist, and a medical anatomist. They are not biologists, not scientists that have specialized training in the field of evolution. If we are not careful, the term *scientists* may mislead us into thinking expert scientific opinion has it that evolution did not occur.

c. Hard Cases and Soft Experts   On some questions we find it hard to know who the experts are or even whether there are any. Consider the question of abortion. Some think whether abortion is morally acceptable depends on when human life begins, and it seems obvious to them that scientists such as biologists and medical doctors are the experts on this underlying issue.

What can these experts tell us about the beginning of human life? They can tell us that from the moment of conception the fertilized ovum is both alive and human. But the sperm and the ovum each by itself was alive, as is any individual cell of a moose, a mushroom, or any other living creature. The scientific sense in which the fertilized ovum is *human* is just that it is the product of the species *Homo sapiens* and could, under just the right circumstances, become another member of the species. The fertilized ovum is not the product of, and could not grow into, a cat, a shark, or an oak tree.

Surely these scientific facts were not what we were uncertain about when we asked about the beginning of human life. We knew these facts all along; we didn't need to consult biologists or physicians to tell us such commonplace truths. Thus, when we are concerned about abortion and ask when human life begins, we must be wondering about something different.

What we really want to know is whether we should regard the fetus as a *person*, whether we should treat it in ways we must treat individuals we take to have rights and privileges. The scientific facts do not answer this question. Indeed, the real question is not a scientific one at all, and it cannot be answered from the perspective of the expertise of the biologist or physician.

Where should we look for expertise on whether we should consider a fetus a person? Or, more generally, on whether abortion is justifiable? Are there any experts on these issues? For that matter, are there experts on whether the god of Moses exists, life has a meaning, the *Mona Lisa*'s smile has any significance, or it is morally right to kill a person in self-defense? Can there *be* any experts on such matters?

Our first response may be to say no, and that would be partly right. Probably there can be no experts on these matters in the way there are experts on mathematics, physics, the history of sports, or television repair. The issues about god, art, and morality are, in some sense, less straightforward. As a result, we are not nearly so inclined, for instance, to defer without question to the word of the "expert" art critic about the meaning of Picasso's *Guernica* as we are to defer without question to the word of a physicist about the meaning of the Second Law of Thermodynamics. We all believe we are entitled to our own opinions in religion or politics in a way that we are not entitled to our own opinions about the square root of 225 or whether a bandicoot is a marsupial.

While this view is correct, it would be a serious mistake to conclude there are no experts in any sense on matters of art, morality, and religion. It would be an even more serious error to conclude that in such areas everything is "all a matter of opinion" or "one person's opinion is as good as another's." Art historians and critics are in a position to have better-informed views on the *Mona Lisa* or *Guernica* than the rest of us. Those trained in philosophy are unusually qualified to evaluate the validity and significance of arguments about the existence of god. Psychologists, philosophers, religious scholars, and those with knowledge and experience in other fields of study may be in a better position than most of us to think clearly about questions regarding the meaning of life.

These people are not "hard experts," authorities to whom those of us with less training must entirely defer in the way the nonphysicist must defer to the physicist. They are what we can call "soft experts," people whose views on certain matters are more informed and more carefully considered than the views of the rest of us.

We should not defer entirely to their views, however. We must finally think for ourselves about abortion, the existence of god, the meaning of life, whom to vote for as president, and so on. Yet if we try to think for ourselves without first learning from those who are most knowledgeable, we almost guarantee that our conclusions will be naive, ill informed, and quite possibly incorrect.

2. Bias Being in a position to know is not enough to make someone a reliable source. We should distrust even experts and careful observers if they have a stake in a claim's truth or falsity. We wonder about the fairness of a judge in a diving contest who awards her son the highest number of points. We are suspicious of an expert on respiratory diseases who is a paid spokesman for a tobacco company and claims cigarette smoking has not been shown to be a factor in developing emphysema. In such cases, we don't so much think the people are lying as suspect they are *biased,* that their interests prevent them from having objective views on the subjects.

Bias can affect anyone. The trained expert, the most thorough reporter, the most careful eyewitness may all turn out to be unreliable authorities if their interests interfere with their objectivity. Hence, we should be especially careful about accepting a claim from someone whose expertise may be compromised by a conflict of interest.

We should also stay aware of our own biases and not allow them to distort beliefs. Am I in favor of an airport bond issue because the community airport needs improvements or because the company I work for may get the contract? Do I reject the evidence showing a certain surgical procedure is pointless because I'm a surgeon who makes money from performing the procedure? Becoming aware of the possibility of bias in a particular case is the first step toward grounding beliefs on reasons and evidence.

3. Deliberate Deception Our experience indicates that people most often tell the truth, so far as they know it. Yet in some situations we think it likely that a person would lie. We expect that someone accused of a serious crime will deny his guilt, regardless of whether he is the perpetrator. We think the first price quoted to us by an auto salesman will not be the price we must actually pay for the car. And white lies told to hosts are a matter of simple politeness.

None of this means we can assume any particular person is lying in any particular situation. But it does suggest that whenever someone may have special reasons for not speaking the truth, we should be suspicious.

New Claims, Background Beliefs, and Rationality

Before we accept a new claim, we must do more than evaluate the nature of its support. We must also consider the extent to which it fits in with the reasonable beliefs we already hold.

Suppose

> A neighbor tells you a dog is pulling your laundry from the line; or a neighbor says seven hippopotamuses have knocked down your clothesline poles.

> You look out over a foggy bay and seem to see a sailboat tacking against a difficult wind; or you seem to see a boat sailing above the water as grinning skeleton passengers wave you closer.

> You reason that since most automobiles cost less than $30,000, you can buy a Dodge minivan for less than that; or you conclude you can get the Porsche convertible you like for less than $30,000.

In each of these pairs, we are given exactly as much reason for believing the second claim as the first. Yet in each case, it is reasonable to believe the first claim but not the second, because the second of each pair of claims is contrary to our background beliefs.

At a given time, each of us holds a complex set of beliefs we take to be rational. Any *new* candidate for belief that comes from argument or observation, or is the claim of another, must be considered against this background of previous beliefs. Even a supposedly self-evident claim coming to our attention must be considered against this background.

Our background beliefs about natural habitats and the security of the local zoo make it incredibly unlikely that hippos should appear in our yard. These beliefs are so well grounded they make it much more likely that our neighbor is mistaken in his claim (he could be drunk, a practical joker, and so on) than that the hippopotamuses are there. What we know about physics and "living skeletons" makes it more likely that seeing a boat flying above the surface and inhabited by bony ghosts is a visual illusion. Our background knowledge is quite contrary to any notion that one can buy a Porsche convertible for less than $30,000.

If we fail to recognize that we must consider new candidates for belief in relation to background beliefs, we are likely to make serious mistakes. We will be too credulous and believe many things we should not believe. Consider some cases:

> People at séances have often maintained they feel the table floating in the air, hear voices from beyond the grave, and see spirits of dead loved ones.
>
> People have insisted they have seen mentalists bend sturdy metal spoons by stroking them lightly.
>
> Others claim to have witnessed "psychic surgery" in which the "surgeons" reach through the flesh of the patient and remove diseased tissue with their bare hands.

Those who think they have observed such occurrences, or who believe the accounts of others who claim to have observed them, often become indignant when faced with doubters. "All the witnesses there say the same thing. No witnesses deny it. You doubters are just being close-minded and dogmatic. And that is irrational."

But it is the believers who are irrational. They are credulous to the point of gullibility because they have not taken into account the importance of background beliefs. We do not need eyewitnesses who say, "I was there and I saw that what the 'psychic surgeon' said was diseased tissue from the patient was really a piece of chicken liver he had palmed." We have a very well-grounded set of background beliefs that rules out the possibility of performing surgery with a bare hand without leaving so much as an external mark on the patient. Our background beliefs also give excellent reason to deny that spirits were present at the séance and that spoons were bent by psychic means.

A failure to recognize the importance of our background beliefs may also lead to the mistake of thinking that all claims coming from the same source must be equally believable. It is an error to hold that since I have known my friend for a long time and believed him when he told me of his service in the army and his year as a law student, I must now believe him when he insists he was an astronaut and became a double agent for the CIA and the KGB.

Similarly, we often hear that it is inconsistent to accept some parts of a basic religious document (the Hebrew Bible, the New Testament, the Koran, and so on) and not others. Both fundamentalist Christians and religious skeptics sometimes maintain that it is a mistake to accept the New Testament accounts that Jesus was born in Bethlehem, was trained as a carpenter, and threw the money-changers out of the temple, but not accept that he literally walked on water or turned water into wine. All of these, after all, are based on the authority of the same document, and so all must be accepted or rejected together. The fundamentalists' aim here is to support their view that everything in the New Testament should be accepted quite literally. The skeptics' aim is to discredit the entire document in the minds of anyone who would doubt the literal truth of stories about walking on water or changing a liquid of one chemical composition into one with a quite different composition.

Both sides are mistaken here, just as I would be if I thought that because I believed my friend was in the army, I must believe he is a double agent. Our background beliefs indicate that the latter is simply less likely than the former, and so we need better reason to believe it. My friend's word is quite enough for me to accept the commonplace claim that he served in the army. We have the background belief that many people have done so. The very same word is not enough for me to believe the extraordinary claim that he was a double agent. In the same way, we do not have to take an all-or-nothing approach to the Hebrew Bible, the Koran, or the New Testament. It may well be that we should accept their more usual claims while remaining skeptical about those that conflict sharply with our background beliefs. The failure to appreciate the importance of background beliefs leads to such common mistakes.

Finally, what about the charge of dogmatism? If no witnesses deny the accuracy of claims that tables floated or that spoons were bent by mental powers, is it just irrationally close-minded to refuse to believe these events happened? It *would* be dogmatic and entirely irrational to say that no new claim that conflicts with our background beliefs could ever be rationally accepted. But that is *not* what is being said.

The point is that the more a claim accords with our background beliefs, the less strong its own credentials must be. (The claim that it snowed in Minnesota in December does not need strong credentials to be accepted.) The less a new claim is in accordance with these background beliefs, the stronger its own credentials must be. (The claim that it snowed in Florida in July needs very strong credentials.) Any new claim, no matter how outlandish (that is, no matter how much it conflicts with our background beliefs), could conceivably turn out to be true. But some claims are so outlandish they must have extraordinarily strong credentials if they are to be taken seriously.

When we stand in the supermarket aisles and read the tabloid headlines I WAS KIDNAPPED AND OPERATED ON BY SPACE-MEN and STATUES WEEP AFTER COUPLE DIVORCES, we should adopt a critical stance and consider each such claim in the light of both the reputation of the publication *and* our background beliefs. Lacking a mass of further evidence in favor of the claims, it is not dogmatic to reject any of them without further investigation.

That is exactly what a reasonable person will do.

Exercises

A. *Consider whether each of the following is analytically true, analytically false, or not analytic. Explain each of your answers. (#12–#16 may be controversial and particularly in need of discussion.)*

  1. Baseball players are ball players.
 *2. If this is a triangle, it has three sides.
  3. All three-sided things are triangles.
 *4. 10 less 4 is 5.
  5. Water is the best thirst quencher.
  6. Albert's dog is not a canine.
  7. All soft, disgusting things are disgusting.
  8. A banana is a fruit.
  9. Helping the helpless is praiseworthy.
 *10. Every effect has a cause.
  11. Her bachelor uncle is an only child.
 *12. All persons feel pain.
 *13. Pornography degrades women.
  14. Some machines can think.
  15. It is bad to be a coward.
 *16. Solitaire is not a game.

B. *Evaluate the justifiability of "your" decision (action/conclusion) in each of the following.*

  1. From somewhere in the trees beyond the fence you hear a "mooing" sound, and you conclude that a cow is nearby.
 *2. Three different mechanics tell you that to make your 1968 MG drivable, you must have a new engine that will cost you $3,000. You conclude that you will have to come up with that amount or stop driving the car entirely.

3. You are somewhat nearsighted and have lost your glasses. A person runs out of your neighbor's house and right by you. Later you tell your neighbor that the person who ran out was wearing a parka the same color as the red one her ex-husband usually wears.

*4. Testifying at a criminal trial, a respected citizen swears that there were three holdup men, each wearing a ski mask and carrying a gun. But because she does not know the color of the masks or anything about the sort of guns, you convince the other members of the jury that she is an unreliable witness and none of her testimony can be relied on.

5. A respected physicist at a famous aeronautical laboratory tells you that you can lose weight by eating foods that are themselves lighter in weight than most others. You buy a food scale and adjust your diet accordingly.

*6. Last week you sipped a Courvoisier VSOP cognac at the Ritz-Carlton. The cognac you ordered at the Plaza tastes the same. You conclude it is Courvoisier VSOP.

*7. Your college English professor insists that *Catch-22* is a finer antiwar novel than *All Quiet on the Western Front*. You have no doubt that this is correct because she holds a Ph.D. in literature.

8. Your mother is eighty-eight years old and incurably ill with a very painful malignancy. Your minister advises you against prolonging her life by the use of artificial breathing devices. You defer without question to his expert opinion.

9. "Our steak knives cost a little more, but, unlike any others, they never need sharpening," the salesman at your door tells you. That sounds good to you, and you purchase a set of twelve.

*10. You live in a central Florida neighborhood that is built around a pond. Everyone is concerned about the recent disappearance of several cats and smallish dogs. One evening at twilight you see what appears to be a vague reptilian outline with eyes just above the surface of the pond. You take your poodle inside and call the wildlife authorities to report a dangerous alligator.

*11. The situation is the same as in #10, but you, the pond, and the neighborhood are in Alaska.

12. The manager of your local National League baseball team appears in a series of radio and television commercials in which he praises a nearby Ford dealership for its prices, service, and straightforward way of dealing. You admire the

manager and are convinced that he is honest and intelligent. You plan to buy your next car from that Ford dealership.

13. Your best friend, a sober and reliable person you have known for years, swears that she clearly saw a saucer-shaped object moving back and forth over the mountains at such incredible speed that it could only have been an alien spaceship. You conclude your friend is hallucinating.

14. You look over the mountains and are struck by the sight of a saucer-shaped object moving back and forth at incredible speed. Seeing is believing, you think. You can only conclude that the object is an alien spaceship.

15. Wondering whether you should rely on the automobile ratings in *Consumer Reports*, you consult an automotive expert friend, an upper-level executive with the Ford Motor Company. Your friend tells you that *Consumer Reports* is biased against American-made cars. You pay no attention to the magazine in making your car-buying decision.

C. *Taking into account the cited sources and your background beliefs, consider whether each of the following is probably true, probably false, too close to call, or so unclear in meaning that it is not possible to evaluate its truth.*

1. The Konica Z-up 135 Super has 38–135mm *f*/3.6–9.8 lens and shutter speeds of 3.2–1/280 sec. It features an infinity lock, single self-timer, night flash, TV mode, and more. The list price is $550. —*Popular Photography* (August 1995, p. 21)

*2. "There are some monstrously large cockroaches in Central America." —Told to you by a pest exterminator in Chicago

3. "Nudists come from all walks of life. They are doctors, lawyers, housewives, laborers, businesspeople, and even members of the clergy. They are just like other people." —*Nudist Park Guide*, 16th ed., The American Sunbathing Association, Kissimmee, Florida (1988, p. 7)

4. "Penalties against [tennis player] Jeff Tarango were reduced yesterday after he apologized for accusing an umpire at Wimbledon of corruption last summer. . . . After today's apology, the [governing] committee reduced the total fine from $43,756 to $28,256." —*The New York Times* (December 20, 1995)

5. "Making money in the stock market is more difficult than you might think." —A stockbroker's comment on a radio program

*6. Ninety-eight percent of households in the U.S. have at least one TV set. More than half have cable. The typical person watches at least four hours per day. —Howard Rosenberg, *The Los Angeles Times*

*7. "There is a medical conspiracy to prevent the dissemination of the truth about curing cancer. It can be cured very easily, but doctors do not want this known since that would deprive them of a large portion of their inflated incomes." —Ralph R. Rafael, *The Truth About Cancer*, RRR Press

8. "Until the mid-1960s, most women didn't know how crucial the clitoris was. . . . Learning about the clitoris increased sexual enjoyment for countless women and freed many of us from years of thinking we were 'frigid.'" —*The New Our Bodies, Ourselves*, The Boston Women's Health Book Collective (New York: Simon & Schuster, 1984, p. 169)

9. Each of the following appeared as a front-page headline in the April 4, 1989 *Weekly World News* (a "supermarket tabloid"):

    a. ELVIS TRIBE FOUND IN JUNGLE: They wear Presley wigs and sing "Hound Dog" just like The King!

    b. BABY BORN WITH A WOODEN LEG! SHOCKING NEW PROOF OF REINCARNATION! Tiny peg leg is just like pirates wore in the 1700s, say experts.

    c. RAPIST DIES OF A HEART ATTACK WHILE ATTACKING HOUSEWIFE

    d. BAFFLING! RABBIT BURSTS INTO FLAMES FOR NO REASON!

    e. PSYCHIC CAN PREDICT THE DATE YOU'LL DIE

    f. VISION OF LIBERACE FLOATS OUT OF UFO

Chapter 10

DEFINITION

Definitions can be crucial to understanding. If the meaning of a key word is uncertain, it may be impossible to understand properly a claim, argument, rule, or explanation. After discussing the nature of definition, we consider two types of definition, then examine definitional methods and standards.

Definition of *Definition*

A **definition** is an explanation of the meaning of a word. The meaning of a word is the set of rules or conditions governing the word's use. Thus, to define a word is to state the rules or conditions for using the word. The rules may be ones followed in actual practice or ones adopted for some special purpose. Hence, we may say that to define a word is to explain how the word is actually used or is going to be used.

We define words, terms, expressions, symbols, and other linguistic entities. We also define the concepts and ideas that the linguistic entities represent or express. For convenience, we shall speak here of defining only words.

Two Types of Definition

Definitions can be divided into types on the basis of whether the account of meaning they give is a report or a stipulation about a word's use.

1. Reportive Definitions

Definitions intended to explain how words are actually used are called **reportive definitions**. They are offered as factual reports to the effect that the word defined is used in accordance with the conditions mentioned.

For example, we may define "great aunt" as "a sister of one's grandmother or grandfather." According to this definition, the expression "great aunt" is properly used to refer to someone who is the sister of a grandparent. Anyone meeting this condition (satisfying this description) may be called "great aunt."

Like other factual claims, reportive definitions may be true or false, accurate or inaccurate. A definition of "great aunt" as "the brother of one's grandparent" is simply false. Similarly, defining "uncle" as "the brother of one's mother" is inaccurate. In our society, the word also refers to the brother of one's father, as well as to the husband of one's aunt. To be both correct and complete, we might define "uncle" as "the brother of one's parent or the husband of one's aunt."

Most words have several meanings that may be quite distinct. For example, the word *plate* has some twenty meanings. It is used in sports, printing, photography, metal manufacturing, geology, biology, electronics, and other fields. A definition is not defective if it fails to report on all distinct uses of the word. Although we might fault a dictionary for not informing us about the variety of meanings, a definition intended to explain only one of the meanings can be correct and complete. Thus, the definition of "plate" as "a shallow dish in which food is served or from which it is eaten" is a good explanation of one of the ways in which the word is properly used.

Reportive definitions are used to explain both ordinary and special meanings and on this basis may be divided into three types. The distinctions remind us that a report about a word's use in one area need not hold true for other areas.

a. Lexical Definition A **lexical definition** is a report about the way a word is used in everyday life. The definition explains the word's ordinary or usual meaning. The above definition of "uncle" as "the brother of one's parent or the husband of one's aunt" is a correct lexical definition.

b. Disciplinary Definition A **disciplinary definition** is a report about the way a word is used in a particular discipline or special area. The definition is an explanation of the word's accepted meaning within that discipline.

Often a word has both ordinary meanings and disciplinary meanings. Consider the expression "acute pain." In ordinary usage, an acute pain is a sharp, stabbing pain, and the description "sharp and stabbing" must be met before we can properly call a pain an acute one. However, in medical terminology, an acute pain is one that occurs suddenly and without warning signs. Whether the pain is sharp, cramping, burning, or aching is irrelevant to whether it is acute.

"Acute" has still other meanings in other disciplines. In geometry, "acute" applies to angles of less than 90 degrees, and in poetics it designates a stressed sound in a metrical scheme. (Many of the twenty meanings of "plate" are special or technical ones.) Disciplines also have technical terms (*prion, afferent,* and so on) that have no ordinary uses.

c. Historical Definition A **historical definition** is a report about how a word was used during a particular historical period. The definition may be lexical or disciplinary. If lexical, the explanation will be of the ordinary use of a word at a specific time. If disciplinary, the explanation will be of the use of a word in a specific discipline at a specific time.

Words, like other expressions of human culture, have a history. Some words come into being; others pass away. Some retain meanings for long periods; others shed old meanings and acquire new ones. Still others alter their meanings, acquiring new conditions without wholly losing the old ones. Without a grasp of the historical meanings of words, we cannot correctly interpret the literary, political, religious, scientific, and personal documents of the past.

Even when words are familiar to us, we must be certain their meanings have not significantly changed. For example, in the eighteenth century, to say someone was a *flasher* was to say he dressed in an ostentatious manner. Someone knowing only the current meaning might get a very wrong impression from an eighteenth-century letter.

The need for historical understanding also affects technical areas. The disease referred to as syphilis during the sixteenth through the nineteenth centuries included a variety of skin diseases, but now we limit the term to a particular disease caused by a certain spirochete.

A common error to avoid in connection with historical definitions is the assumption that an earlier or original meaning of a word is its "true" meaning. That the word *alternatives* was once properly used only in cases of just two options does not mean that it is now incorrect to speak of, say, "three alternatives." Current use and earlier use are merely different.

2. Stipulative Definition

To stipulate is to lay down a rule or condition. A **stipulative definition** is a statement of the rule that will be followed in using the word defined. A stipulative definition is a resolution to use a word in a certain way, to assign the word a particular meaning. Hence, stipulative definitions, unlike reportive definitions, cannot be true or false. Depending upon whether the meaning assigned is arbitrary or a modification of an accepted meaning, we can distinguish two types.

a. Arbitrary A new word, abbreviation, or symbol is typically introduced simply by laying down a rule for its use. Since we are free to choose any rule we like, such stipulative definitions may be regarded as **arbitrary**. Here are typical examples:

Let "D" stand for "disposable income minus savings."

I shall use "!" written after a letter to mean "all letters in the Roman alphabet up to and including this letter." Thus, "C!" will mean "ABC."

"BASIC" will stand for "Beginner's All-purpose Symbolic Instruction Code."

Words introduced by arbitrary stipulative definitions may later come to be accepted into the language and acquire a standard meaning. This happened with Thomas More's "utopia," Karel Čapek's "robot," and Francis Galton's "eugenics." In such cases, the conditions of the word's use may resemble those laid down by the inventor, but typically the meaning undergoes substantial change. "Utopia" is no longer just the name of More's ideal society, but has also come to mean any ideal society.

b. Precising **Precising stipulative definitions** restrict the ordinary meaning of a word to make the meaning more exact in a certain context. For example:

For tax purposes, "head of household" will mean "the member of the household with the highest earned income."

"Savings," according to my theory, is money invested.

Herein, a "crash" should be understood as a total loss of computer programs and data.

Precising stipulative definitions are ways of turning ordinary words into technical terms. The more precise meaning assigned to a word is connected with the word's standard meaning, yet the assigned meaning is not a report on the word's standard use. A phrase like "head of household" has a common meaning broader than that required by the specialized needs of tax collectors.

Even though stipulative definitions cannot be true or false, they are not beyond criticism. A definition may be faulted for introducing a term that is unnecessary, misleading, awkward, or otherwise ill considered. For example, critics have suggested that the introduction of "adience" (liking) and "intense adience" (love) to describe human relationships was not needed. The social sciences, in particular, have often been accused of engaging in unnecessary naming.

Precising stipulative definitions also present the possibility of intentional or accidental deception. It is easy to assume when reading the text of a contract, solicitation, insurance policy, or law that crucial words have their ordinary meanings. So, when the words have restricted meanings, even if they are spelled out in the document's fine print, a naive, uneducated, or careless reader may be misled. To get a "free trip," an unwary consumer may have to sign a contract agreeing to pay expenses and "handling fees" in excess of normal costs. The free trip involves taking the consumer for a ride.

Methods of Definition

Any way the use of a word can be explained to someone counts as a method of definition. Accordingly, there is no set number of methods. The five traditional methods discussed here have met the test of experience and been found helpful. No single method is best for every word in every situation, and no one should hesitate to use new methods that might be equally effective.

1. Synonym

Definition by **synonym** requires providing a word or phrase equivalent (or approximately equivalent) in meaning to the word defined. This is perhaps the most common method of definition:

> "Flat" means the same thing as "apartment."
>
> "Heliocentric" means "sun centered."
>
> A "bicameral" legislature is one with two houses.

Probably no two words are exactly equivalent in meaning. In some contexts, one of the words cannot be substituted for the other without altering the meaning of the sentence. In practice, this possibility rarely presents a difficulty. We recognize that in offering a definition by synonym we must choose a word having roughly the same meaning in the same context. Thus, "flat" may be substituted for "apartment" when the reference is to dwellings, but "apartment" may not be substituted for "flat" when the reference is to tires.

2. Genus and Species

The method of **genus and species** consists in mentioning a feature of an object to which a word refers that places the object within a class, then mentioning another feature that places the object within a subclass. The general class is the genus, and the (proper) subclass is a species. In the definition of "democracy" as "a form of government in which people govern themselves," the genus is "a form of government" and the species is "people govern themselves."

The terms *genus* and *species* are relative ones. If "people govern themselves" is treated as a genus, then we can establish species consisting of "people govern themselves directly" and "people govern themselves through representatives." These subclasses correspond to the distinction between direct and representative democracy.

Sometimes we mention only the feature that places the object in a general class, saying nothing about the feature that would place it in a subclass. (Perhaps we are ignorant of such a feature or do not consider the species important.) For example, it may be enough in some situations to tell someone that "gorgonian" refers to "a kind of coral," that a "rondo" is "a musical form," or that "monetarianism" is "an economic policy."

3. Complete Enumeration

Some words can easily be defined merely by **enumerating (listing)** all the items to which the word refers. For example:

Arabic numerals: 1, 2, 3, 4, 5, 6, 7, 8, 9, 0

Baltic republics of the old Soviet Union: Estonia, Latvia, Lithuania

The Axis powers: Germany, Italy, Japan

Defining by enumeration is useful in providing stipulative definitions. The potential vagueness of terms like "southwestern states" or "European economic community" can be eliminated by naming exactly the items the phrase is supposed to refer to.

The way in which a definition is phrased is usually adequate to determine whether a list of items is a complete enumeration. A phrase like "for example" indicates an incomplete list.

Although reportive definitions can be given by this method, most words cannot be defined by complete enumeration because they refer to things that belong to a potentially unlimited class. For example, it is impossible to give a reportive definition of "tree" using this method, for it is not possible to provide an enumeration of every tree past, present, and future. Other sorts of words, such as "political power," do not clearly refer to anything in the direct fashion that words like "tree" do.

4. Ostention

An **ostensive definition** consists in pointing to an object correctly designated by the defined word. If I gesture toward the proper sort of animal and say "jaguar," I give its meaning by demonstrating how the word is used in a paradigm case—that is, a noncontroversial and straightforward instance.

The demonstration might be helped by indicating that some animals that might be confused with the jaguar (cheetah, puma, and the like) are not correctly referred to by the word. The ostensive definition itself, however, consists in nothing more than pointing and naming.

Some words, such as color words like "red" and "yellow," can be defined only by means of ostensive definition. Although "red" may be identified with a certain wavelength in the electromagnetic spectrum, this identification is not a definition of the word *red*. Not only may we have the experience of seeing red when the wavelength is absent, but we must also be able to name the color red to identify the wavelength associated with it.

Words that function the way proper names do are the best candidates for definition by ostention. In the same way that we can point to a person and say, "That's Richard Ford," we can point to the proper objects and define words that name colors, trees, animals, plants, chemicals, bridges, geological strata, and so on.

5. Example

When we cannot literally point to an example, we can define some words by mentioning examples of the sort of things they designate. For instance:

> A "deficiency disease" is one like scurvy, pellagra, or beriberi.
>
> "Even numbers" are ones like 2, 4, 6, and 8.

Some words do not lend themselves to definition by ostention or example. This is true of words like "sad," "happy," and "pain" that are used to characterize subjective experience. Although such experiences cannot be pointed to in a direct way or examples of them cited, we can describe the circumstances that produce them. In this way, their correct use can be indicated by describing a paradigm case: Pain is what you feel when you are walking in your bare feet and you stub your toe on something.

We can employ the same method to define words that do not refer necessarily to subjective experience. Again, a paradigm example is imagined or described:

> What is the "chilling effect" that censorship is likely to have on us? Imagine you are writing something and you pause to search for the right word, idea, or image. If while you are thinking it occurs to you, "Am I likely to be jailed or fined or humiliated by the choice I make?" that is a chilling effect. The thought itself is likely to interfere with the choice actually made.

Other ways of using examples to define words are familiar from ordinary life: pointing to pictures, inviting others to smell or taste something, describing modes of behavior, circumstances, situations, people, and so on.

These five methods are useful and frequently employed, but any method at all that helps explain the meaning of a word is a legitimate method of definition.

Standards of Definition

A definition appropriate for one purpose is not necessarily appropriate for another. The reader of a popular article on biology may need to know only that the "Hardy-Weinberg law" is "a law about the way genes in a population change in frequency," but a student of population genetics needs a definition that states both the law and the parameters of its application. However, the definition in the popular article is not defective even though it does not meet the needs in some other context.

No matter what our purposes are in offering a definition, certain errors should be avoided.

1. Avoid Complete Circularity

The definition of *arbitrageur* as "one who engages in arbitrage" is unhelpful because it is almost wholly uninformative. It is unlikely that someone would know the meaning of *arbitrage* and not know *arbitrageur*. Since the aim of definition is to explain the meaning of a word, a definition that assumes an understanding of a key part of the meaning is a failure.

2. Avoid Obscure, Metaphorical, or Ambiguous Language

The language in which a definition is expressed can frustrate the aim of explaining the meaning of a word.

The way in which **obscure language** may render a definition useless is well illustrated by Ambrose Bierce's satirical definition of the simple word *eat:* "to perform successively (and successfully) the functions of mastication, humectation, and deglutition."

Metaphors have their place in explanation, but defining a word solely by metaphor is of little help in understanding the word's meaning. A computer manual that defines "DOS" as "the policeman who directs the traffic inside the machine" does very little to explain the meaning of "disk operating system."

A definition fails when it is **ambiguous** because it is impossible to determine which interpretation of the definition is the right one. The definition of "minuscule" as "a form of writing developed during the

Middle Ages" leaves unclear whether handwriting or literary composition is intended.

3. Avoid Accidental Conditions

A definition involves stating conditions that govern the use of a word. But in some cases words are associated with additional features that are not really part of the definition. These features are called "accidental" to contrast them with ones that are "essential" to determining the word's use.

For example, the definition of "women" as "members of the more exploited sex" makes use of an accidental feature. As a matter of fact, the conditions mentioned happen to be satisfied by women at the present time. Yet we can imagine a social revolution that would reverse the situation and make men into the more exploited sex. If this happened, the meaning of "women" would not change. Hence, being exploited is an accidental feature, not a defining characteristic, of women.

4. Avoid Definitions That Are Too Broad or Too Narrow

The conditions governing a word's use establish a class of items to which the word correctly applies. The conditions governing the use of the word *cat* (a mammal with certain feline characteristics) establish the class of things referred to by "cat."

A definition may fail by being *too broad*, by making a class so large it includes items not properly characterized by the word. A definition may also fail by being *too narrow*, by making a class so small it excludes items properly characterized by the word. Thus, a definition of "apple" should establish a class that includes all and only apples. One that includes oranges is too broad, and one that fails to include Red Delicious apples is too narrow.

Even for words that cannot be defined with this sort of precision, it still makes sense to talk about the class established by a definition as being too inclusive (too broad) or too exclusive (too narrow). An accurate definition of "art" has eluded generations of thinkers, but we can still say with confidence that Tolstoy's famous definition of "art" as "that which communicates the religious sentiments of mankind" is too narrow. It excludes, for instance, most nonrepresentational art. We can also see that Tolstoy's definition simultaneously manages to be too broad. It could include such heartfelt expressions of sentiment as undertaking a pilgrimage, which none of us would be willing to think of as art.

Tolstoy's doubly defective definition can be used to illustrate a final point. Words and their meanings are important. Merely calling an object a work of art accords it a certain status. We come to look at it in a different way: We may put it in a museum or sell it for a much higher price at auction. Similarly, when we call someone a "hero," pronounce a defendant "guilty," describe a scientist as a "genius," or condemn abortion as "murder," we are making crucial judgments that turn partially on the meanings of "mere" words. Words do make a difference.

Exercises

A. *A definition may be defective by being too broad or too narrow, employing an accidental feature, using obscure, metaphorical, or ambiguous language, or being completely circular. Consider the definitions below and explain on what (if any) grounds they might be criticized.*

1. Chair: a four-legged piece of furniture

2. Money: the root of all evil

*3. Triangle: a geometrical figure with equal sides and equal angles

4. Triangle: a closed three-sided plane figure with equal angles

*5. Gouda: a cheese made in the Gouda district of Holland

*6. A neonatologist is someone who specializes in caring for neonates.

7. "Truth is the shadow that existence casts across the realm of essences." —George Santayana, *Skepticism and Animal Faith*

8. "Saw: dentated instrument, by the attrition of which wood or metal is cut." —Samuel Johnson, *Dictionary of the English Language*

*9. Cow: an animal sacred in India

*10. Parfait: a layered ice-cream sundae or pudding served in a tall glass

11. A singletree is the same as a whiffletree.

12. Something is "harmful" if it is capable of causing harm.

13. "Informal logic" is best defined as a travel guide to the world of correct reasoning.

*14. Ensign: a standard of a military unit

15. Oxygen: a chemical element usually sold in cylindrical tanks

16. "[Poetry] is language whose individual lines, either because of their own brilliance or because they focus so powerfully on what has gone before, have a higher voltage than most

language has. It is language that grows frequently incandescent, giving off both light and heat." —Lawrence Perrine, *Sound and Sense*

B. *Reportive definitions may be subdivided into lexical, disciplinary, and historical, while stipulative definitions may be subdivided into arbitrary and precising. Use these categories to classify the following definitions.*

1. "To qualify as a writer (and hence for membership) a candidate must have had at least one work of at least 5,000 words published by a newspaper, magazine, or professional journal (church or club sponsored publications are excluded)." —Serial Writers Guild

*2. "A set we shall define as any group or collection of entities." —G. W. Holton, *Basics of Statistical Inference*

3. In poker, a full house is a hand consisting of a pair and three of a kind.

4. "Serendipity" means making a lucky discovery by accident.

*5. "I am bound by my own definition of criticism: a disinterested endeavour to learn and propagate the best that is known and thought in the world." —Matthew Arnold, *Essays in Criticism*

*6. "The word *antibiosis* was first used by Vuillemini in 1889 to describe the phenomenon where one organism is in opposition to the life of another." —P. R. Burkholder, "Antibiotics"

7. "Orthopedics" is the medical specialty that treats disorders of the skeletal system.

8. According to the alchemists, "calx" was the ash or fixed part of a substance remaining after it was burned.

9. "An element is a substance, a sample of matter consisting solely of atoms with the same atomic number." —W. A. Kieffer, *Chemistry: A Cultural Approach*

10. "To 'barbados' a person meant the same in the seventeenth century as to 'shanghai' him meant in the nineteenth." —Sidney W. Mintz, *Columbia Forum* (Spring 1970)

C. *Words may be defined by these methods: synonym, genus and species, enumeration, ostention, and example. Examine the definitions below and identify the method used.*

*1. If you imagine a line extending directly out from the dipper of the Big Dipper, then you will see that at the end of the line is Polaris, the North Star.

2. Old-world animals are those such as the horse, the water buffalo, the camel, the tiger, the pig, and the cow.

*3. "Back office space is nonexecutive space. It is the supply room, the broom closet, the computer installation, the library, the Kafkaesque desk grid of clerical and sales personnel." —C. B. Horsley, *The New York Times* (June 18, 1980)

4. A perfect number is a number that is the sum of its divisors.

5. "Howitzer: a cannon with a barrel longer than a mortar that delivers shells with medium velocities against targets that cannot be reached by flat trajectories." —*American Heritage Dictionary*

*6. The letters *t.i.d.* on a medical prescription mean "take three times a day."

7. "The term 'mortgage,' when used herein, shall include deed of trust, trust deed, or other security instrument." —American Land Title Association Standard Form 3360

8. "By a *fallacy* is commonly understood any unsound mode of arguing, which appears to demand our conviction, and to be decisive of the question in hand, when in fairness it is not." —Richard Whately, *The Elements of Logic*

9. "For our purposes language may be defined as systematized combinations of sounds which have meanings for all persons in a given cultural community." —Thomas Pyles, *Origin and Development of the English Language*

10. "Cure: a method or course of medical treatment used to restore health." —*American Heritage Dictionary*

11. In this paper, I shall make use of the expression "DSP" to abbreviate "different senses of possible."

12. A "curette" is a spoon-shaped surgical instrument used to remove tissue from a body cavity.

Chapter 11

VAGUENESS AND AMBIGUITY

Vagueness and ambiguity are often confused with one another, but they are distinct concepts. In general, **vagueness** involves a term's lack of precision, whereas **ambiguity** involves different possible meanings, each of which may be quite precise.

We begin by defining and illustrating two types of vagueness, then discuss how vagueness can sometimes be desirable. We next turn to ambiguity and distinguish and illustrate three types. Our focus throughout is on situations in which vagueness and ambiguity may create problems.

Vagueness

We discuss vagueness as fuzziness and vagueness of quantity and type. We then consider reasons for deliberately employing vague expressions.

Vagueness as Fuzziness

This is the basic and probably the logically most important sense of *vagueness*. Terms are vague to the extent that they have blurry boundaries—are fuzzy at the edges—so there are borderline cases to which they may or may not apply. (Since 1965 a whole new field of "fuzzy logic" has been developed about the use of terms that are vague in this sense.)

A classic case of a quite vague term is *bald*. Clearly a person with a full head of hair is not bald, and a person with a head like an egg is bald. But what about someone with just fringes of hair around the sides? Or someone with a large bare spot on the top of the head? *Bald* is not precise enough to give any clear answers to such questions. The more such borderline cases, the more vague a term is. Vagueness, then, is a matter of degree.

It is often said that virtually all terms in ordinary language are somewhat vague, and that may be true. Still, some terms are much more vague than others. *Blue*, *vegetable*, and *can opener* are not nearly as vague as *tall, large, smart, democracy,* or *obscenity.* We are far more likely to be unsure whether something is obscene than whether something is blue.

Generally the use of vague terms does not cause problems. Saying that she is *smart* and *well educated* and a *hard worker* gives a picture that may be all that is needed for many purposes. But consider the following:

> Every player who comes to camp *overweight* will be fined $100 a day until he makes his *proper weight.*

> I don't need so many *blond* actresses. Fire all the *blond* extras.

> Anyone posting *child pornography* on the Internet is subject to arrest and a minimum of ten years in jail upon conviction.

Each of the italicized words has fuzzy edges, although in many cases their applications will be clear enough. A 500-pound human is surely overweight, but how heavy can one be without being overweight? Just how blond is *blond*? What ages count as a *child*? When is something *pornography*? We just do not know how to apply the terms in some cases.

An easy way to solve the application problems is simply to stipulate some precising definitions of the vague terms.

> The *proper weight* for any player is the average weight of the starters at his position on other teams last year.

> A *blond* is someone whose hair is naturally a very light yellow throughout.

> *Child pornography* will be understood as any pictures or descriptions of any person under the age of 18 in any state of undress.

Such a procedure is much too simple because it decides important issues in arbitrary ways. Why, say, should a quarterback who is 3 inches taller than the average weigh the average? What difference could it make whether a movie extra is naturally blond or has skillfully lightened hair? Any picture of a less than fully clothed baby becomes child pornography by this stipulation.

It is entirely appropriate to try to alleviate problems of vagueness by stipulating precising definitions. But the definitions should be carefully considered and to the point. Suppose, for instance, that we must accomplish a task and are blocked from doing so because (1) we are uncertain about whether some term applies in a particular case, (2) we need to decide whether the term applies, and (3) we cannot resolve the doubt by acquiring additional facts. More particularly, suppose we must administer a law granting price-support payments to producers of what the law calls "agricultural products." Growers of wheat, corn, and rice apply for payments, and we have no doubt their crops make them eligible to receive the payments.

Then a grower of Christmas trees applies. Should Christmas trees be considered "agricultural products"? Christmas trees were not specifically included or excluded in the legislation; we cannot act until we decide whether they count as "agricultural products." Given the problem at hand, "agricultural products" is a vague phrase.

We easily recognize some cases to which the term *agricultural products* applies (rice, wheat, and watermelons) and some other cases to which it obviously does not apply (cars, coal, and computers). But does it apply to Christmas trees? How are we to decide? Finding additional factual information does not seem promising. We already know that Christmas trees are trees planted and cultivated by "tree farmers" who harvest them to sell around Christmastime. Nothing else we can learn about Christmas trees is likely to help in determining whether they should count as "agricultural products." So, to perform our task in a reasonable and defensible way, we must find a way of resolving the vagueness of this phrase.

We may do this by devising a set of criteria for applying the term *agricultural product* to items offered as candidates for price supports. The criteria cannot be chosen arbitrarily or with prejudice. Rather, they must be developed and tested by considering how they handle the obvious and uncontroversial cases.

Consider how we might do this. The term *agricultural product* obviously applies to soybeans and squash, but not to petroleum and fish. Thus, to be acceptable the criteria must include beans and squash and exclude petroleum and fish. Criteria that excluded beans from the class of agricultural products would obviously be defective; they would be too narrow (too exclusive). Criteria that included fish would be defective because they would be too broad (too inclusive). Ideally, the criteria should define a class that *includes* all undoubted agricultural products and *excludes* all undoubted nonagricultural products.

Suppose that through this process of examining the consequences of proposed criteria and revising them when needed, we arrive at the following criteria. To be correctly designated by the phrase *agricultural product*, something must be (1) a plant or part of a plant (leaf, root, nut, or berry) that is (2) cultivated (as distinct from wild-growing) and is (3) harvested (4) for use as food or as raw material in manufacturing a food product.

The four criteria seem to reconstruct properly the differences between agricultural and nonagricultural products in cases about which there are no doubts. Ordinary vegetables are in the agricultural class. Timber for lumber is excluded, and so are flowers and ornamental shrubs. If the criteria are acceptable, we can now use them to resolve doubtful cases. They make it possible to decide in a *nonarbitrary* way whether to include or exclude disputed cases from the class of agricultural products.

Christmas trees, according to the criteria, are not agricultural products. Although they are plants that are cultivated and harvested, they are not used as food or for raw materials in making a food product. In these respects, they are more like flowers than vegetables. Consequently, we must turn down Christmas tree growers who apply to us for subsidies under the agricultural products support plan.

Growers may disagree with our decision and claim it was the legislature's intent that the law cover their industry. However, unless they can demonstrate that our criteria are flawed by being too inclusive or exclusive in undoubted cases, our position is sound. Seeking a specific directive from the legislature to include Christmas trees in the class of agricultural products is their only recourse.

We can use similar sorts of procedures in contexts where we want or need to identify and rationally resolve vagueness involving terms such as *literature, conservative, rich, corrupt, incompetent,* and thousands of other useful but occasionally troublesome terms in ordinary language.

Vagueness of Quantity and Type

This sort of vagueness is resolved by supplying more specific factual information. Alice says to the clerk at the delicatessen counter, "I would like a pound or two of sliced meat." The clerk's questions are obvious: "Just *how much* do you want? *What kind* of meat would you like?" The clerk has to ask these questions because Alice has *not* been *specific* enough about the quantity or the kind of what it is that she wants. What she said is too **vague** in the sense of being too *general* in both respects.

In the strict sense, vagueness has to do with the fuzziness just discussed. But in ordinary life and language we often accuse others of being too vague, meaning that they are being overgeneral. ("Come on! Don't just say that you will be here *in the afternoon*. Exactly when?") We do not know what really happened when a newspaper tells us vaguely that the robber had "a weapon." (A knife? A gun? A grenade? What?) Vague statements of this sort may tell us less than we want to know, but they are misleading only if we think they are telling us more than they are (if we wrongly assume that "in the afternoon" means before 3:00 p.m. or that the robber's "weapon" was a gun).

In fact, this sort of vagueness often is quite acceptable. We are not likely to reprimand someone who says "The Sahara Desert is a vast expanse of sand" for using a term like *vast* instead of providing exact quantitative information. In the context, the term is unobjectionable. Similarly, expressions like *big, tall, short, fat,* and *very high* might offer all the precision required. We may need to know only that a crowd was a *large* one, not that 80,000 people were present. Someone making a shopping list for another person may write down "small loaf of bread" rather than "1-pound loaf of bread." For practical purposes, numerically expressed measures, even when available, sometimes are not required, and to employ them might seem pedantic.

In some circumstances, though, we either need or want exact information. A cartographer drawing a world map could hardly be satisfied with the knowledge that the Sahara is vast. To do her job, she needs the answer to "How vast is it?" The answer can be provided in terms of some appropriate system of measurement—square miles, hectares, or whatever. In the context of mapping, then, the term *vast* is unacceptably vague. In the same way, a demographer may want to know how many people live in the Nile Valley. Because he wants a number, he would consider "quite a few" unacceptably vague.

In some cases, using comparative expressions is the best way to increase precision because we have no measuring systems to provide us with a numerically precise account. We have no metric for love, charm, or friendliness; we cannot assign a number to represent how bored we are or how tasty the ice cream is. Still, in most cases, we get by with little difficulty with expressions like "The lecture was terribly boring" and "I love you more than I can say."

In summary, a quantitative word may be considered unacceptably vague if we need or wish for a more exact description than the word provides. The vagueness may be resolved by replacing the word with a more precise description. The description may be a comparative one (not so heavy, rather heavy, very heavy) or a quantitative one expressed in the terms of some measuring system (118 pounds). A word considered unacceptably vague with respect to a particular aim or need may not be considered such with respect to some other.

Parallel considerations apply for vagueness of type. I may need to know only that the object in your pocket is a screwdriver (rather than, say, a knife). But in some cases *screwdriver* will be too general. According to the instructions I will need a screwdriver to assemble the desk. Do I need a Phillips-head screwdriver or a flat-blade one? What size would be best, or will any do? As with vagueness of quantity, lack of specifics regarding type may or may not result in unacceptable vagueness in a given context. If the vagueness is unacceptable, we must get more specific information.

Deliberate Vagueness

Ordinarily, anyone who says or writes something wishes to be as clear as possible. Yet in special circumstances we consider it desirable or expedient to use language that is **deliberately vague**. A computer manufacturer being interviewed for an article in a trade publication may not wish to provide his competitors with information that could be used to his disadvantage. Hence, in speaking of the number of engineering defects in a new model, he may use a phrase like "several important, but not ruinous, ones," even though he could say exactly how many defects have occurred and precisely describe them and their significance.

Someone wishing to be kind in refusing an invitation may do so by giving a vague response. The question "Would you like to go out to dinner tomorrow?" may be answered by, "I'm sorry, but I have other plans." It would usually be considered rude in our society to press for a more detailed answer.

The language of agreements, treaties, laws, and resolutions is often what may be described as *studiedly vague*. That is, not only is the language deliberately vague, but certain crucial words or phrases have been carefully chosen so as not to offend the doctrines or principles of those who must approve the document.

These carefully chosen words are typically ones that avoid precision and are open to various interpretations. Thus, a congressional resolution directing federal agencies to provide "help and support" to refugees from "politically oppressive foreign governments" leaves open the crucial questions of how much and what kind of help and support should be provided and just which governments should be considered politically oppressive. This wording leaves room for much political maneuvering by federal agencies, members of Congress, and the executive branch.

Sometimes words are chosen to permit the expression of an agreement-in-principle, leaving to a later time the problem of replacing vague language with precise terms. Hence, the United States and the former Soviet Union more than once agreed to work toward a "substantial reduction in the number of nuclear weapons in the world today."

Vague language may often cause puzzlement and aggravation, but in the right circumstances it can be a valuable tool.

Ambiguity

To avoid both practical and intellectual confusion, three types of ambiguity are important to recognize. The types are not offered as exhaustive or exclusive.

Word Ambiguity

With the exception of a handful of technical terms, virtually every word in a language like English has more than one meaning, but this fact alone is not what leads us to say a word is ambiguous. A word is **ambiguous** when (1) it has more than one meaning and (2) it is not obvious which one is intended in a situation in which the word is used.

Ordinarily, the intended meaning of a word is so clear from the context that we may have to make a special effort to recall another possible meaning. It sometimes happens, though, that more than one meaning makes sense in the situation, and which one we are supposed to choose is not so obvious.

Suppose the head of a physics department tells a professor, "We cannot request an increase in research funds from the university until the end of the year." What does *year* mean here? Does it mean academic year, calendar year, or fiscal year? We have no way of knowing which is the intended meaning without knowledge of the university's budget-request procedure.

Ambiguity of this sort is most often easily resolved. In this case, all the professor has to do is ask which of the possible meanings is the proper one. However, the ability to ask this kind of question depends on being aware of possibilities. Someone who has never heard of a fiscal year obviously cannot ask whether this meaning is the appropriate one. Someone whose career has been in industry may not consider that a university might budget on an academic-year calendar. Consequently, someone may get the wrong idea about what is said without even being aware of the possibility of being wrong. When we are in doubt about what is meant, clearing away confusion is comparatively easy. Yet when we think we know what is meant and are mistaken, trouble may later arise in an unexpected way.

An error in reasoning that involves treating two distinct meanings of a word as though they were the same is traditionally called the **fallacy of equivocation.** Suppose someone argues:

> It is a well-founded constitutional principle that all men are entitled to due process of law. Ms. Walters, however, is not a man. Thus, the Constitution does not guarantee her this protection.

In the first sentence, *men* clearly refers to human beings, while in the second, it is taken to refer exclusively to males. So, the argument is really this:

> It is a well-founded constitutional principle that all *human beings* are entitled to due process of law.
> Ms. Walters is not a *male*.
> _____
> The Constitution does not guarantee her this protection.

Properly spelled out in this way, without the equivocation, the argument is obviously worthless.

Political and moral terms like *free*, *able*, *obligation*, and *can* easily lend themselves to the error of equivocation in reasoning, as do terms like *personality*, *society*, *intelligence*, and *culture*.

Referential Ambiguity

We use words and descriptions to refer to particular people, objects, or states of affairs. We generally rely on context and shared information to make clear exactly what we intend to designate. Hence, we say such things as "Your car key is on the table," "The person who talks too much was fired for insubordination," and "Poor George has not been quite right since the war." We assume that the listener will know what table, what person who talks too much, and what war we are referring to.

Referential ambiguity occurs when this assumption fails and the referring expression can be interpreted as designating more than one thing. This may produce two possible results. First, the other person may be in doubt about what we are referring to. Your car key is on the table, but which table—the dining table, the kitchen table, or the coffee table? Second, the listener may wrongly believe we are referring to something that it is not our intention to refer to. Because it does not occur to him that we might be referring to the dining table, he assumes we mean the coffee table.

Once aware of ambiguity, we need only ask for clarification. Yet someone mistakenly believing he knows what is being referred to may fall into whatever sort of error such a mistake may lead to. The consequence may be as trivial as a few minutes' delay in finding a key or as profound as death.

Grammatical Ambiguity

We can read the mathematical expression $2 \times 3 + 4$ as $2 \times (3 + 4)$ or as $(2 \times 3) + 4$. Read the first way, the expression is equal to 14, and read the second way, 10. The expression is ambiguous, and parentheses are needed to make clear which possible reading is intended.

The grammars of languages like English permit similar sorts of ambiguity. A sentence is **grammatically ambiguous** when (1) it has a grammatical structure allowing it to be understood in more than one way and (2) it is not clear from the context which understanding is the intended one.

If someone in an ordinary context says, "So you like target shooting? I like to shoot myself," we can see the possibility of interpreting the second sentence as asserting that the speaker likes to fire bullets into his body. However, this is so obviously not what is meant that we do not give the possibility a serious thought, if we notice it at all.

The case is different with a sentence like "All men are not sexist." Exactly what is being asserted here? The sentence can be understood in two quite different ways: (1) "No men are sexist" and (2) "Not all men are sexist," that is, "Some men are not sexist." The difference in meaning between these sentences is considerable, and how the original claim is interpreted may mark a major political or ideological difference. As important as the difference is, we have no way of telling from the sentence itself which of the two possible readings is the one intended.

As this example shows, even sentences that are grammatically correct may be grammatically ambiguous. In some cases, though, grammatical errors introduce the possibility of ambiguity. Consider this example: "After returning from a long trip, the dog did not recognize him." Who took the trip? Who did not recognize whom? In this case, despite the error of a misplaced modifier, we have little doubt of the intended meaning of the sentence.

Yet is the meaning of this headline equally clear: "COURT UPHOLDS MAN'S RIGHT TO DIE IN CALIFORNIA"? It is possible that a court ruled that a certain man has the right to go to or stay in California to die. This interpretation seems unlikely, though. In defending euthanasia, many have argued that individuals have a right to die, but no one has argued they have a right to choose where to die. Presumably the headline should be interpreted as "COURT UPHOLDS CALIFORNIA MAN'S RIGHT TO DIE" or as "CALIFORNIA COURT UPHOLDS MAN'S RIGHT TO DIE." Yet without more information, we cannot say which possibility is intended.

We can usually resolve puzzles produced by the use of a vague word by substituting a precise expression or providing additional information. If this is not an appropriate solution and a matter of importance is at stake, we may have to face the task of developing a satisfactory set of criteria for applying the word in disputed or borderline cases.

A difficulty with ambiguity is that we may not notice it, and, as a result, we may fail to grasp the intended meaning of a sentence. The meanings of a word, the way a word is used to refer, and grammatical structure may each render a sentence ambiguous. Knowing how this may happen is a way to guard against becoming confused or misled by ambiguity.

Exercises

A. *Identify the words or phrases that might be considered vague, and explain the sort of information that could be supplied to resolve the vagueness.*

   1. Rebel forces suffered limited casualties and captured a large number of Ethiopian armaments.

   2. Yes, I really do like the Beatles a great deal.

   *3. We noticed something was wrong when we saw a number of people gathered and looking down at something on the pavement. Then a handful of men ran out the door of a café and starting throwing things. We couldn't see what they were throwing at first, but each threw several. Then the explosions started.

   *4. Save up to 50 percent throughout the store during our annual sale.

   *5. Get BETTER TRACTION and LONGER WEAR at LESS COST. Buy Brophy Tires today.

   6. Sam was repeatedly disruptive of the classroom despite frequent warnings. He should be punished severely.

   7. Question and answer about a power paint sprayer in a television commercial: "Does it clean up quickly?" "Yeah. It is quicker than you think."

   8. Three horoscopes in one day:

      Suppose that you are a Gemini (born May 21–June 20), a Scorpio (born October 24–November 22), or a Taurus (born April 20–May 20). What could you learn about yourself or what you should do this day from the following?

      GEMINI: Intuitive intellect at work! Unorthodox procedures, methods succeed. Lunar position emphasizes ability to rise above the crowd. Spotlight on direction, motivation, marital status.

      SCORPIO: Those who shunned you will now seek your counsel. Be realistic, remember the aphorism, "A leopard doesn't change its spots!" There also could be a proverbial snake in the grass.

      TAURUS: Shake off lethargy. This is the time for originality, daring, creativity, new start, fresh concept of love. Correspondence with one in foreign land could lead to overseas journey. —Sidney Omarr, many newspapers (December 26, 1995)

9. For a brighter smile and fresher breath, brush with Ultra-Zyme Toothpaste after every meal.

10. The press reported that Elvis Presley had been using drugs before his death.

11. The president of the republic, a short, overweight, balding man, left by the last train from North Station.

12. In the first year of his reign, the emperor Tiberius spent much of his time attempting to consolidate certain warring factions.

*13. "The first time I laid eyes on Terry Lennox he was drunk in a Rolls-Royce Silver Wraith outside the terrace of The Dancers." —The first sentence of *The Long Goodbye*, by Raymond Chandler

B. *In each case, identify the problem caused by vagueness. When the problem has been resolved, evaluate the solution offered and identify some of the issues with which you had to deal. When the problem is unresolved, propose and consider some criteria that might be used to solve the problem.*

*1. These categories were established by Executive Order on April 2, 1982: *Top Secret:* Information that could cause "exceptionally grave damage to the national security" if made public; *Secret:* Information that could cause "serious damage to the national security" if made public; *Confidential:* Information that could cause "damage to the national security" if made public.

2. The U.S. Supreme Court upheld 6 votes to 3 the search of a motor home without a warrant in a controversial 1985 decision. In *California v. Carney*, the Court held that although the vehicle at issue possessed "some if not many of the attributes of a home" for which a search warrant is typically required, it most closely resembled a car. Police can search cars without warrants. The motor home had beds, a sink, a stove, and other furnishings.

3. Has the concept of addiction become useless? As the term is used, it is now possible to be described as addicted to drugs (cocaine, crack, heroin, marijuana, and so on), alcohol, coffee, cigarettes, food, exercise, sex, shopping, role-playing games, computer games, gambling, and work.

4. a. It is 1972 and you are the chief prosecuting attorney of a small city where a number of citizens have complained that a film being shown at a local "art theater" is obscene. You

do not consider yourself much of a film critic, but you see the movie and discover that it does contain strong language, female frontal nudity, and scenes of sexual intercourse that may or may not be simulated. It also contains some rather clever sexual humor and two brief discussions of the role of pleasure in the good life. Showing obscenity is illegal, so it is your duty to prosecute the theater owner if the movie really is obscene. Should you prosecute on the basis of your viewing of the film and your understanding of "obscenity"?

b. It is today and you are still the prosecuting attorney. A similar film is being shown, but there is frontal nudity of males as well, and the sex acts are clearly not simulated. You remember your problems with the vagueness of "obscenity," but now you can turn to the U.S. Supreme Court's 1973 decision in *Miller v. California* for guidance. To determine whether a work is obscene,

> the basic guidelines for the trier of fact must be: (a) whether "the average person, applying contemporary community standards," would find that the work, taken as a whole, appeals to the prurient interest; (b) whether the work depicts or describes, in a patently offensive way, sexual conduct specifically defined by the applicable state law; and (c) whether the work, taken as a whole, lacks serious literary, artistic, political, or scientific value.

Do the 1973 criteria resolve the earlier problems?

C. *Explain how each of the following may be ambiguous. Classify the ambiguity as* word, referential, *or* grammatical.

*1. Saying: "It is always in the last place you look."

2. Official advice to those in the vicinity of a flood: "Boil your water north of Interstate 10."

*3. Supermarket sign: "Candyless Checkout Lane"

*4. News item: "The economic downturn was caused by the recent tax increases passed by the U.S. Congress."

5. Personal criticism: "You are not a good looker."

6. Publicity release: "Professor Berman, a nationally known authority on leadership from Harvard University, has joined the Brenton College faculty."

*7. Headline: "Norman Goes on Run, Is Shot Behind Waldorf"

8. Academic announcement: "Conference on reasoning at Flanders University"

9. Heard on the radio: "Eugene Futo is grilled by county police."

10. Heard on the local news: "An Illinois man accused of shooting his mother from St. Louis will be brought to trial next week."

11. Line in an ad for a photofinishing outlet: "Refund for prints not made."

12. Headline: "A City Sold Dirt Cheap"

13. Detective's order: "Yes, make the arrest now. It was the parent who molested the child."

14. News item: "In a lawsuit filed yesterday, McGraw-Hill charges that a company it hired to shred and recycle books illegally resold $12 million worth of [the books]."

*15. From a biography of Janet Leigh: "Ms. Leigh was reportedly upset upon hearing that Alfred Hitchcock had wanted 'a much bigger actress' for the role she played in *Psycho*."

16. Overheard:

    Rudolph: I definitely want to marry the woman I went out with last week.

    Marilyn: I know you had at least three dates with different women last week.

17. Sports item: "Now-retired tennis player Miloslav Mecir said of Boris Becker: 'Boris is never so bad that he cannot beat anybody.'"

18. Headline: "S. Florida Illegal Aliens Cut in Half by New Law." —*The New Yorker* (June 15, 1987) responded, "That'll teach 'em."

19. Historical claim: "Misconduct by the emperor is what finally caused the Roman Empire to collapse."

20. Text from restaurant ad: "Join us in the lounge for 10-cent oysters and shrimp at 18 cents each."

21. Columnist's comment on the firing of a certain football coach: "He lost to a team he had to beat by 37 points."

*22. Animal advice columnist: "Your dog may have kidney problems. If her kidneys check out fine, then you could restrict her water intake, but I would only advise this after 7 p.m."

*23. Beginning of a joke for children: "How do you get down from an elephant?"

24. A question with at least two sorts of answers: "Where did she shoot him?"

25. Refusing an invitation: "No, sorry. I can't play baseball."

26. An unhappy fact: "Bob told Bill he did not pass the test."
*27. Signs posted in hallways near the Criminal Justice Department of a university:

Understanding

Law Enforcement

Camp

28. Small-town news item: "The thief stole three matched dinner plates, some cups, and a pair of glasses."
29. Newspaper headline: "Scientific Committee Defends Fat Report"
30. Mildly unfortunate fact: "Steve scratched his chest while moving into his new apartment."
31. Canine news: "All pit bulls aren't vicious."
32. Newspaper headline in the science section: "How Do Insects Smell?"
33. Library Notes and News: "The last volume of the *Worldbook Encyclopedia* was stolen."
*34. Newspaper headline: "Lucky Man Sees Pals Die"
35. Houses-for-sale section: "Four-bedroom home, custom-built for owner. Large trees and a full bath on the first floor are among the many fine features."

D. *What is the fallacy in each of the following? Restate the arguments without the fallacy and then evaluate the arguments.*

1. Logic is usually considered to be a topic in philosophy, but it really should be seen as a topic in interpersonal relationships. This is obvious when we realize that *logic is the study of argument. When people disagree and shout at one another, they are having an argument. So, logic is the study of people disagreeing and shouting at one another.* What could be more about interpersonal relationships?

2. "... *discrimination.* Frankly, I'm getting tired of the word [as always used for something bad]. . . . Sometimes, discrimination is a good thing.

"For instance, I've been searching for a new place to live. . . . I have loved some and I have found others to be lacking. In other words, I have discriminated. . . . Therefore, discrimination is not always bad, is it? . . . Liberals have . . . the idea that discriminating . . . for any reason is wrong." —Rush Limbaugh, *See, I Told You So*

EXERCISES:
SOME ANSWERS, HINTS,
AND COMMENTS

Some exercises have straightforward answers, but others may depend on interpretations of meanings, intentions, or situations. The answers here are based on reasonable interpretations, but other reasonable interpretations may be possible and may yield different answers. More important than getting the "right" answer in such cases is being aware of the possibilities and approaching them with a questioning and analytical attitude.

As the chapter title indicates, sometimes we give not so much an *answer* as a hint or comment on the exercise.

Chapter 1

A. *(p. 13)*

1. Not an argument.

2. *Premise 1:* Smallpox is no longer a threat to anyone in the United States.

   Premise 2: The vaccination against it is unpleasant and, in rare cases, life-threatening.

   Conclusion: We were wise when we ceased the routine vaccination of our children.

3. There are two inferences in this argument.

   Premise: Herbert had the highest score on the qualifying exam.

   Conclusion: Herbert will get first consideration for the job.

   The above conclusion is a premise in the second inference.

   Premise 1: Herbert will get first consideration for the job.

   Premise 2: The person who gets first consideration almost always does get the job.

   Conclusion: It is pretty sure that the job will go to Herbert.

8. We take this to be an argument: "There are plenty of jobs for decent women on land. So, a decent woman would not want to work on an oil rig with a bunch of men." Although expressed in the form of a question, "Why would a decent woman . . . ?", is actually closer to a statement of opinion.

B. *(p. 15)*

1. The unstated *premise* is "Anything that deliberately leads us to see an ordinary object in a new and interesting way is rightly regarded as a genuine work of art."

3. The unstated *conclusion* is "Melvin should be publicly disgraced."

6. The unstated *premise* is "Anything that kills a living human being is murder." This is a good example of the importance of recognizing unstated premises. The original argument, without the unstated premise, is a common one and may look plausible, but the unstated premise it needs is surely not true. Killing in self-defense or in war is not murder. So, the apparently plausible argument must be rejected because it relies on a false unstated premise.

12. The unstated *premise* is "Any film that has a lot of nudity and almost no plot is pornographic." Here again (as in #6) the argument relies on a very implausible unstated premise. On this premise, a medical film on childbirth might be deemed pornographic.

15. Although a good bit of this argument is unstated, clearly it goes this way:

    Premise 1: We have a simple choice: the defendant should or should not be convicted.

    Premise 2: It is not true that the defendant should not be convicted.

    (Unstated) *Conclusion:* The defendant should be convicted.

17. The unstated *premise* is "If at one time there was nothing in existence, even now there would be nothing in existence."

Chapter 2

A. *(p. 27)*

1. Explanation. We seldom *argue* that we have particular likes and dislikes. But we often *explain* why we have them.

2. Argument. Reasons are given here to accept the moral claim about how you should behave.

4. Neither. This just gives us several facts about Hobart. We may well think someone has made a terrible error in expecting him to become a normal member of society, but there is no argument to that effect here.

11. We must be very careful here. This *only* tells us how long Jan has been sleeping in a tent. We can guess that she has been in the tent *because* her house burned down, but this sentence does not say that. It gives neither an argument nor an explanation.

19. The first sentence must be an explanation, a single explanatory claim. If we mistakenly take it as an argument (an inference), then the whole argument would be: "(a) Allen was bitten by a rattlesnake, so (b) he is very ill. Since (b) Allen is very ill, (c) he will survive only if snakebite antitoxin serum is made available immediately." But the inference from (b) to (c) makes almost no sense. Being ill does not in itself indicate a need for antitoxin (rather than, say, antibiotics). What does make sense is to take (a) as the *explanation* for Allen's illness. He is *ill on account of being bitten,* which does support the need for antitoxin.

21. Is this an argument for the existence of God or an explanation of why I believe that God exists? Compare with #20.

B. *(p. 28)*

2. The inference indicator is "since." This is a simple (one-inference) argument, so we do not need to number the lines.

The Cat90 is the best lawn mower you can buy.
You want the best.
_____
You should buy the Cat90.

3. The inference indicators are "thus" and "that means that."

1. Without a tax increase, there will soon be runaway inflation.

2. Congress refuses to raise taxes.

3. Before long, there will be runaway inflation. 1, 2

4. You should borrow all the money you can right now. 3

C. *(p. 29)*

3. [1][We should go for a hike in the canyon this weekend.] [2][The air is crisp,] and [3][the leaves are turning to lovely reds and

yellows.] And ⁴[the exercise will be good for us,] (since) ⁵[we haven't been out all week.] (So), ¹[let's take the hike.]

$$5$$
$$\downarrow$$
$$\underline{2 + 3 + 4}$$
$$\downarrow$$
$$1$$

The last sentence essentially repeats what is said in the first, so it is also numbered "1."

6. ¹[A meter is longer than a yard.] (Therefore), (since) ²[this ship is 100 meters long,] ³[it is longer than a football field.]

$$\underline{1 + 2}$$
$$\downarrow$$
$$3$$

Notice that "Therefore" and "since" are separate inference indicators, one indicating that a conclusion is about to be given, the other indicating that a premise will be given before the conclusion.

This argument very obviously has an unstated premise. We can easily diagram unstated premises and conclusions by writing them in and assigning them letters to distinguish them from stated claims.

[A = A football field is 100 yards long.]

$$\underline{1 + 2 + A}$$
$$\downarrow$$
$$3$$

8. ¹[If the detective really is a racist—²[which he is]—then he never should have been allowed to testify at all,] (since) ³[white racists are especially unreliable witnesses when the accused is a person of color.] (So), ⁴[the detective should not have been allowed to testify at all.]

$$3$$
$$\downarrow$$
$$\underline{1 + 2}$$
$$\downarrow$$
$$4$$

The "which he is" is a separate claim and must be bracketed separately.

9. [1][The eighteenth-century philosopher David Hume was undoubtedly a finer thinker than his even more celebrated successor Immanuel Kant.] [2][Hume was by far the more lucid writer.] [3][His contributions were more diverse than Kant's,] (for) [4][he was a first-rate historian as well as a philosopher.] Further, [5][Hume's ethical thought did not suffer from the rigidity of Kant's.] [6][Hume, unlike Kant, would never have said the duty not to lie is so absolute that we should answer truthfully even when a would-be murderer asks where his intended victim is hiding.] (Thus), there can be little doubt that, [1][of the two, Hume was the superior thinker.]

$$
\begin{array}{cc}
4 & 6 \\
\downarrow & \downarrow \\
\end{array}
$$
$$
\underline{2 + 3 + 5}
$$
$$
\downarrow
$$
$$
1
$$

Is being a better writer a cogent reason for being a better thinker? Possibly not, but it seems to be offered as such here.

18. [1][Most people are surprised to learn that, overall, capital punishment is more expensive than life imprisonment.] Of course [2][we could make capital punishment less expensive by greatly limiting the number of possible appeals for someone convicted to death.] [3][A result of limiting the number of appeals would be that more innocent people would be executed.] [4][This is not acceptable in a civilized society.] (So), [5][appeals cannot be limited much.] [6][Capital punishment must, (then), remain the more expensive alternative if it is kept at all.]

$$
\underline{2 + 3 + 4}
$$
$$
\downarrow
$$
$$
5
$$
$$
\downarrow
$$
$$
6
$$

The first sentence gives some relevant information, but it seems to be more an introduction than a part of the argument itself.

Chapter 3

A. *(p. 38)*

1. Valid. There is no conceivable way the same person has read this book by Kant and has never read a word by Kant.

4. Not valid. Even if most sex criminals have watched pornographic movies, so have millions of others who are not sex criminals. (Compare: Most sex criminals have eaten hot dogs, so most hot dog eaters are sex criminals.)

7. Valid. Completely spelled out, the argument is: "According to physics, no object can go faster than the speed of light. So a spacecraft cannot go faster than the speed of light if physics is right." That is obviously valid. Notice that the argument would not be valid without the words "if physics is right." (Be sure you see why these words are required for the validity of the argument.)

10. Not valid. Just as it is *conceivable* that Crombie survived his ordeal, it is *conceivable* that this person (if the "he" is a person) suffered not so much as a bruise or a broken bone. (Think, for instance, of Superman.)

17. Not valid. The students who work hard and the ones who get good grades could be entirely different groups of students.

19, 20. See the discussion on pp. 35–36.

B. *(p. 40)*

1. Deductive but not valid. This is meant to be a simple, mathematical (valid) inference, so it is deductive reasoning. But it is incorrect. (Since .6 miles = 1 kilometer, 1 mile is longer than 1 kilometer. So, there must be a greater number of kilometers than miles in any given distance. That means 48 kilometers has to be wrong.)

4. Deductive but not valid. The words "must be" are a clear indication that this is meant to be a valid inference. Obviously it is not.

9. The reasoning in #8 is clearly meant to be valid and is valid. Here we have just the same kind of reasoning, but a mistake is made. So, this is deductive but not valid.

C. *(p. 51)*

2. The premises of this inductive generalization make the conclusion very likely. The sample is rather large and is randomly selected, and the conclusion is modest.

3. This is a plausibility argument. Even though there are many reasons why she might fail to do well (she could be sick on the day of the exam, for example), Xaviera's high IQ and her test experience together count strongly in favor of the conclusion. Overall, the conclusion is a good bit more likely than not.

5. Is the sample here likely to be large? Is it random?

6. There are two inferences in this argument. The first is non-deductively successful (as strong as the vagueness of "most" will allow); the second is valid. Overall, the argument is nondeductively successful (again, as strong as "most" will allow).

12. This variation on a statistical syllogism is nondeductively successful. (Just how successful depends on how we under-stand "usually.")

16. Modern technology (900 phone numbers, computer services such as Prodigy and America Online, and so on) has made unscientific polls more popular than ever. Considering each conclusion in turn should make clear why such polls are not to be relied on for important information about public opinion.

17. Polls such as this one often rely on what seem to most of us to be astonishingly small samples. When carried out by ex-perts, the polls are usually very accurate. Most of us are, in effect, appealing to the authority (expertise) of the pollsters when we trust their conclusions.

    One often hears "I don't believe in those polls. I have never in my whole life been asked for my opinion." This reflects no understanding at all of the polling procedures or even of the very notion of *generalization.*

19. Be sure to notice that there are two inferences here.

20. Without at all minimizing the dangers of smoking, we should recognize that this common argument is a bad one. Suppose that billions of people smoke heavily, 1,000 people die of lung cancer, and 800 of them smoke heavily. The premises are true then, but billions of smokers are left who do not die of lung cancer. So, these premises do not make it more likely than not that a heavy smoker will die of lung cancer.

21. Whether the inference to "Most smokers eventually die of lung cancer" is successful depends on how we take "a large majority" and "most" in the premises. (Be sure you under-

stand this.) But in this case, whether the inference to "*Most* smokers eventually die of lung cancer" is successful is relatively unimportant. Suppose that all we are justified in concluding is that 30 percent of smokers die of lung cancer, and we know that almost no one else does. It would still be incredibly stupid to begin smoking.

D. *(p. 54)*

3. Known, relevant information is left out of the argument. Most intellectuals who are also professors of mathematics do know about Goldbach's Conjecture.

4. The conclusion ("Your cat can't fly") is obviously true, but the argument is a bad one because "No mammal can fly" is false.

6. A tempting and entirely unsatisfactory answer is "Being strong and quick and tall *does not mean* he can play basketball." This is a very poor explanation of the problem here because it can be understood in at least three different ways: (a) being strong and quick and tall does not *guarantee* he can play. That is, the argument is *not valid;* (b) being strong and quick and tall does not support at all that he can play. That is, the premises are *not relevant* to the conclusion; (c) being strong and quick and tall does not make it very likely that he can play. That is, the support is *not adequate.* Which is it? (Answers like "Maybe he can't play basketball" are unsatisfactory in the same way.)

   One much better way of explaining the situation is "Being strong, quick, and tall are relevant to being a good basketball player, but it could be that he has no experience at the game or he does not like sports or he is a convicted felon who is in jail or. . . . So, we have some support for the conclusion but far from enough. The support is not adequate."

11. The premise is probably false. And that something would make you happy is not relevant to its being true. #12 is much more interesting. Give it careful thought.

15. "What you don't know can't hurt you" seems to be just foolishly false. (Not knowing your food has been poisoned can certainly hurt you.) But we hear this a lot and somehow it sounds plausible. Is there some way of understanding it that would make it plausible?

Chapter 4

A. *(p. 59)*

3. $E \rightarrow (A \rightarrow B)$
   $A \cdot E$
   _____
   B

5. $(B \vee L) \rightarrow {\sim}D$
   L
   _____
   ${\sim}D$

B. *(p. 65)*

1. Answers would be pointless here, since the forms can be determined by checking pp. 60–64 in the text. Of course the idea is to come to know the forms so that it is not necessary to look them up.

C. *(p. 66)*

1. ${\sim}F \rightarrow {\sim}G$
   G
   _____
   F MT (*modus tollens*)
                Valid

3. S
   _____
   $S \vee P$ Add
              Valid

9. $B \rightarrow {\sim}T$
   ${\sim}T$
   _____
   B Affirming the Consequent
               Not Valid

D. *(p. 69)*

1. 1. ${\sim}H \rightarrow (B \vee L)$
   2. ${\sim}H$
   3. $B \vee L$ 1, 2   MP
   4. ${\sim}L$
   5. B 3, 4   DS

E. *(p. 70)*

    1. 1. $E \rightarrow (A \rightarrow B)$

        2. $A \cdot E$

        3. E 2   Simp

        4. $A \rightarrow B$ 1, 3 MP

        5. A 2   Simp

        6. B 4, 5 MP

    5. 1. $K \rightarrow W$

        2. $W \rightarrow H$

        3. $\sim H$

        4. $K \rightarrow H$ 1, 2 HS

        5. $\sim K$ 3, 4 MT

    Here is a second way of doing #5:

        1. $K \rightarrow W$

        2. $W \rightarrow H$

        3. $\sim H$

        4. $\sim W$ 2, 3 MT

        5. $\sim K$ 1, 4 MT

    6. 1. $P \vee \sim M$

        2. $P \rightarrow K$

        3. $\sim M \rightarrow D$

        4. $\sim K$

        5. $K \vee D$ 1, 2, 3 CD

        6. D 4, 5   DS

    Do not forget to look for another way.

    9. 1. $P \rightarrow Q$

        2. $P \vee R$

        3. S

        4. $S \rightarrow \sim Q$

        5. $\sim Q$ 3, 4 MP

        6. $\sim P$ 1, 5 MT

        7. R 2, 6 DS

F. *(p. 76)*

    2. b, d

G. *(p. 77)*

   2.   1. $\sim E \to L$
        2. $\sim L \to E$ 1   Contra

   4.   1. $\sim(A \bullet D)$
        2. $\sim A \vee \sim D$ 1   DM

   6.   1. $\sim S \to O$
        2. $S \vee O$ 1   Imp

H. *(p. 78)*

   1.   1. $B \to L$
        2. $L \to P$
        3. $B \to P$ 1, 2   HS
        4. $\sim P$
        5. $\sim B$ 3, 4   MT
        6. $\sim B \to I$
        7. I 5, 6   MP

   3.   1. $F \to (T \to \sim L)$
        2. L
        3. $(F \bullet T) \to \sim L$ 1   Exp
        4. $\sim(F \bullet T)$ 2, 3   MT
        5. $\sim F \vee \sim T$ 4   DM

   6.   1. $(P \bullet J) \to D$
        2. $P \bullet \sim D$
        3. $P \to (J \to D)$ 1   Exp
        4. P 2   Simp
        5. $J \to D$ 3, 4   MP
        6. $\sim D$ 2   Simp
        7. $\sim J$ 5, 6   MT

Do not forget to look for another way.
Hint: Use MT and DM.

  11.   1. $Q \vee (R \bullet S)$
        2. $\sim Q$
        3. $S \to (T \vee U)$
        4. $R \bullet S$ 1, 2   DS
        5. S 4   Simp
        6. $T \vee U$ 3, 5   MP
        7. $\sim T \to U$ 6   Imp

Chapter 5

A. *(p. 85)*

1.

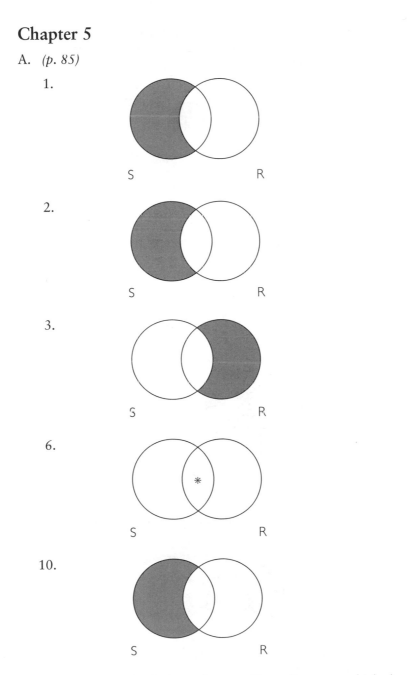

2.

3.

6.

10.

#1, #2, and #10 have the same Venn diagrams, which shows that they are equivalent (mean the same).

We have to be careful to notice that #10, "Only reptiles are snakes," means that "*Nothing but* a reptile is a snake," which is the same as "All snakes are reptiles." Ordinary language has many different-sounding ways of wording logically equivalent statements.

#6. "A few reptiles are snakes" is another ordinary language way of saying that *some* reptiles are snakes.

B. *(p. 92)*

1.

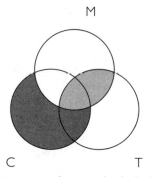

Since sections 3 and 6 are shaded, the argument is *valid*.

2.

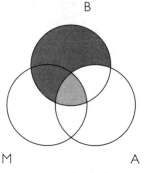

Since section 6 is not shaded, the argument is *not valid*.

9.

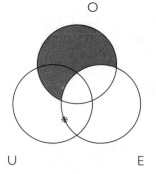

The asterisk is on the line rather than inside section 5, so the argument is *not valid*.

11.

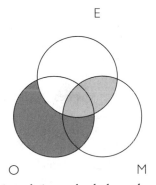

Sections 3 and 6 are shaded, so the argument is *valid*. (Compare this to #1. Why are the Venn diagrams the same?)

14.

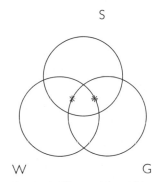

No asterisk is wholly within either section 3 or section 6. The argument is *not valid*.

Chapter 6

A. *(p. 109)*

4. A controllable condition is a factor we can modify in a set of conditions jointly sufficient for an event. For example, an increase in poverty is often mentioned as being responsible for increases in the crime rate, usually in conjunction with the suggestion that if we want to reduce crime, we should reduce poverty.

6. A triggering condition is the condition completing a set of conditions sufficient for the occurrence of an event; for example, a pistol shot starts an avalanche.

B. *(p. 109)*

2. Freedom is a necessary condition for creating art.

4. Triggering condition, given existing economic and political factors.

7. "One of the causes" is usually understood as a sufficient condition (one of several). Viral infection is also "one of the causes" of fever. (Being cautious, one might say bacterial infection is one of the factors that with others forms a set of conditions that is sufficient for fever.)

9. "Partly responsible" is perhaps best construed as one factor in a set of conjointly sufficient conditions. The factor might be mentioned by a historian as a controllable condition. The interpretations are compatible.

11. Sufficient condition. Earthquakes may also result from volcanic activity and land subsidence, so plate activity is not a necessary condition.

C. *(p. 110)*

1. a. When salt and snow are mixed, the mixture has a lower freezing point than that of snow alone.

   b. When the temperature remains the same, the snow in the mixture will turn to slush.

   c. Salt was sprinkled on snow on the sidewalk, producing a mixture of snow and salt.

   d. The temperature remained the same.

   Thus, the snow on the sidewalk turned to slush.

3. [1]Light travels in straight lines. [2]When light strikes an object, it is reflected from the object's surface. [3]We see objects when light reflected from them enters our eyes. [4]Light reflected from the part of the stick in the air travels in a straight line, but light reflected from the part below the water emerges at a different angle. Thus, light rays from the two segments enter our eyes at different angles, and the stick looks bent.

D. *(p. 110)*

4. The joint method of agreement and difference indicates that faulty batteries are the reason one of the flashlights produces no light. We need only three cases to determine this, but this is a complete list of the possibilities:

   flashlight *A*, batteries *A*: Light

   flashlight *B*, batteries *B*: No light

   flashlight *A*, batteries *B*: No light

   flashlight *B*, batteries *A*: Light

   In both cases in which batteries *A* are employed, the flashlights produce light. When batteries *B* are used, the flashlights do not produce light.

E. *(p. 110)*

1. Goldberger reasoned that if pellagra is infectious, injecting or ingesting materials likely to contain the agent will produce the disease. Doing so did not. Thus, by a *modus tollens* argument, he concluded that pellagra is not an infectious disease.

4. The method of difference. The only (apparent) difference between the two cases is that air was excluded from one but not the other. So, air (or something in it) is the cause of the growth, and life does not arise spontaneously.

7. The method of agreement. Those convicted of murder are similar in having suffered early head injuries, even though they differ in other respects.

Chapter 7

A. *(p. 120)*

1. Moral. An interpretation of the argument: The AMA says physicians are committed to preserving the life of human beings, and because executions involve taking such a life, it is wrong for a physician to execute someone. But abortion involves taking the life of a human being, and since the AMA forbids physicians to perform executions, it ought to forbid physicians to perform abortions.

   In this interpretation, the analogy at first seems to be between execution and abortion, and the argument gains psychological appeal from the implicit suggestion that abortion is an execution of the innocent. (If physicians cannot justifiably execute the guilty, they certainly cannot execute the innocent.) However, the core of the argument actually rests on an analogy between a fetus and an adult human being. The implicit claim is that since it is held wrong for physicians to kill an adult human, it ought to be held wrong for them to kill a fetus.

   The argument would be persuasive if the case could be made that an adult human and a human fetus are sufficiently similar to warrant similar treatment. But the ways in which they are supposed to be relevantly similar are not specified. Indeed, the question of their similarity is begged (that is, their similarity is taken for granted without demonstration).

   A second way to interpret the argument is to see it as trying to establish the claim that physicians ought to be allowed to perform executions. In this interpretation, the analogy between abortion and execution becomes relevant: Abortion involves taking an innocent human life; execution involves taking a guilty human life; hence, since physicians may perform abortions, they should also be allowed to perform executions.

These possibilities reflect the writer's view that the AMA position is "highly incongruous." The present social context and tone make the first interpretation the likely one.

5. Factual. Earth and Mars are said to be alike in that both have an atmosphere with clouds and mists, seas, land, and snowy polar regions. Earth has inhabitants. Thus, Mars must have them as well.

   We now know that some of the claimed resemblances either do not exist or are not as close as once thought. Mars has no seas and no (free) atmosphere. Even when this was not known and even granting the resemblances asserted, the conclusion ("Mars must have inhabitants") is much too strong for the premises to establish as likely, much less as virtually certain.

6. Moral. The claim is that because Saunders's GPA is lower than the GPA of students admitted to the Honors Program, she should not be admitted. The argument is weak. Saunders's GPA is only slightly lower and was earned at an institution giving fewer As and Bs. Hence, her case actually is similar to the cases of those at Whitman who are admitted to the Honors Program.

B. *(p. 122)*

1. Mental illness is still diagnosed in terms of the behavior and subjective reports of afflicted people. This is true of the two major psychoses: manic-depressive disorder and schizophrenia. Schizophrenia, for example, may involve visual or auditory hallucinations (seeing or hearing things not present), flattened affect (little or no emotional response), inappropriate affect (laughing upon hearing a friend has died, for example), or paranoid delusions (thinking people are talking about you or plotting against you).

   With animals, we have no way of knowing whether they are hallucinating; we may judge some animal behavior as indicating depression, and for some animals (such as the primates), we may judge inappropriate affect. However, we have no way to determine whether animals are subject to delusions. In general, the range of traits we identify as manifestations of mental illness has not been identified in animals. Consequently, we are in no position to test most causal hypotheses.

Compare this situation with the study of somatic diseases. We can identify diabetes (for example) in rats and investigate the mechanisms involved in producing changes that distinguish normal sugar metabolism from abnormal. We can breed the rats and track the genes involved, and we can feed the rats special diets and observe the outcomes. We cannot identify schizophrenia in animals and so are stopped from additional direct inquiry.

Chapter 8

A. *(p. 130)*

1. Appeal to ignorance
3. Appeal to popular attitudes and emotions
7. Appeal to inappropriate authority

B. *(p. 135)*

1. False alternatives. (The correct answer is "You lose the point.") Since the false alternatives are embedded in a question, it is also a loaded (complex) question ("Either the point is replayed or I win the point. Which is it?"). The basic source of the problem is the false alternatives, however.
6. Begging the question. Circular reasoning in this case.
7. False alternatives. One student was quoted as saying, "If I wear jeans, I am an unequivocal supporter of gay rights and all attendant social and political positions. If I do not, I am a reprehensible bigot. I am comfortable with neither of these positions." —*Princeton Alumni Weekly* (November 22, 1989)

C. *(p. 140)*

2. Straw man. Buckley gets it exactly right as he continues: "To say there are too many regulations in life is not the same thing as saying you are against any regulation. To say there are too many people farming in America is not the same as saying we could get along without any bread."
5. The talk show host's *ad hominem* (against the person) attack to show that he does not use *ad hominem* attacks would be unintentionally funny if not for the great number of people taken in by such nonsense.
6. Loaded words. The strong language takes the place of any real reasons here.
10. This is not an *ad hominem* or any other fallacy. Why not?

D. *(p. 142)*

2. *Ad hominem.* One partial paraphrase of Hunter's position would be "Steinem, Greer, and others had inadequate childhood experiences so they must be wrong in their beliefs and choices, choices which in turn have led other women to wrong beliefs and choices, which in turn have led to children feeling adrift and homeless." The convoluted reasoning is not easy to sort out, however. Hunter might reply that she just means that Steinem and others had inadequate childhood experiences and they have been bad influences. But then why bring up their childhoods at all if not to try somehow to discredit them?

9. Hasty generalization. Compare with C #5 in Chapter 3. This sort of generalization is so enticing and so dangerous that the point bears repeating. Most of us do not know that many people, and those we know do not constitute a random sample.

10. No fallacy. A person does not need to be an expert in mathematics to know about and understand the meaning of Goldbach's Conjecture.

11. False alternatives. The conditional that Cal Thomas offers here means the same as "Either all human life is valuable, or no human life has value." This dilemma is, at best, in need of justification. (Does the life of a person who has been brain dead for years have value?) Many people recognize immediately that conditionals such as the one Thomas gives here are, in effect, *either/or* statements. We state this formally in the equivalence rule "Definition of Implication" on p. 73.

13. Pooh-pooh. This is a response to an argument that a tree should not be cut because it is the world's tallest. The comment is clever, but it is a refusal to deal with the basic issue.

14. This is a fallacy, but it is not a hasty generalization. What is it, and why is it not a hasty generalization?

16. Note: Grizzard died shortly thereafter. We leave it to you to decide what to make of that.

18. Look for the unstated premise and then the fallacy.

24. False alternatives. Look carefully at the conditional "If great art is good for us . . . " and compare with #11. A similar argument has been given by others in recent years. The argument is difficult, influential, and important. Spend some time thinking about and evaluating it.

27. At the end of this inspirational story, we are told, as if it is not of much importance, that doctors said that the boy awoke at about the time they had initially expected, given the nature of his injuries. Consider how that matters.

33. Straw man. The implied argument here is something like "If people always married others of the same sex, there wouldn't be any children, and pretty soon there wouldn't be any people left in the whole world. It is very undesirable that there should be no people. So, it is very undesirable that people always marry others of the same sex." Even if this argument is acceptable in itself, it is not an argument against the original assertion that people should be *allowed to* marry others of the same sex. Allowing people to marry others of the same sex and everyone in fact marrying others of the same sex are entirely different. The original claim is distorted into another that is easier to argue against.

Chapter 9

A. *(p. 160)*

2. Analytically true.

4. Analytically false.

10. Analytically true. (Be sure to notice the difference between this and "Every *event* has a cause.")

12. A difficult case. Is it analytically true or not analytic? Think about what can be said on each side of the question.

13. "Pornography" is notoriously difficult to define, but we probably would not expect a definition to include *degrades women*. In some cases, however, *degrades women* does seem to be included. See the discussion of "Definitional Dodge" on pp. 139–140.

16. Must a game involve competition between opponents? Are there other (supposed) games that do not involve competition between opponents? Are there *any* characteristics that all games share, so that statements like "If this is a game, then it has such and such characteristics" are analytically true? (The great twentieth-century philosopher Ludwig Wittgenstein used "game" as an example of a word/concept that does not have any necessary characteristics. Of course, Wittgenstein could be incorrect in this.)

B. *(p. 160)*

2. Unless there is reason to think the mechanics are conspiring together, your conclusion is well justified. Notice that when the second mechanic gives the same diagnosis as the first, the degree of support goes up a great deal. The agreement of the third also multiplies the likelihood that they are correct. If they were just incompetent or cheats (operating independently), it is very unlikely they would all give the *same* incorrect assessment.

4. You are wrong. The number of men and the masks and guns are *functionally* important and the things an observer would notice. Not noticing the further details that do not matter in the heat of the moment does little to undercut the recognition of the masks, guns, and so on. Compare with the discussion of seeing there is a chair if one wants to sit, but not noticing its shape (p. 152 above).

6. This is a hasty judgment (unless your palate is much more cultivated for cognacs than are most of ours).

7. Your English professor's view is certainly relevant to your decision, but you seem to be treating her as a "hard expert" on a matter in which there may not be hard experts.

10, 11. Be sure to explain very clearly just how the situations in #10 and #11 are and are not different, and how the differences affect the correct decision(s) in the two cases.

C. *(p. 162)*

2. How big are these cockroaches supposed to be? An inch and a half long? A foot and a half? This is too unclear (too vague in this case) to evaluate.

6. There is no reason to doubt this, although one would like the reference to be more specific. (The actual date is April 10, 1989.)

7. There is little reason to take this claim seriously. It is unlikely, given our background beliefs, and the source appears to be a self-published book without even a date. (NOTE: We made up this example to be representative of many "basement publications" by eccentric authors.)

Chapter 10

A. *(p. 173)*

3. Too broad; includes squares, for example. Also too narrow; excludes nonequilateral triangles.

5. Too narrow; restricts *gouda* to cheese made in Gouda. This may also be seen as an accidental feature.

6. Circular.

9. Accidental feature; being sacred in India is true of cows but not a feature governing the use of the word *cow*.

10. Both too narrow and an accidental feature. Explain.

14. One meaning of *ensign* is "flag of a military unit." *Standard* does mean "flag," but it also can mean "principle." So, the definition is ambiguous.

B. *(p. 174)*

2. Stipulative, precising. Were this a report about the use of "set" in statistics, it would be reportive, disciplinary. But it is a resolution, not a report, even though the resolution parallels ones made by many others.

5. Stipulative, arbitrary. Arnold gave "criticism" a meaning it never possessed before, even though his meaning was connected with ordinary uses of the word.

6. Reportive, historical. The historical context is the discipline of biology. The report is of a stipulation.

C. *(p. 174)*

1. Ostention.

3. Genus (space) and species (nonexecutive). Also by example: "supply room," and so on.

6. Synonym.

Chapter 11

A. *(p. 185)*

3. "Number" (specify how many); "something" (describe); "handful" (specify how many); "things" (describe); "things" (describe); "several" (specify how many); "then" (specify how long after the throwing started).

4. The common advertising phrase "up to . . . " is hopelessly vague. In this case, all we know is that we will not save more than 50 percent on any item. Possibly we would not save anything anywhere in the store.

5. Another common advertising gimmick is the use of unspecified comparisons. Better than what? Longer than what? Less than what? Unless the comparisons are filled in, these phrases are too vague to tell us much of anything.

13. If you found anything vague here, you are looking too hard. This is a model of lucid and powerful writing.

B. *(p. 186)*

1. When it is decided that some governmental information ought not be public, the problem is to determine who should have access to what information. This approach establishes categories of damage to security that might result from information being public. Using the categories requires specifying criteria and using examples to determine (to start with) what would constitute an "exceptionally grave danger to national security." The codes needed to fire missiles with atomic warheads would fall into the category, but the speed of the missiles might cause only "serious damage," and the type of guidance system (but not its design) used might cause only some "damage." Once criteria for the categories are established, who should have access to information in each category must be determined.

C. *(p. 187)*

1. Word. Does "the last place you look" mean the *last place there is to look* (for instance, #10 on a list of ten places to look) or *the last place you do in fact look* (because once you have found it you stop looking)? We find that many people know the phrase and never thought it was ambiguous at all. Interestingly, about half of those we've asked about the phrase always thought it clearly had one of the meanings, but the other half thought it clearly had the other. We know of no better evidence that it is genuinely ambiguous.

3. Grammatical. "Why are you in this long line? That one is shorter?" "I know. But I have some candy in my cart." (Note: "Candyless" means *without candy* in any case. So, this is not word ambiguity.)

4. Referential. Which economic downturn? Which recent tax increases?

7. Word. What is this supposed to mean? A good guess would be that a criminal fled and was shot behind the famous Waldorf-Astoria Hotel. Actually the headline is over a story about the golfer Greg Norman hitting a hot streak and catching up, so he is only one shot behind tournament leader Duffy Waldorf. (There are many grammatical differences between these readings, but the source of the problem seems to stem from the different meanings of *goes on run, shot,* and *behind.*)

15. Word. Ms. Leigh was upset because she thought Hitchcock wanted a bigger actress in the sense of one with a bigger reputation or a better actress. In fact, Hitchcock had in mind a physically bigger person.

22. Grammatical. We just wonder what he would advise if we asked him in the morning.

23. "You don't. You get down from a duck."

27. We have no idea what these signs meant. There was to be a camp about understanding law enforcement? If so, was it about coming to comprehend law enforcement? About law enforcement of an understanding (compassionate) nature? Or is it an understanding camp (no mean wardens here!)? Something else? This (we think) is a mixture of word and grammatical ambiguity.

34. The line could be read as (1) Man who is generally lucky (for example, won the lottery) sees pals die; (2) Man lucky not to have died himself sees pals die; or (3) Man is lucky to get to see pals die. The intended answer is presumably #2. The case is not easily classified, but "lucky" does not have different meanings here. So, this may be best thought of as grammatical ambiguity.

INDEX